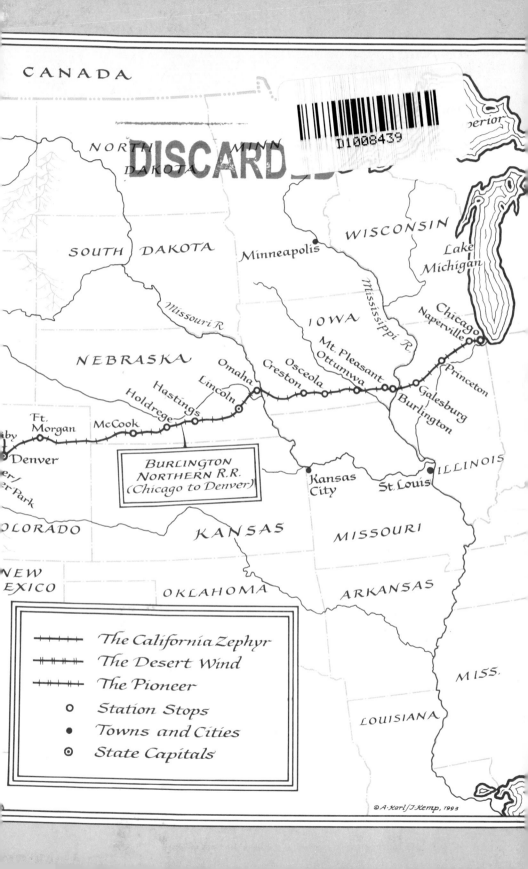

CANADA

NORTH DAKOTA

DISCARDED

D1008439

Superior

SOUTH DAKOTA

MINN

Minneapolis

WISCONSIN

Lake Michigan

Missouri R.

IOWA

Mississippi R.

Chicago
Naperville

NEBRASKA

Omaha

Creston

Osceola

Mt. Pleasant
Ottumwa

Princeton

Hastings

Lincoln

Galesburg

Holdrege

Burlington

Ft. Morgan

McCook

ILLINOIS

by

Denver

BURLINGTON
NORTHERN R.R.
(Chicago to Denver)

Kansas
City

St. Louis

er/
er Park

OLORADO

KANSAS

MISSOURI

NEW
EXICO

OKLAHOMA

ARKANSAS

MISS.

LOUISIANA

The California Zephyr
The Desert Wind
The Pioneer
○ Station Stops
● Towns and Cities
◎ State Capitals

ALSO BY HENRY KISOR

What's That Pig Outdoors?:
A Memoir of Deafness

ZEPHYR

ZEPHYR

TRACKING

A DREAM

ACROSS

AMERICA

HENRY KISOR

TIMES T BOOKS

RANDOM HOUSE

Library of Congress Cataloging-in-Publication Data

Kisor, Henry.
    Zephyr : tracking a dream across America / Henry Kisor. — 1st ed.
        p.   cm.
    ISBN 0-8129-1984-X
    1. United States—Description and travel—1981– 2. Railroad travel—United States. I. Title.
    E169.04.K55 1994
    917.304'929—dc20   93-26880

Manufactured in the United States of America
9 8 7 6 5 4 3 2
First Edition
Design by JoAnne Metsch

FOR COLIN AND CONAN

ZEPHYRUS

Whan Zephirus eek with his swete breeth
Inspired hath in every holt and heeth
The tendre croppes, and the yonge sonne
Hath in the Ram his halfe cours y-ronne,
And smale fowles maken melodye
That slepen al the night with open yë
(So priketh hem nature in hir corages):
Than longen folk to goon on pilgrimages,
And palmers for to seken straunge strondes,
To ferne halwes couthe in sondry londes. . . .

GEOFFREY CHAUCER, *The Canterbury Tales*

When, with a gentle warmth, the west-wind's breath
Awakes in every wood and barren heath
The tender foliage, when the vernal sun
Has half his course within the Ram to run—
When the small birds are making melodies,
Sleeping all night (they say) with open eyes
(For Nature so within their bosom rages)—
Then people long to go on pilgrimages,
And palmers wander to the strangest strands
For famous shrines, however far the lands. . . .

LOUIS UNTERMEYER, *after Chaucer*

ZEPHYR

The names and identifying characteristics of some of the passengers on the train trip described in this book have been changed.

INTRODUCTION

At about age six, when I was making my first mental maps of the world, trains branded my brain. For three years I had been totally deaf, after a near-fatal bout with meningitis. Other children in that postwar year of 1946 thrilled to the din of DC-4s and Constellations. I could feel vibrations from the airliners' piston engines, but I could not locate the source, and had to search the sky. Nor, closer in, was the cause of the thrumming apparent, except for the propellers, whirling almost invisibly.

I knew, however, that the machine making the ground reverberate so deliciously down at the depot in Ho-Ho-Kus, a small town in northern New Jersey, would appear from just around the curve of the tracks. In a moment I could *see* what made that almighty rumble: a big black Ten-Wheeler bringing my father home from Manhattan on the Erie Railroad. Smoke, soot and cinders belched from the locomotive's stack, and clouds of steam seethed from its cylinders. *Chuff! Chuff! Chuff!* In time with the phlegmy bark of the great iron mastiff, massive steel rods pumped the driving wheels, three times taller than me. Shiny valve gear churned with purpose, like the elbows of a race-walker. The locomotive announced its presence with the thunderous majesty of the Book of Revelations. The memory seared me deeply.

Time passed. Other boys grew up in synchrony with advancing technology, progressing from electric trains and rubber-band-driven balsa-wood planes to gas-powered radio-controlled model aircraft and primitive miniature rockets. So did I, for the most part. As an adult I plunged first into photography, then tropical fish, spending small fortunes on those obsessions. I became a husband and a father. I grew older, grayer, balder and heavier.

All the while I felt the tug of the train. As a young man living in Evanston, Illinois, I would stop, turn and gaze whenever a North Western commuter express glided into the Central Street station to discharge its passengers from Chicago. My eyes caressed the smooth green-and-yellow flanks of the diesel locomotive, and I mightily envied the men who sat high in the cab of the Electro-Motive E8.

A few years later, in our car idled at a grade crossing by a slow freight, my wife and our toddlers would fidget, but I silently thrilled to the legends on the boxcars and hoppers. Some of them were ghosts from a romantic corporate past: NICKEL PLATE ROAD. CHICAGO, BURLINGTON & QUINCY. NEW YORK CENTRAL. COLORADO & SOUTHERN. GREAT NORTHERN. WESTERN PACIFIC. MONON. PENNSYLVANIA. LACKAWANNA. Others bore fresher and still-surviving heralds: CONRAIL. UNION PACIFIC. COTTON BELT. BURLINGTON NORTHERN. SOUTHERN PACIFIC. SANTA FE. SOO LINE. Even CANADIAN NATIONAL and CANADIAN PACIFIC and, once in a long while, an N DE M, for NACIONALES DE MEXICO. As the caboose disappeared into the gloaming, I wished myself into its cupola. Even in my late forties, I dreamed of being a conductor, even a brakeman, if not an engineer.

But I couldn't, and for an obvious reason: I am deaf. I can't hear shouted orders or radio transmissions. I read lips but not well enough for me to deal with the traveling public as a conductor or trainman. Nor is my speech sufficiently precise for such a task. So

I took up newspapering, a slightly more hospitable craft for people such as I, and became a critic and book-review editor. I have never regretted it, although from time to time, when a headlight splits the night and a quartet of diesels bellows past with fast freight for the West Coast, *I want to be on that train.*

"Oh, you're a rail buff," people sometimes say in condescending amusement when I confess my passion for the high iron. Yes, though that is not the preferred term in our fraternity. We call ourselves *railfans.* Despite what others may think, there is nothing homogeneous about us. The one similarity railfans share is an affinity for what has been loosely called "the romance of the railroads," and, like love between human beings, that romance is manifested in many ways.

Admittedly, some of those manifestations border on the obsessive. Many railfans are so deeply smitten with hardware—locomotives and cars—that their craving substitutes for human contact. They wall themselves off from ordinary travelers with barriers of jargon. I once heard a railfan across a lounge-car aisle announce, as our train crept past a long freight on a siding, "That's an essdeefortyteedashtwo."

"A what?" his companion replied.

"A tunnel motor," the first speaker declared.

"A how much?" the second man said with a touch of irritation.

"A *locomotive,*" his tormentor replied, with the air of a parent explaining a simple matter to a small child.

The "essdeefortyteedashtwo" enthusiast, a skinny, brush-cut man in unpressed denim and a baseball cap bearing the herald of the Southern Pacific Railroad, was holding forth on the SD40T-2, a class of diesel locomotive built to haul freight trains through long tunnels. "See," he said, although whatever there was to see had long since disappeared aft, "your tunnel motor has its air intakes down low on the long hood, instead of up top, so it can draw in cooler air from down near the tracks to keep the engine from overheating." His companion nodded politely and a little

5

distantly. "You find your tunnel motors only on the Rio Grande and Southern Pacific . . . ," continued the first man, working up a good froth.

The fellow was a "foamer," a species you'll find everywhere flanged wheel encounters steel rail. A foamer—who bubbles at the lips when discussing his favorite subject—is what a professional railroader calls the hyperenthusiastic railfan, often with a touch of irritation and sometimes contempt. ("Fern," for "F.R.N.," or "fucking rail nut," is gaining popularity among railroaders in the West.)

Most railroaders are tolerant, although some can be stirred to fury by foamers with the effrontery to compare their book-learned knowledge with the professionals' on-the-job experience. Some of these hyperkinetic railfans clamp radio scanners to their ears the way freeway commuters affect car phones, eagerly listening in on the conversations of train crews and dispatchers. Some engineers and conductors hate the idea of such casual eavesdropping, although in most states it's perfectly legal.

And "some foamers just get in the way all the time," an apoplectic conductor on a Western train told me after slamming shut a vestibule window that a camera-bedecked railfan had opened at seventy-nine miles per hour. There is an airborne peril in the watery toilet residue sprayed on the track from the car ahead, as well as a real danger of being struck by gravel ballast and other missiles kicked up by the train's wash.

A few highly visible railfans often display an unfortunate tendency to endanger themselves by poking around mindlessly on passenger trains and trespassing on the tracks and in busy freight yards with Pentaxes and Minoltas, video cameras, tape recorders and scanners. Members of this variety tend to be overweight blue-collar types in engineer's caps encrusted with railroad pins. Many of them strew droppings in the form of beer cans, Big Mac boxes and film wrappers, and some are outright thieves—more than one Amtrak crewman has told me that no "builder's plate" containing construction information remains in the vestibule of any Amtrak passenger car, thanks to these light-fingered "collectors." Many

foamers of this kind are socially dysfunctional, too, unable to inter-
act in any meaningful way with the rest of humanity.

Many more railfans, however, are extraordinarily gregarious
creatures, attending meeting after meeting of railroad historical
societies and riding every special steam-engine excursion they can
find. One subspecies of this kind is the "mileage collector." Identi-
fiable by his expensive but well-worn sport coat and slightly out-
dated necktie, he always occupies the best seat in his coach or the
lounge car. From time to time he will jot a note in his bulky
logbook, and a quiet expression of interest will persuade him to
open it and display the columns of data representing all the railroads he has ridden. The late Rogers E. M. Whitaker, a sports-
writer, nightclub columnist and copy editor for *The New Yorker*,
perhaps was the most industrious mileage collector of all.

Writing under the pseudonym E. M. Frimbo, Whitaker billed
himself as "the world's greatest railroad buff." He was a tall, pink-
faced man in a Homburg who, his friends said, looked "a little like
Samuel Johnson and a lot like a conductor with his eye on a small
boy dangerously close to the emergency cord." His ambition was
to ride every single foot of passenger trackage in the United States,
and he achieved this goal in 1957, after riding more than 100,000
miles a year, chiefly on weekends and during vacations. Before he
died in 1981, he had racked up an official 2,748,636.81 miles on
railroads throughout the world. (And he claimed to be at least
several years behind in his arithmetic.)

In his view he was only doing something sensible and practical.
"If I rode around in a Buick all weekend," he liked to point out,
"no one would say a word." During the 1960s this dry sense of
humor led him into an attempt to persuade American railroads to
fight the airlines by adopting the slogan, "Go Through the Mountains, Not Into Them." So whimsical was his approach to trains
that in the days when the New York Central's *Twentieth Century
Limited* had a barbershop on board, he would gather his friends for
a ride as far as Albany just for a shave and a haircut.

Unlike the more famous Paul Theroux, a cranky traveler who
rides railroads in order to map the underbellies of societies he

despises, Frimbo never met a train he didn't like. As amiable toward his subject as he was eccentric in personal habits (a cat buff also, he shared a Greenwich Village apartment with thirteen Persians), Frimbo once wrote of a Spanish dining car: "You were never quite sure what the devil you were eating, but it was all absolutely magnificent, especially when embellished with large drafts of Spanish wine." He collected exotic moments; the Bengada Railway in Angola, for instance, burned eucalyptus logs in its steam locomotives as well as in its dining-car stoves, yielding "the most life-enhancing incense I have ever inhaled."

He regularly reported his rail journeys to all parts of the world in *The New Yorker*'s "Talk of the Town" section. In 1974 he and his colleague Tony Hiss brought out *All Aboard with E. M. Frimbo,* a collection of those "Talk" essays. It's a grand compendium of train rides from the Casbah to the Caspian, from Buffalo to Kyoto, and limns what Frimbo called "the most nearly perfect way of moving from one place to another." I consider it the most nearly perfect book to take on a train ride anywhere in the world. Pity that it's out of print.

Some railfans—more conventional ones—are employees of railroads, including Amtrak. I have encountered Amtrak crewmen who are pillars of railroad clubs. One, a quiet, personable and witty young chief of on-board services, is beloved by crews and passengers alike. He admits to being both a railroad professional and a railroad hobbyist—seemingly a rare combination, although I suspect many more like him simply never have come out of the closet. Another chief, a garrulous wretch with the soul of Cliff Clavin, the know-it-all letter carrier on the television comedy "Cheers," irritates passengers and crews alike with endless foamer lore over the PA systems of the trains he oversees.

But the railroads do not generally recruit their employees from among railfans. "Sometimes buffs want to work for Amtrak because they love the railroad," a chief once told me. "That's fine and dandy, but you've got to be concerned with your job. You can't be involved with what signal are you at or what the engineer is doing.

That's *his* job. You have to be concerned with your passengers. People who are *not* railroad buffs make better employees because they care more about what's going on in their cars rather than watching something else."

Civilian buffs root for individual roads as if they were sports teams, often continuing their love affairs long past the demise of their beloveds. The old New York Central attracts as many diehard fans as do the old Brooklyn Dodgers, and they utter the words "Water Level Route" with the same hushed reverence as Dodger enthusiasts say "Ebbets Field." Central devotees accumulate hardware and ephemera with the "NYC" stamp the way Brooklyn worshipers collect baseballs autographed by Jackie Robinson and Pee Wee Reese.

Some railfans even swap railroad trading cards, a cheap and booming new hobby. A typical introductory set of fifty bubble-gum-set-sized cards features photographs of shapely locomotives and brawny boxcars from a variety of railroads, with "lifetime statistics" printed on the backs. Each set is printed in limited numbered editions and costs about fifteen dollars.

Collectors of more authentic (and therefore more expensive) railroadiana favor suburban houses with paneled basement "rec rooms" converted into shrines to their passions, and their collections can be more pridefully specialized than the practice of a Park Avenue plastic surgeon. I have seen rec rooms filled with brass switchmen's lamps, oak chests full of switch stand locks, sideboards groaning with dining-car crockery, desks stuffed with timetables. This particular subspecies of railfan likes to hang out at flea markets. Many other railfans consecrate entire bookcases to volumes dealing with their favorite railroads; most of these, of course, are picture books with cliché three-quarter shots of charging locomotives, but some are thoughtful academic works and a few are interesting little specialized histories. On one train I met an author working on his third volume, published by an obscure regional house, on small-town Western railroad stations; in decades to come, these thin books are likely to prove valuable sources for architectural and industrial historians. Still other railfans have become video addicts, collecting taped epics of their favorite modern railroads as well as old rail movies that have been converted to videocassette form.

Then, of course, there are the model railroaders, whose passion for true-to-life detail is legendary. They are the ones who examine boxcars and gondolas with tape measures, meticulously counting and entering into little notebooks every dimension and rivet they find. God help them with their modeling peers if their miniature cars should sit on the track six scale inches higher than the real thing. I used to be a model railroader, too, until computers came along and I could pain my family and friends with a fresh dialect of technobabble. Of course, many model hobbyists run their empires with computers; *Model Railroader* often publishes articles on interfacing one's PC with one's pike. I don't have that kind of money and don't expect I ever will.

At heart I am a fellow traveler with the largest subspecies of American railroad buff—those who probably do not think of themselves as railfans, those who do not give two hoots for arcane technology. Like E. M. Frimbo, we simply like to exercise our imaginations by riding trains. Perhaps we ride for the sheer tourist joy of traveling somewhere and seeing where we're going. Perhaps we ride for nostalgic reasons, recapturing warm memories of childhood train trips with our parents or grandparents. Perhaps we just want to wrap ourselves in a little Fourth of July historical bunting, the remnants of nineteenth-century Manifest Destiny. In some cases we ride for other emotional reasons—restlessness, the hope of finding love or friendship, or opening new frontiers in our deeper selves. Whatever our intention in taking a train trip, it is a journey of dreams and reality, of imagination and perception, of heroes and yeomen. Sometimes it is difficult to distinguish one from the other, and that is part of the joy.

The passenger train is the last relic of the great age of travel, before prepackaged tourism took over after World War II. Ironically, our romantic memory selectively recalls not the slow, hard-class locals by which most of our forefathers moved west between 1865 and 1890, but the grand long-distance luxury expresses of the early twentieth century—trains for the wealthy few such as the all-Pullman *Broadway Limited* of the Pennsylvania Railroad, once known as "the Standard Railroad of the World," and the similar *Twentieth Century Limited* of the New York Central, the Pennsylvania's most intense competitor on the New York–to–Chicago run. Both these railroads are "fallen flags," their names consumed by consolidation and merger into the misbegotten Penn Central, heart of today's successful Conrail. Yet the names of their classic passenger trains live still in the Amtrak namesakes that ply the same routes.

Amtrak runs America's passenger trains with infamously mixed success. From its birth on October 20, 1970, when Richard Nixon signed the act incorporating the National Railroad Passenger Corporation, it has never had enough money to perform services that will satisfy all the passengers, all the politicians or all the professionals. Its route network is paltry compared even to that of the last days of private rail passenger service. There never are enough cars and locomotives in decent condition to serve the trains that do exist. So far as smooth and fast track is concerned, Amtrak remains at the mercy of the freight railroads over which its long-distance trains run, and some stretches of rail rattle the fillings in riders' teeth. Except on the rails it owns between New York and Washington, Amtrak does not field high-speed trains, and the ones it does are hardly comparable to those in France and Japan.

By any standard, however, Amtrak of the 1990s is far superior to the Amtrak of the 1970s, the decade when government-owned passenger service got a bad name. Since then, most of the shabby hand-me-down cars and locomotives from the failed passenger roads have been cut up into scrap, and replaced by more modern coaches, sleeping cars and locomotives. There aren't enough of them, of course; Amtrak still has to send out on the line cars and engines in less than perfect repair simply because there are no reserves. And although surly and uncaring people sometimes weigh down its crews, especially in the East, as a whole Amtrakers have become far more motivated and courteous, thanks in great part to changes in American travel habits and attitudes during the last decade.

The changes began during the early 1980s, when the bloom faded from the airline industry after deregulation. Air fares skyrocketed. Carriers abandoned marginal routes. Competition intensified. Revenues plummeted, resulting in service cutbacks and loss of pride among flight and ground personnel. Airports grew crowded and hectic. Baggage disappeared between flights. For many Americans, air travel was no longer the pleasant adventure it had been from the 1940s through the 1970s. They began to take another look at trains.

Short-distance train travel on the East Coast, they found, was much cheaper than and nearly as fast as flying, especially when city-center-to-city-center times were compared; trains arrived at and departed from downtown terminals instead of airports an hour away in the boondocks. On long-distance trains, especially the sleek, comfortable new double-deckers Amtrak had put into service on its Western routes, Americans discovered that they could recapture a historical adventure they thought had been lost. People who hadn't taken a train in years gave Amtrak a try, and while some suffered unpleasant experiences, many more found the train a surprisingly agreeable way to travel.

In the 1970s, like most American travelers, I avoided Amtrak if I could. Rail buff I may have been, but masochist I was not. If I had to go to New York, I flew; why, I reasoned, should I pay for the privilege of viewing the rusting industrial backside of America through the dirty windows of a ramshackle sleeper whose peevish attendant always seemed to disappear when I needed him? Rail travel, to me, meant the fast and clean trains of Europe, especially the exhilarating speed of the *TGV*s of the Société Nationale des Chemins de Fer between Paris and Lyon and the crisp, efficient Deutsche Bundesbahn along the cliffs high above the Rhine between Frankfurt and Cologne.

Then, during the winter of 1983–84, I heard surprisingly cheerful reports from friends who had ridden Amtrak's new Superliners, the two-story-high silver ships that had begun plying the Western routes in 1979 and 1980. The sleepers were clean and comfortable, they said, the dining-car fare inexpensive and acceptable, the scenery of the High Plains and Rocky Mountains glorious.

So, like many Americans of the generation that still remembered how good train travel could be, I took my wife and two sons, then aged eleven and fifteen, on a two-day trip aboard Amtrak's *Empire Builder*, our destination Glacier National Park in northwest Montana. For all of us the twenty-eight-hour overnight trip was a pilgrimage into history as well as a reawakening of my affection for American passenger trains. I am only a little embarrassed to confess that somewhere in western North Dakota, when the engineer announced over the PA system that we were approaching a herd of buffalo to the north of the tracks, I reverted to an adolescent fantasy. I imagined myself flinging up the window, Sharps rifle at the ready, onto an endless brown sea of bison, slavering and wild-eyed at the thundering approach of the iron horse. It mattered not at all that the herd turned out to be half a dozen scrawny beasts huddled forlornly in the lee of a downed willow. So memorable was the experience of riding the *Empire Builder* that we repeated it twice, in 1986 and 1989. Today, whenever I travel within the United States, I take the train—when time permits.

Time: That's what appeals to me most about a long train journey. Despite the railroads' history of diminishing time and increasing speed, time on today's long-distance train no longer means haste—at least for me. Exactly the reverse, in fact. Train time means large blocks of leisure to rest, to read a book cover to cover, to write a few thousand words on my laptop computer in the warm privacy of a sleeper compartment, or simply to woolgather, letting my imagination carry me where it will.

Just as important, a subtle alteration in the perception of time occurs aboard a long-distance train. Everything seems to run more slowly, including my emotional and intellectual metabolism. Arrival at my destination is many hours, even days away; without the pressure of the clock, I feel more relaxed, patient, confident, ready to open myself to new adventures and connections. Much of my sometimes crippling shyness, rooted in my deaf person's imperfect speech, drops away. I feel poised, self-assured, ready for anything.

And so, I suspect, do most other passengers, especially when they encounter me for the first time. Confronting one who does not hear can be unsettling for those uninitiated in the special problems of the deaf and hearing-impaired. How can we communicate? Do we even speak the same language? But when both sides have all the time in the world to listen to each other, such a meeting can be a marvel instead of an embarrassment.

The same phenomenon occurs between passengers and Amtrak crews on long-distance trains. Sleeper attendants have time to learn your name instead of just your compartment number. Often, I find, the best of them work for the railroad because they have an affinity for service: They're simply good at taking care of people. In these more democratic times, many of them no longer feel distanced by racial and social considerations from those they assist. They know their human worth matches that of their passengers, and that gives them poise and confidence.

It used to astonish me that my deafness never seemed to faze Amtrak crews, that by and large they reacted to it with casual and relaxed interest, rather than the sweaty consternation I have encountered in so many other hearing people. But I shouldn't have been surprised. Every day, railroaders as a matter of course encounter humanity in all its glorious (and shameful) manifestations. Nothing amazes them; they've seen it all.

That's part of the wonder for long-distance train passengers, too—the joy of encountering humankind in its endless variety. Some friends and acquaintances of mine who have traveled by train just once, during the summer when riders tend to be families on vacation, have complained of meeting only what they call "middle Americans" of minimal intellectual stimulation, small-town or suburban blue-collar and mercantile types. At any time of the year one is unlikely to run into the wealthy and well-connected on a long-distance train, unless they're afraid of flying. But the frequent rail traveler—especially one who rides in the off season—will meet professors and novelists as well as vacationing Europeans, South Americans and Australians, and, thanks to the luxury of time, come to *know* them.

I met many of them in the course of traveling on a single train, one that bears one of the most honored names of American railroad history: the *California Zephyr*. Today it's the most representative, as well as one of the most popular, of Amtrak's long-distance trains; each month it carries more than seventy thousand passengers between Chicago, traditional hub of America's railroads, and California, traditional destination of the westering spirit. No other American train traverses such a variety of terrain: the industrial backside of Chicago, the Midwestern breadbasket of Illinois, Iowa and Nebraska over the Mississippi and Missouri rivers to the high plains and towering Rockies of Colorado, the intermountain desert of the Great Basin of Utah and Nevada, the high Sierra of California, the shore of San Francisco Bay.

The pre-Amtrak *California Zephyr* is the grand old American train I remember most fondly, having ridden it during the early spring of 1956 from Chicago to Winter Park, Colorado, with two dozen other high-school skiers from the YMCA in Evanston. We stayed up all night and luxuriated in glass penthouses bulging upward from the middle of many of its cars. High up we sat, mesmerized by the bright yellow beam of the locomotive's Mars headlight, sweeping in wide figure-eight strokes through the darkness ahead as if it were Zorro's sword slashing aside night-riding bandits.

The old *California Zephyr* was one of the last and best of the nation's celebrated luxury trains. Its tale began in 1937, when executives of three railroads first conceived of cooperating to run a daily diesel-powered streamliner 2,525 miles between Chicago and Oakland on San Francisco Bay. The Chicago, Burlington & Quincy would run the train from Chicago 1,034 miles west to Denver, where Denver & Rio Grande Western locomotives would take it over for the 570 miles from Denver to Salt Lake City. Finally, the Western Pacific would haul the train from Salt Lake City to Oakland, 921 miles distant.

The business dip of 1938, however, caused the executives to shelve the notion of a streamliner, although that year the railroads did field a conventional steam-powered train—the *Exposition Flyer*—over the route. Still the idea percolated in railroad minds during the course of World War II, and scarcely a month after the war ended in 1945, the three railroads dusted off their plan and ordered equipment from the Budd Company, the nation's premier streamliner builder. Budd, however, was choked by a huge backlog of war-delayed orders, and it was not for four more years that the *California Zephyr* would set out on its maiden voyage.

The name *Zephyr* had been used by the Burlington Route since 1934, when the first stainless-steel, diesel-hauled streamliner was introduced. In 1933 Ralph Budd, president of the Burlington (no relation to Edward G. Budd, Sr., president of the Budd Company) wanted to christen the new train with a word starting with *z*, because it was the "last word" in high-speed passenger service. Budd, the story goes, reached the end of his desk dictionary and laughed. The last word was "zymurgy: the practice or art of fermentation, as in wine making, brewing, distilling, etc." An aide found in *his* dictionary "zyzzle: to sputter," which was even less appropriate.

Budd, however, had been rereading Chaucer's *Canterbury Tales*, in which Zephyrus, the god of the west wind, signifies renaissance, rebirth. Ah, there was the name! When the new *Zephyr* reached 104 miles per hour on its first run between Omaha and Kansas City, it indeed became a symbol of revival, of hope that the Depression would soon be over. In 1935 the Burlington fielded the *Twin Cities Zephyr* between Chicago and Minneapolis and the *Mark Twain Zephyr* between St. Louis and Burlington, Iowa. The same year it renamed the original *Zephyr* the *Pioneer Zephyr*. The train survives still, on display outside the Museum of Science and Industry in Chicago, after carrying more than a million passengers over three million miles. Later there was a *Denver Zephyr* between Chicago and Denver, and a *Nebraska Zephyr* between Chicago and Omaha.

I can still remember this last train sitting derelict, yet still stainless-steel shiny, on the dead line in the Burlington coach yard below Chicago Union Station in 1968, when I was a commuter from west suburban La Grange. It ended up in a museum, too.

When the *California Zephyr* entered service on March 20, 1949, it immediately captured the nation's imagination, and not because of its speed—a leisurely 51 hours 20 minutes westbound and 50 hours 30 minutes eastbound between Chicago and Oakland. The *Overland Limited*, which bypassed the high Rockies through Wyoming on the tracks of the Chicago & North Western, Union Pacific and Southern Pacific railroads, was more than ten hours faster. The difference lay not in the inherent speed of the trains, but in how they got there. The spectacular Colorado Rockies and California Sierra route was only part of the attraction. Five of the *Zephyr*'s ten sleek, silvery, air-conditioned fluted stainless steel cars featured glass-enclosed penthouses that gave the rider a fish-eye lens's 180-degree vista. The Vista-Domes, as they were called, were the brainchild of Cyrus Osborn, a General Motors executive. In 1944 Osborn was riding in the cab of a Rio Grande locomotive (some sources say the cupola of a caboose) through the heart-stopping scenery of Glenwood Canyon in the Colorado Rockies when he had a bright idea: Suppose similar vantage points, made of glass, could be built atop passenger cars—what a view they would afford! The Vista-Domes became the *Zephyr*'s most popular feature.

Significantly, none of the twenty-four seats under each Vista-Dome was reserved; they were for the use of any passenger who wanted to stretch his legs away from his reserved coach seat, roomette or bedroom, and watch the countryside passing above and below. This was a *democratic* luxury train.

Most important, the *Zephyr* represented a new conception of rail travel: the train as tourist cruise ship through a sea of scenery, not merely as a means of transportation from city to city. The new train pulled in flocks of riders eager to see the dramatic tunnels and alpine valleys of Colorado and the Feather River Canyon in the California Sierra. Moreover, unlike the schedules of most of the transcontinentals, the *Zephyr*'s time card was designed to allow passengers to sleep during the long, boring hours across the flat, featureless Great Plains and the arid Great Basin of Utah and Nevada, and enjoy the mountain scenery during daylight hours.

The Vista-Dome was a brilliant idea, helping make the late 1940s and early 1950s the golden age of streamliners. Briefly it seemed as if the new trains might revive the railroads' passenger fortunes, which had slowly declined from their peak in 1929, when they carried 78 percent of intercity travelers. Moreover, the train's appointments were unmatched. The interior of the buffet cars replicated San Francisco's cable cars; their carpets were woven to resemble the cobbles and rails of Powell and Market Streets. Historical murals graced the coaches and carved bar fronts pictured sage hens and wild turkeys. Coaches took on such names as Silver Dollar and Silver Feather, lounge cars Silver Club and Silver Shop, diners Silver Cafe and Silver Banquet.

A good part of the train's personality lay in the Zephyrette, an on-board factotum who, like an airline stewardess, was a mix of hostess, paramedic, tour guide, secretary, nanny, security guard, purser, public relations agent and ombudswoman. While the other service crew were almost all black (lounge car attendants tended to be Filipino), the Zephyrette was white—and pretty. "In order to deal with crews and passengers," wrote a Burlington executive in a confidential 1961 memo that is revealing of the sexual and racial mentality of the time, "she must have a better than average intelligence, make a fair appearance and have a desire and willingness to serve. Her character must be above reproach. An attractive and refined girl sets a standard of behavior for all crew members and creates a wholesome atmosphere." Part of her job, the memo continued, was to pipe commercial radio into the public address system. "Who would trouble to monitor stations were she not aboard? She also regulates reception of World Series and other events of national importance. Were the colored boys running it there would be games of 'Podunk' versus 'Podunk' or some fight."

Of course black service crew, as late as the 1960s, still were the unsung heroes of American passenger trains. When the *Zephyr* was born, the invisible stringencies of class and caste still separated them from the middle-class white traveling public. Not until the civil rights revolution and the failure of the passenger railroads did the industry achieve more than token integration of the crews.

Meanwhile, though labor was cheap, a good deal of it was required; the labor-intensive level of service helped make the train a celebrated one, but it also helped do it in. For 280 passengers, the 1949 *Zephyr* provided twenty-two service crew. (On today's Amtrak *Zephyr*, sixteen crew members service more than five hundred passengers.) By 1960, just eleven years after its birth, the *Zephyr* was losing money during the off season, even with crew cutbacks, and the Burlington president proposed merging the *Zephyr* with another Burlington train for part of its journey. Nor could the three railroads keep the *Zephyr* on schedule; in August 1961 alone, the *Zephyr* arrived in Oakland on time only ten days out of thirty-one. That month it was usually an hour or more late, and once limped in four hours, thirty minutes behind. Unreliable and unprofitable, long-distance passenger trains like the *Zephyr* could not compete with the Boeing 707 or the booming interstate highway system, and the end came for the hemorrhaging *Zephyr* on March 21, 1970.

Amtrak revived the *California Zephyr* in its present form in 1982, but today's *Zephyr* is to yesterday's as, say, an '82 Buick is to a '49 Rolls-Royce. One Western Superliner train is much the same as any other. Except for its length, the *Zephyr* is identical to Amtrak's *Empire Builder, Southwest Chief, Coast Starlight* and *Texas Eagle*. The cars and locomotives are the same; indeed, they're often interchanged among the routes. So are the crews; every six months they bid for their runs, and senior chiefs and attendants often choose another route just for variety. The services they perform are identical. Only the scenery is different. Whether or not you agree that the price was worth paying, that democratic homogenization of equipment and crew was a necessary cost of rejuvenating America's passenger trains.

During several trips aboard the *Zephyr* in the early 1990s, I discovered that the people who worked on the train often could show an old-fashioned mettle. In many instances, their resourcefulness and creativity would have delighted their predecessors in the golden age of American passenger trains, proving that courtesy and service are not lost arts. And the frequently enthusiastic and caring spirit of professional railroaders—as well as that of the civilian buffs who follow their fortunes—helped persuade me that despite the vast changes in railroading, and indeed in American life itself during the last two decades of the twentieth century, the long-distance passenger train is a part of our heritage worth preserving.

ONE

At 10:30 on a frosty morning in early April I arrived at the cinder-block "crew base" in Amtrak's sprawling 14th Street yards four-fifths of a mile south of Chicago Union Station. I had asked the cabbie to drop me on the Roosevelt Road overpass a long city block away at the entrance to the yards so that I could saunter down to the crew base past the coach yard, getting a good look at the trains.

On the fourteen ready tracks sat half a dozen of the day's departing long-distance trains, silently awaiting their locomotives like headless silver serpents. Shining double-decker Superliners that would head west and southwest loomed over older single-level trains bound for the lower clearances of the east. One, a mix of faded, straight-sided traditional sleepers from the 1950s and gleaming, rotund Amcoaches from the 1970s, still dripped and steamed from the car wash building. During the next few hours, maintenance workers and cleaning crew would swarm over the trains before their locomotives coupled on and pushed them backward into the station to board passengers.

Walking down the ramp into the yards, I expected to be challenged by an Amtrak cop, but none was about. It was one of those famously cold spring days that always seems to follow a mild winter in Chicago, one last malicious slash from the Hawk, as Chicagoans call the savage northeast wind that bullets in off Lake Michigan. Like a falcon after a squirrel the wind dipped, swooped and rolled, its trajectory upset by the tall buildings of the Loop nearly a mile north, yet retaining enough velocity to claw through the back of my down vest.

Maybe that was why almost no one was visible in the yards. Indeed, at this late-morning hour I saw not a soul except for the hard-hatted engineer of a battered little switcher, shunting out a sleeping car from a single-level train on a far track and replacing it with another, presumably fresh from the car shops.

I chose to begin my journey to Oakland in the yards rather than Union Station so that I could watch the behind-the-scenes preparations for the *California Zephyr*'s departure that afternoon at 3:35. Much of the success of a good long-distance rail trip depends on the alacrity and ingenuity of three key service crew members during the six hours before departure, and I wanted to see them at their tasks.

Service crews, responsible for the comfort and feeding of their passengers, travel all the way from Chicago to Oakland and back over a six-day run with their trains; the operating crews responsible for the mechanical running of the trains—engineers and conductors—change seven times each way. On each train the ranking service crew members are the chief of on-board services, the steward and the chef. In Amtrak's order of battle, the chief is like an Army platoon lieutenant, the steward and chef his sergeants, the lounge-car bartender, dining-car waiters and car attendants his corporals and privates. Besides performing hundreds of routine tasks, they often must overcome irritating obstacles—human and mechanical—before leaving on a run.

"NEVER TRUST A SKINNY CHEF," proclaimed the baseball cap from its perch atop John Davis. John, who is not skinny but short, compact

and wiry, stood in the cavernous cold room of the crew-base commissary otherwise resplendent in freshly pressed dress uniform:
starched white tunic and black-and-white checked slacks, white
linen kerchief knotted around his neck. A shiny steel meat ther-
mometer peeked out from under his lapel, next to an array of
service award pins. His breast bore the embroidered green-and-
gold badge of the Culinary Institute of America, evidence that
Amtrak had dispatched him to that illustrious gastronomic institution for a refresher course in creativity with standard-issue provisions.

Sending its cooks to "Chef College" was one of Amtrak's smarter
moves in the early 1990s. Another such decision was to resurrect
genuine china and white linen napery on a few trains (not, alas, the
California Zephyr at this writing) as an experiment, replacing the
paper napkins, plastic tablecloths and foam plates and bowls that
so often give eating in Amtrak's diners all the ambience of a picnic
without ants. While the new dining-car experience hardly rated
four stars, it suddenly had passengers marveling over how good
relatively inexpensive meals could be on the train. A well-fed traveler, Amtrak reasoned, echoing the principles of the old passenger
railroads, is much less likely to fret over all the things that can go
wrong on a train, from delays to air-conditioning breakdowns.
Pride returned to many of the once defensive dining-car crews,
lubricating their amiability, as I discovered that morning in the
commissary.

"John, you'll have to talk white for Henry," the steward, Lela
Janushkowsky, said with a sly grin. "He's deaf. He can't read your
lips very well."

"White? Me?" John demanded. "Ah ain gon tawk lak no white
folks!" He chuckled at his own exaggeration. It was true, however,
that John's soft Mississippi accent was sometimes difficult to lip-
read. As a suburb-bred middle-class Midwestern white, I'd grown
up familiar with only one of many American dialects—my own—
and sometimes had a tough time with others. But with Lela's
impromptu interpreting and John's amiable patience, we
managed to connect.

"What did you learn at the Culinary Institute?" I asked, to break the ice. John had been one of the first Amtrak employees sent there the previous year.

"Nothing."

John grinned as I jotted his answer in my notebook. I should have known better than to ask such a question. A chef with as many years of experience in the restaurant business as he counts isn't going to admit that his techniques might have needed sharpening. To be sure, John's ego is commodious, as a creative chef's should be, but in his case leavened by great dollops of self-mockery.

John had joined Amtrak three years before, after three previous years as executive chef at Walker's Seafood, an upscale restaurant in Wilmette, a tony North Shore suburb of Chicago. While working there, he told me more than once, "I got a three-and-a-half-star writeup in the *Sun-Times*." Before then he had been *sous-chef* at Chicago's Mercantile Exchange Club after eight years at the Hilton in Denver.

He is a graduate of Lyndon Johnson's much-maligned Job Corps, the Great Society program founded to train and employ impoverished youths. At age sixteen, in 1967, John had left his Mississippi home to join the Job Corps.

"They put me in the kitchen and I discovered that's what I wanted to do and I been doing it ever since," he said. Once he had learned the basics, the Job Corps found him a slot at a Denver cafeteria, "and they said I was the best cook that was. They started me out as a vegetable cook. Every day I had to cook my eighteen vegetables, and all of them had to be done precisely. Before we started serving, the manager would come by. He would taste everything. If you done anything wrong, you would have to do it over again. It was a *hot* kitchen. All us cooks wore white pants, white jackets, white bow ties. And we had to stay clean at all times."

John soon stepped up to the Denver Hilton—and down. "I started as a runner, supplying all the main commissaries for the Hilton restaurants, because they said I was too young to be a cook. But they also said I was too good to be just a runner. I got thirteen promotions in three months. They couldn't find a job that tied me down."

A combination of footloose ambitions and a teenage dream brought John to Amtrak. It wasn't the money—"I could make more on the street"—but a growing awareness that he could pursue his trade and travel at the same time. In the beginning, Amtrak offered no attractions. While at the Denver Hilton, John said, he had listened as older chefs talked about working on the railroad. As will veterans of any institution, they groused about their employers. "They never give you the right information," John said. " 'They comin' out with new microwaves,' they would say. I was just getting excited about culinary stuff and I didn't want nothing to do with microwaves."

One particular friend complained constantly about Amtrak. "He says he wasn't happy there," John said. "He would never give me the positive side. He'd only give me the negative side. But he would never miss a trip. He was always out on the road. Soon I really did want to see for myself. As a teenager I had wanted to ride cross-country and get paid for doing what other people only dream about. So when I saw the ad in the paper, I mailed Amtrak my résumé, and here I am."

With Lela at his side, John turned to his Form 896. A seven-page, eight-foot-long, twelve-inch-wide computer printout, it "sets the pars," or informs the chef what and how much of it Amtrak's electronic brain thinks he will need to feed his passengers. ("Just like the Army, everything's done by paper," John said.) And it'll be a long run: three days and two nights from Chicago to Oakland on the *California Zephyr*, or Number 5 as its crew calls it. (It's Number 6 on the eastbound leg.)

Among themselves, railroad crews identify their trains by numbers rather than names. In the beginning I considered train numbers merely part of the shamanic argot with which members of any industry set themselves apart from the rest of society, but I came to learn that they do serve a practical purpose as a kind of precise shorthand. On Amtrak, odd train numbers are usually westbound (or southbound), even numbers eastbound (or northbound). For everybody concerned with the movement of a train—dispatchers, engineers, conductors, service crew—referring to it by number rather than name is quicker.

"I'm missing a hundred and ninety-six orders of eggs!" John growled suddenly. Lela peered about for them, but in vain. Each order consists of two eggs, so John was short thirty-two dozen and change.

"The main thing is to make sure all the revenue items the chef is accountable for are here," Lela said as John disappeared in the direction of the foreman's office. "Otherwise out of his pocket he'll have to pay."

Lela had arrived at ten o'clock, she said, an hour ahead of her scheduled reporting time, to get an early start on helping John verify the counts of those revenue items: fish, chicken, steaks— whatever carries a price tag on the meal checks proffered to pas- sengers at the end of meals. "Saves a lot of madhouse if we don't have to rush," she said.

She fanned open the Form 896. "See," she said. "One hundred forty-four chickens, one hundred thirty steaks, seventy-two fish. That means they expect a busy time in the diner." Thirty-one articles made up the revenue-item list: dry cereal packets, bacon, sausage, pizzas, chicken breasts, cheesecakes and more, including an unidentified "Chef's Special." The rest of the form ran to 114 items, from "Bread, White Loaf, ea. 22" to "Vinyl Tablecloth, ea. 24."

Provender of all kinds, stacked tall on skids and trolleys, sur- rounded us. Crates of potatoes, lettuce and tomatoes leaned against the wall. Through glass-windowed doors opening upon a large zero-cold room nearby, I watched a hard-hatted young woman with clipboard and voluminous parka directing operations as two muscular young men hoisted crates, displaying their massive arms in sleeveless undershirts. Next to us a now unlocked steel cage protected the revenue items, including dining-car bar supplies: a case each of Heineken, Miller, Bud Light, Scott Fetzer California chardonnay, the same brand of zinfandel and burgundy, Bloody Mary mix, two Cokes, one Diet Coke. At my dubious expression— three cases of beer for the diner seemed woefully inadequate pre-prandial libation for today's scheduled departing load of four hundred passengers—Lela said soothingly, "Those will be replen-ished at Denver and Salt Lake City."

"Heads up!" At the steward's warning gesture I jumped aside as a tractor chugged past, briskly towing trolleys of crated potatoes. Chastened, I looked about. Slogans covered the walls: "ON THE JOB SAFETY BEGINS HERE." "THINK AND WORK SAFELY." John, who by now had returned with his missing eggs, noticed my glance and pulled out his keys. On the fob was stamped: "SAFETY PAYS." "If you get hurt, you get paid," John said nonchalantly.

This was, I thought, a deceptive flippancy, part of the lingering macho of the railroad trade—a macho that today is more surface than substance. Like most every other railroader I would notice the rest of the morning, John kept a weather eye out for perils, looking about carefully before he made a move. Railroading always has been dangerous work, and railroad managements—Amtrak's in-cluded—constantly nag the rank and file about safety in this litiga-tion-mad age. All commissary workers wear hard hats and safety spectacles, though in a place like that it seems to the uninitiated that the greatest danger must be a low-flying can of peas knocked out of a stack by a passing forklift.

"What *is* the chef's special?" John asked, turning to the stacks of revenue items. "Barbecued ribs." He pulled a face. "Mmmm. I feel like *prime* rib." Again he disappeared.

"What John wants, John gets," Lela said. Amtrak bureaucracy, ever seeking to squeeze the last drop of revenue out of its federally subsidized turnip, discourages arguments with the wisdom of its computers. Nonetheless, its chefs and stewards are masters at twist-ing, bending and confounding the Form 896. Their main weapon is the "backorder," a smaller computer form that allows some creativity—and safety—in obtaining supplies. It is filled out and sent to the commissary headquarters as soon as the stock supplies are checked against the 896. Once a commissary supervisor approves the backorder, workers then trundle to John and Lela's station the supplies listed on it.

"I always backorder five hundred 'four-in-ones,'" Lela said. Those are cellophane-wrapped plastic knife-fork-spoon-napkin combinations. "Just in case the dining-car dishwasher breaks down. It's one of the most important backorders," she said. "You never know what's going to happen."

"Got the prime rib!" John sang gleefully upon his return. He examined the backorder. "Put on it extra A-1 and Worcestershire sauce, Spanish and white rice, spices, garlic, broccoli, carrots, Italian veg, mixed veg. Ninety extra baking potatoes. And bowls. Last trip they lost my backorder and we run out of bowls so I couldn't serve soup. Now where's the fish?"

John donned white cotton gloves and pulled from a stack three boxes of frozen stuffed Idaho trout, each containing ten fish, and a large crate of frozen red snapper. "They don't look good," he said, although to my untrained eye they looked fine. "Snapper sometimes is not a very high quality fish," he added.

Just then the foreman from the zero-cold room walked by, her sleeveless hunks trailing behind. "Sweetie baby honey . . . ," John said in a wheedling tone, trotting after her with the snapper. The foreman stopped and gazed at the ceiling in mock exasperation. Lela winked at me. In a few minutes John returned smiling with a large box of frozen catfish fillets. "Had a choice of this or lemon sole," he said. "I took the catfish 'cause I can grill it. You'll see."

It was now 11:00 A.M., and a tall and princely figure in his mid-thirties, neat in blue blazer, gray slacks and maroon Amtrak necktie, joined us. He was Reggie Howard, today's chief of onboard services. After shaking my hand with grave and courteous dignity—a mien he rarely drops, except for his friends—he turned to John and Lela. "Everything on the money?" he asked. "Need help with anything?" When they shook their heads, he added, "Backorder forty extra lasagnas. We have a group of forty with a prepaid order for lasagnas."

I trotted behind Reggie's long legs around the corner to another array of steel cages, where Noel Prell, a hefty, bearded lead service attendant—the official Amtrak term for lounge-car bartender—labored amid tall stacks of his own supplies: liquor, beer, wine, soft drinks, sandwiches, cookies, pizzas, Danish pastries, frozen hamburgers—everything one would find in a well-stocked corner tavern, except for pool cues and a dart board. "Up the par on the soft drinks and potato chips," Reggie told Noel. "We'll have a lot of thirsty riders today." Noel bent to his backorder, and Reggie and I stepped upstairs.

Train chiefs have existed only since 1983. Before then, stewards headed the on-board passenger service. They were subordinate to the conductors and trainmen, whose employers on the long-distance Amtrak runs were the freight railroads over which the trains rode. From time to time, a roving Amtrak on-board inspector would hop aboard the train to check the quality of the service, but there were few. Some of them are now chiefs.

A train chief is more than a steward with lieutenant's bars. Though most of the job is routine, much of it is also challenging and sometimes even requires heroics. One *Zephyr* chief won fame throughout Amtrak when a suicidal passenger threw himself into the Colorado River from a train halted at a siding. The chief dove in after the passenger, only to be grabbed in a fierce headlock as the rushing, icy waters tumbled them downstream. The chief sank his teeth into the passenger's thumb, releasing the death grip, and wrestled him safely back to the bank.

More often a chief will have to step into the breach when a crew member falls ill or fails to show up at the last minute. Chiefs must be able to perform any service job aboard a train, from cooking and making up bunks to cardiopulmonary resuscitation and mechanical repairs. Many carry their own tool kits. They must be diplomats, swift to mediate disputes among an on-board population of more than five hundred passengers and crew. They must be patient with children. And they must have steady nerves.

The most unpredictable peril that faces a train chief is the passenger tanked on liquor or drugs. On one memorable *Zephyr* trip, chief Curtis Keeton had a violent encounter with a passenger zonked mindless on PCP. "This was about the time Greyhound went on strike," he said, "and we were taking aboard a lot of bus passengers. There was a lot of shooting, you remember, and people didn't want to ride Greyhound. They didn't want to take a bullet in the head. I don't know if it's a good idea to say it, but you can tell the difference between somebody who rides the bus and somebody who rides the train. It's a different class of people."

The addict "was in a sleeping car, and he didn't belong there. We asked him to leave. He cussed me and cussed the conductors out, and one thing led to another. It took six of us to get him down. I got bit twice and thrown against the baggage rack and kicked in the knee, and my knee swelled up. I weigh about two hundred fifteen pounds, and this guy weighed only about one hundred forty, but he had me by the throat up against the luggage rack. We radioed the dispatcher, and the dispatcher called police to meet us at the next town."

Two years after that encounter, Curtis was still suffering from its aftereffects. At the time I spoke with him, he had just returned from a three-month leave after undergoing surgery to repair a torn ligament in his knee, and surgeons told him that a pain in his neck was being caused by two disks pressing upon his spinal cord. "They tell me that I can either live with it or have it operated on," he said. "I'd rather not go under the knife again."

That experience, Curtis said, taught him to be wary about passengers. "You watch passengers as they're coming down the platform to board the train. If they're staggering, you don't want them on the train. A lot of times they still get on the train, and then you have to talk to them and tell them how things are going to be. 'Gotta be cool, this is the program,' we tell them. 'Now if you do that, you're going to make it where you're going. If you don't, we're going to have to put you off, and I don't want to do that.' Sometimes it happens that way, but most times we just try to get them away from other passengers so they don't see their behavior, to maintain a certain atmosphere aboard the train."

Drugs also led to Reggie Howard's worst on-board experience.

"It was two trips ago I had two passengers OD," he said. "Two young men, one seventeen and the other twenty-seven years old. They had a sleeping car room in the Seattle section, and in the middle of the night they used all their alcohol and all their drugs together. The crew woke me up at one o'clock in the morning and told me they needed me back there.

"It was just chaos. They were going into convulsions, eyes rolling into the back of their heads. One vomited right on my foot and died. The other one was taken off the train and died on the way to the hospital. You know, everything was perfect that day, but that night some person sees something like that. . . ."

Reggie Howard takes strength from his deep roots in railroading, roots that give him a combination of memory and experience rare among today's Amtrakers. Not only was his father a railroader, but his sister is a sleeper attendant and her husband is president of an Amtrak union local. His brother is a former railroader. And Reggie is married to another Amtrak train chief. ("She still has to practice her PA announcements," he said, "because she's from Cape Town, and even though she's been in this country for twelve years now, she still has a heavy South African accent.")

The Howards are a huge Oakland family with two sets of twins. (Reggie is not a twin but the eighth of nine children.) His father, a sleeper attendant, began his career as a Pullman porter and retired from Amtrak after thirty-nine years as a railroader. "I got to work one year with him before he retired," Reggie said fondly. Reggie himself is the father of four.

Despite his father's profession, Reggie as a child felt no tug from the high iron. He and his brothers were basketball enthusiasts, and in high school and college—he completed two and a half years at the University of New Orleans—he played all three major sports, basketball, football and baseball. As do so many talented young athletes, he had no doubt he would soon turn professional.

During the midyear college break of 1980, however, he let his father obtain him an Amtrak slot as a summer train attendant working out of Oakland. The work "just got into my blood," Reggie said. He enjoyed the job, he added, because he'd been riding trains with his father throughout his childhood. The lore about railroading he had unconsciously learned dropped into place, like tumblers at last driven home on a lock long left open. In his dozen years on Amtrak, Reggie worked as a car attendant, a waiter, a second cook and a lounge-car bartender before being tapped for a chief's job.

Because his memories and those of his father root Reggie in the days of traditional railroading, he can compare today's quality of service to that of the heyday of passenger trains. "I remember the linen tablecloths, the china, the silver, the fresh fruit," he said. "The dining car was real elegant back in the late sixties. All the waiters were male, and they would dress in white jackets and big blue bow ties with a long white apron and a towel over their arm."

To work together efficiently in the tight little diner "and give that high quality of service—that was real excellence," Reggie said. "And it was amazing that in this tiny kitchen with wood-burning stoves the chefs could prepare such good food, caring how it looked as well as how it tasted."

Now most of the old-timers are gone, and, Reggie says, management has mixed feelings about their departure. At its birth Amtrak faced serious woes, and had to rely on whatever pride was left in the sometimes demoralized service crews it inherited. Thanks to the old roads' deferred maintenance, the locomotives and cars creaked with age and decrepitude. Kitchen air conditioners never worked and the cooks often had to labor in heat well over 100 degrees Fahrenheit.

"When a train went by," Reggie said, "you'd see the chef with the little dining car door open, sitting on a couple of milk crates fanning himself with hot air. It was real tough in those days, and I think management has a soft side for these old chefs and attendants and waiters who stuck it out and made the railroad what it is today. They *are* set in their ways, though. Even though management is trying to go with fresh new young blood and bring in new ideas and start new policies, some of these old-timers just don't want to do it management's way."

Reggie had signed in at 10:00 A.M., checked his crew roster and assigned rooms in the dormitory coach to the car attendants and waiters, who would report at noon and 12:30 P.M., respectively. We stepped into the train managers' office, dirty off-white Concrete Block Moderne in thrifty Amtrak fashion. Each name train has its own manager, to whom the chiefs report.

Reggie logged on the computer and printed out a manifest, which lists the number of coach riders and the names of sleeper passengers and the rooms they booked. The manifest also reveals special groups or requests. Might this coach rider need a wheelchair at Sacramento? Might that sleeper passenger need meals in his room? Are any of them blind or deaf or aged?

For a week, however, the computer had been troublesome. It would yield only a partial manifest, giving the total numbers of passengers in sleepers and coaches, but not the points at which coach riders board and detrain. The chiefs could, however, make an educated guess about their loads just by the time of year. There would be collegians returning to school after spring break, and late-season snow in the Rockies and Sierras would attract skiers. Since it was the off season, elderly riders would take advantage of lower ticket prices. I ran my finger down the manifest. *Golden Age Club* headed one list of twenty-nine passengers.

When the computer works properly, the chief is able to prepare a complete briefing sheet for his crew. It lists the total number of riders the computer expects on the six-day round trip of the *Zephyr.* Working with a calculator, the chief then breaks down the passenger total into coach and sleeper riders boarding and disembarking at each of the major station stops—Chicago, Denver, Glenwood Springs, Grand Junction, Salt Lake City, Reno and Oakland. Today that couldn't be done, but it still was possible to copy the special passenger requests, then jot down six Safety Rules of the Day, one for each day of the trip. "Let's all work safely at all times," Reggie wrote. "Don't take anything for granted, and always expect the unexpected." On the office Xerox machine, he reeled off twenty copies and tucked them into his briefcase with a sheaf of meal vouchers.

Reggie's preparations actually had begun on his off time the day before, when he dropped by the crew base to pull up the names of the sleeper passengers on the computer. All meals are included in sleeping-car ticket prices, and that causes writer's cramp for *Zephyr* chiefs. Each sleeper passenger gets a meal voucher, and on each voucher Reggie must write the holder's name and sign his own. That's at least sixty vouchers per sleeper; on one six-day round trip, a single sleeper room may be occupied by as many as four parties of one or two passengers. Moreover, besides Number 5's sleeper, Reggie has two others to do: the sleeping cars of Trains 25 and 35.

On its departure from Chicago and for much of its run, the *California Zephyr,* Amtrak's longest Western train, is actually three trains in one: Numbers 5, 25 and 35. The coach and sleeper of Number 25, the *Pioneer,* split off at Denver, where they are coupled to a diner and locomotive for the northwestward trek across Wyoming, northern Utah, Idaho, Oregon and Washington to Portland and Seattle. Number 35, two coaches and a sleeper called the *Desert Wind,* is uncoupled at Salt Lake City to be hooked to a waiting dormitory-coach, diner and locomotive, and heads southwest to Las Vegas in Nevada and Los Angeles. The remaining sleeper, three coaches, diner and lounge car of Number 5 head due west across Utah and northern Nevada to Winnemucca, Reno, Sacramento and finally Oakland.

The phone rang. It was the station agent in Salt Lake City. Both of the toasters in the galley of the eastbound *Zephyr* that had just left Salt Lake that morning had burned out. Its chief would appreciate it mightily if the chief of today's westbound would drop off one of his at Omaha at midnight tonight, for the eastbound chief to pick up at 6:30 A.M. tomorrow. "Sure enough. No problem," Reggie said.

Often, Reggie said, eastbound *Zephyr* chiefs will leave leftover supplies, such as pillow slips, in "a little cabinet we have" at Omaha in case their counterparts on westbound trains find themselves running short. Impromptu supply dumps like these are common all over Amtrak, and they're important to the smooth functioning of passenger trains. "So many Amtrak departments, instead of ordering when they get low on an item so they still have some when replacements get in, don't order until they run out," Reggie said. "It takes two or three weeks to get that order shipped to Amtrak. You find a lot of that—sheets, pillow slips, mechanical parts to fix the refrigeration, things like that. It really gets frustrating."

At last Reggie wound up his loose details. On the copier he ran off a clutch of trivia sheets, each containing eleven questions (such as "What is the highest point on the *California Zephyr*'s route?") for a game passengers play each afternoon in the lounge car, the prize a deck of playing cards or similar souvenir. He stepped into the office next door, picked up several videotaped movies for screening in the lounge car each evening, and stowed them in his case. It was now 11:30, time for me to go out to the train with John. "See you aboard," Reggie said.

I picked up John at the commissary gate while Lela stayed behind to ride with the supplies, keeping an eye on those revenue items, especially the beer and liquor. To civilians the vast Amtrak yards may seem empty, but the cars on the ready tracks actually are full of sharp eyes and light fingers. Some yard workers indulge in a practice called "polacking," in which they fall upon a train when a switcher brings it down from Union Station after the day's run, plundering it of valuable items left behind by passengers. A chief once told me that not twenty minutes after he left in his compartment an expensive leather shaving kit, he returned to find it gone—before the train had stopped rolling into the yards.

Then there is scavenging born of necessity. "I like to get out to my train early to protect it," John said. "Some of those old-timers on the trains that go out before ours, they check out their cars early and if they don't have the proper equipment, they don't have enough pots and pans, they're gonna go take it off my train here."

Fresh and dripping from the car-washing building, the *Zephyr*—or most of it, without mail cars and locomotives—towered over Track 12 in the coach yard. Even after ten or eleven years of hard service, the sleek stainless-steel Superliners gleamed like new. I stowed my bags under the watchful eye of the attendant of Car

3530, the Los Angeles sleeper in the middle of the train. He was a small, thin man who greeted me with a demeanor that was a democratic mix of helpfulness and affability. Meanwhile, John tucked his kit in his room in Car 510, first in line, the coach-dorm. Then we set off for the dining car.

During the age of the great trains, passengers expected to dine not just well but also with elegance. As that era fades, the memory becomes almost mythical. Older people recall the soft chimes with which a passing white-jacketed waiter announced dinner seatings. The stewards, chefs and waiters of the time possessed an *esprit* rivaling those of the finest New York and San Francisco restaurants, and offered a level of service almost never encountered today. The typical old-time dining-car crew of eleven—steward, a chef, three cooks, six waiters—served thirty-six passengers at a time. In our far less labor-intensive day, Amtrak crews of seven or eight—steward, chef, two cooks, three or four waiters—must serve seventy-two patrons at each seating on the Western routes.

In the beginning of America's railroad history, trackside vendors proffered their wares at servicing stops to much hustle and bustle and general confusion. Frederick Marryat observed in 1838 that "the cars stop, and all the doors are thrown open, and out rush all the passengers like boys out of school, and crowd around the tables to solace themselves with pies, patties, cakes, hard-cooked eggs, hams, custards, and a variety of railroad luxuries too numerous to mention. The bell rings for departure, in they all hurry with their hands and mouths full, and off they go again. . . ."

A bit later "news butchers," who could be described as two-legged 7-Elevens, dispensed sandwiches and snacks with their newspapers. By 1860 eating houses had cropped up at division points, many of them inside the stations and others in adjacent buildings. Southwest from Chicago on the Santa Fe Railway, Fred Harvey's Harvey Houses, staffed with pretty young Harvey Girls imported from the East, "kept the West in food and wives," as Will Rogers marveled.

The first recorded food service car rolled out on the Baltimore

& Ohio Railroad in 1842, but meals were prepared elsewhere and carried on board to be served cold. During the Civil War, hospital trains for wounded soldiers contained kitchen cars, and in 1862 a rustic "refreshment car," a fifty-foot-long remodeled day coach, appeared on the Philadelphia, Wilmington & Baltimore Railroad. A contemporary account said that it contained "an oblong counter around the four sides of which patrons ate while seated on high stools. . . . From the inside of the oblong viands were served by colored waiters in white jackets. If memory does not betray me, the bill of fare . . . consisted chiefly of oyster stew, pie, crullers, and coffee."

The first dining car designed for the cooking and serving of meals was born in 1867, when a Chicagoan named George M. Pullman—whose name today is synonymous with the sleeping car, but who also ought to be remembered for his dining cars—kitted out what he called a "hotel car." Named *President*, it combined sleeping accommodations, a lounge, and cooking and dining facilities. A crew of four or five served thirty-six to forty passengers.

The following year Pullman rolled out the first true purpose-built full dining car, named *Delmonico* after the New York restaurant. The only problem was that it had open platforms fore and aft, rather dangerous for travelers entering or leaving the car while the train was in motion. Not until 1887, when closed vestibules and elastic diaphragms shrouding the passageways between cars came along, did the dining car as we know it finally appear.

A menu of thirteen different entrees, six kinds of game and a choice of twenty-five desserts was hardly rare. Some dishes became almost synonymous with the railroads that served them. On the Santa Fe it was baked ham with Llewellyn sauce. On the Chicago, Burlington & Quincy, diners favored individual steak-and-kidney pies, Burlington style. Great Northern patrons delighted in reindeer mulligan, hunter style. Nobody who took the *Twentieth Century Limited* could ever forget lobster Newburg New York Central. The Northern Pacific served baked rabbit pie and "The Great Big Baked Potato," a two-pound monster from Idaho.

At no time did railroads make profits from dining-car operations. They were willing to absorb heavy losses from the superb service in order to attract passengers. And why not? Dinner in the diner almost always was what people remembered after a long train ride, and the tastier it was, the more likely they would be to return.

When John and I found our diner and stepped around a bulging dumpster and into the galley on the lower level, he groaned in dismay. The place was a mess, wrappers and rinds strewn about the rubber-matted floor and dishwashing station, remnants of dry ice clogging the bottoms of the six electric refrigerators, and the twelve-foot-long steam table caked with the previous trip's leftovers.

"Yesterday's second and third cooks supposed to clean up before they sign off," John said. "I'm going to have to write this up, and their chef'll catch the heat. He's the one responsible." John was especially irked because, knowing that the previous trip's kitchen crew had a reputation for inattention to such detail, he had asked the crew-base supervisor to send his second and third cooks to the diner as soon as they arrived so that they could clean up if necessary. But the place was emptier than a pro football stadium on Monday morning after a big game, and about as tidy.

John's mood failed to improve when he picked up the Map 21-A, a thick book that lists every malfunction and repair since the car's construction. He winced as he pointed to the most recent entries. Both elevators—the dumbwaiters that lift food-laden trays from galley to dining area above—were declared "Bad Order." If at least one couldn't be fixed, the waiters would have to run themselves ragged for six long days carrying heavy loads up and down the narrow twisting stairs between the two levels.

And when the diner had reached Oakland on its last run, the previous chef had written: "Left Oven. Bad Order. Thermostat wrong. Burns everything." Next to the complaint was scrawled a three-letter code that, John said, meant, "Not fixed. No parts in stock." "That's what they put down in Oakland when they don't *want* to fix it," he grumbled.

A maintenance foreman arrived for a consultation. He didn't

have the parts either. John would have to make do with the oven on the right. "There's no heat control on the grill either," John told the foreman, who protested that it had been fixed that morning and that it was working. "Yeah, it goes on and off like it's supposed to," John replies, "but you can't control the heat." He showed the foreman the Map 21-A, riffling from page to page. "See, the grill is written up all the time. It's *constantly* bad order."

On his radio the foreman summoned a pair of mechanics, and while we waited for them he brought up the subject of the galleys in the new Superliner II cars, which Amtrak had just ordered for delivery in the mid-1990s. Like their older sisters, the new diners are to be all-electric, but with a difference. "They're to have completely modular construction. If a grill or oven goes bad, it can just be popped out and a new or rebuilt one popped in," the foreman said.

He also gave John a small piece of good news: The malfunctioning refrigerators, whose Freon had run out before the train reached Oakland on the previous trip, had been recharged. He wouldn't need a lot of extra dry ice for his perishables. Then the yard workers arrived. One installed a new thermostat in the grill. John twisted the knobs. "Now it's working," he said with theatrical jubilance. "We can serve dinner tonight!"

It was now noon and his cooks still hadn't shown up, so John got to work. First he plugged his boom box into an outlet behind the steam table and inserted one of two dozen tape cassettes reflecting his eclectic musical taste, from rock to holiday favorites. "I play it all the time," he said. "I can't function without it." Next he brought out what he calls his "doctor bag," a large valise bulging with spices and kitchen tools: knives and spoons, spatulas and ladles, and a huge bottle of his own personal Cajun mix for catfish. "I don't offer my secrets to other chefs," he volunteered as I peered inquiringly inside the bottle. "They're all jealous of me anyway."

Just then the second mechanic slapped the door of one of the elevators. "It's working now," he announced. "Comes with a fifty-fifty guarantee, too." Then, gathering his tools and stepping out the galley door, he added with a wink and a chortle, "Fifty seconds or fifty feet!" Nobody laughed. They had heard that one too often.

Things were looking up, even though it was 12:15 and the second and third cooks still had not arrived. Outside, a pickup truck trundled down the platform with huge duffels of linen for the sleepers. "Need another silverware rack for the dishwasher," John said, apropos of nothing, then doffed his tunic and set to cleaning the steam table. A lump of dry ice slumped in one of the steam table pans, thoroughly stuck. "Someone dumped it here for no good reason," John said, prising it out with a spatula and scrubbing down the surfaces with disinfectant. "I would *never* treat a train like this! A lot of people want to be a chef, but they don't want the responsibility. If you write them up they call you a snitch."

At 12:30 a refrigerated truck delivered the lead service attendant and his provisions to the lounge car next door. Fifteen minutes later the stainless steel steam table and dishwashing counter shone, although the floor needed considerably more than the lick and promise John gave it. That was all the time he had, because a tractor arrived with two wagons laden with supplies, Lela following close aboard. She disappeared upstairs while John and his number-one waiter, a wiry, diminutive young man named Alfredo Gomez, immediately set to work unloading the wagons.

First John manhandled four fifty-pound blocks of dry ice the length of the galley and into the dry storage area. "The FDA says I'm not supposed to use dry ice," he said, "but Amtrak's quality assurance people say I'm supposed to. Who do I obey? The FDA says I'm supposed to defrost chickens by running them under water, which I do, but quality assurance says I'm supposed to defrost them in the refrigerators. How do I do that if we don't have room in the refrigerator to put stuff away that's supposed to be stored there? If I do that it'll be seven o'clock before we could start dinner. Everybody got these big ideas and they just throw 'em at us and say do 'em, but nobody up there ever actually ever does the job." He snorted contemptuously.

John and Alfredo worked fast and hard. They stored most of the supplies in long racks running the length of the car and across one side. John showed me how cardboard milk cartons must be stored in the refrigerator on their sides rather than their bottoms, so the rocking of the train won't topple them. And they must be stored with the arrows on their spouts pointing up so they don't leak. (So *that's* what those arrows are for!) Romaine lettuce, iceberg lettuce, precooked bacon rolled aboard. So did the second cook, Altagracia Romo, a short and rotund young woman. She arrived at 12:45, forty-five minutes past her reporting time. "My car wouldn't start," she said dolefully. John quickly forgave her. He trained her, and she's good. "There's a reporter back there," he told her, pointing in my direction. She stepped over, gravely shook my hand, and favored me with a gnomic secret: "We cook downstairs and serve upstairs."

"Chief, if you're on board I need some pillows lifted!" crackled the loudspeaker.

I dashed upstairs to see what was going on. A coach attendant had complained to Reggie that he was short of pillows and had no time to order more from the commissary. "Go over to Forty-eight and get some," the chief said. "I'll be right behind you—I need trays for the waiters, and the Twenty-five sleeper has no coffeepot." The two stepped off the train and climbed aboard the train on the next track, Number 48, the *Lake Shore Limited*, scheduled to depart for New York and Boston three hours after the *Zephyr*. Number 48 was still dark, empty and awaiting the cleaners, and shortly the two furtive buccaneers returned, laden with booty. Number 48's crew, of course, would have to make up its sudden shortage by plundering whatever train happened to be on the next track. Raiding the neighboring unit to make good shortages of supplies is a time-honored practice the Army calls "dog-robbing," but Amtrak crews have no particular term for such intramural pillage. They just do it.

"When the commissary tells me they have no coach pillows in stock, that means I have to go on another train and take theirs," Reggie said. "What else you want me to tell the passengers? We have no pillows because the company didn't order any? Or do you want me to just hope that before this night train over there goes out, another train will be coming in and the chief can just take from it?"

Coach and sleeper attendants had just arrived in the diner for a splash of coffee before finishing up the squaring away of their cars. Cleaning crew, mostly women, napped in coach seats, their jobs done. Everywhere I saw displays of respect and affection—from hearty handshakes and quick, shy hugs to warm, grinning two-armed embraces—even between members of different races. Amtrak says it makes mighty efforts to recruit and promote minorities and women, and the results it achieves are probably not markedly different from those of other progressive American institutions: Things are better than they used to be, but there's still a long way to go. I've heard plenty of racist and sexist comments, veiled and not so veiled, from both whites and blacks among Amtrak crews. Still, it is difficult not to get the impression from the interracial friendliness of many individual crew members upon meeting for a six-day run that Amtrak, like the military, may be a step ahead of most everybody else.

Lela in particular received, and gave, a great many hugs. A few older crew seemed standoffish, as if they considered such displays undignified. One of the maintenance men, spotting my camera, said to Lela, "You're going to be in *Playboy!*" The on-board crew picked up the joke, snowballing it into japes about centerfolds. Lela laughed in great flashes of white teeth.

An electrician assigned to Number 7, the *Empire Builder* bound for Portland and Seattle, dropped by and embraced Lela. They whispered together for a moment and walked outside, reappearing by the hatch on the side of the dining car that allows access to the air-conditioning machinery. The electrician disappeared inside for a few minutes. He emerged, nodded, hugged Lela once more, and returned to his train.

He's Amtrak's best refrigeration-equipment electrician, Lela told me back in the diner, and he and his wife are special chums of hers. When he completes his work on the *Builder*, he often helps out Lela because, she said, the electricians assigned to the *Zephyr* lack get-up-and-go. Her friend plans to quit Amtrak, she added, and go into business for himself in Wisconsin. He's disgusted that yard electricians who slack off their jobs make the same money he does. "There's little accountability in the yards," she said, "and that's why I depend on all the friendships I've made over the years."

With just an occasional Russian-style locution in her precise but melodious speech, Lela Janushkowsky is sturdy, warm and attractive. Today she is dressed smartly in well-tailored blue Amtrak uniform skirt and jacket, subtly fragrant with Jessica McClintock lilac scent. I asked if she preferred skirts to the slacks worn by most female service crew members. "I don't look good in slacks," she said. "If I lose fifteen more pounds, I'll go back to slacks." I refrained from comment, being rather square-built myself, with a low and broad center of gravity.

Though she appears to be what once was called a classic California blonde, Lela was born in a displaced-persons camp in Germany not long after the end of World War II. She is the daughter of Russian and Polish physicians.

"We emigrated to Sacramento when I was three years old, in the early fifties, and we still speak Russian at home," she said. It was the heyday of the House Committee on Un-American Activities and of Tail-Gunner Joe McCarthy, the vicious witch hunter of the U.S. Senate, and immigrants with Russian surnames were suspect. "I was really proud that my family didn't shy away from our background. They always made me proud of my heritage, and I never knew that it was such a terrible time until I read about it later in school. A lot of families that came over with us never allowed their children to learn the family's native language. They wanted them to become American. 'Don't let anybody know you speak Russian,' they told their children. I'm very thankful to my parents for never burdening their children with that prejudice, and I had a great childhood in Sacramento—two brothers, one sister, the Brownie Scouts."

Her father is still in practice, though on "his brink of retiring," she said. Lela could have become a doctor herself, she said. "I had all the support at home to finish college and go into the medical field." Like so many headstrong young Californians in the 1970s, she chose to drop out during her junior year at the state college in Sacramento to work in a pathology lab. "It was a memorable job," she said. "I enjoyed it, but I'd rather work with people rather than people's parts—you know, tissues. I like being with people, and I enjoy to travel. When the opportunity came to join Amtrak, I jumped at it."

A friend in Amtrak management, a supervisor in Los Angeles whose position was cut during a reorganization, was allowed to choose any job that remained open. Two were as dining-car service attendants, or waiters. "She called me up and said, 'You know, this is a fantastic job. Why don't you think about it? You work on the train for a week, you get a whole week off.' That was perfect for me. So I hired out in September of '75. I went through no training class—you either sunk or swam. They put me on a train with a nice crew and sent me to Chicago the next day."

Lela had never in her life waited on tables, but, she said, that first trip gave her the "best training possible. It was one-on-one. The crew helped me, showed me, and I think I got better training than those I've seen come out of massive three-week classes." (A few years later Lela herself would work as a trainer for new waiters.)

A month after starting, Lela was laid off for eight months. At that time Amtrak had a short busy season, ridership dropping off dramatically during the fall and winter months, "unlike today, where there is no off season—there's just more and even more passengers, you know. Our train is never empty. Numbers Five and Six will always be busy."

The lowest point in Lela's career was the summer of 1981, also one of the nadirs of Amtrak's history, when Congress told the railroad that its dining cars had at least to break even, and in self-defense it decreed microwave cooking in all its diners. "I thought that was the end of my career," Lela said. "I didn't think I could do it anymore. I wasn't proud of the product, I was embarrassed.

"I was the first steward out of Oakland with this new prepackaged microwave product on June 15, 1981, and it was just pitiful. It was during the time of the Irish Republican Army hunger strikes, when Bobby Sands starved himself, and I envisioned a headline in the *National Enquirer:* 'The Day the Passengers Went on a Hunger Strike.' I couldn't believe they would eat this stuff. It was horrible. Here we had them trapped in the dining car, and we were feeding them this terrible product."

Lela is proud of her role in pulling Amtrak cuisine up from the pits. As the early eighties wore on, management realized its mistake. It asked for a steward and a chef from each crew base to attend a conference in Washington to design new meals. Lela was one of those stewards. They demonstrated how a pre-plated microwave meal actually cost more to serve than if each item on the plate was prepared separately in the oven or on the grill. For instance, it was much cheaper, Lela said, "to buy a big pan of lasagna and cut it into separate pieces and assemble the plates."

In 1983 Amtrak returned to full-service dining cars, and anyone who dines regularly on the train will agree that it has continued to improve the "product" by sending its chefs to the Culinary Institute, as well as encouraging them to be creative with stock-issue ingredients rather than cook to rigid recipes. Occasionally a passenger can suffer an indifferent meal prepared by a mediocre chef on the verge of retirement, or perhaps by an inexperienced second cook serving as chef when Amtrak is shorthanded. But the bad old days of terrible Amtrak dining-car meals are, thank heaven, gone forever.

Down in the galley John, Alfredo and Altagracia had been stowing for an hour, squeezing everything carefully into the limited space. Tucking nine 37½-foot rolls of heavyweight aluminum foil next to the grill, John said, "Many chefs don't put their own stuff away, but I do because I want to know where it is so I can get at it fast. Besides which, I have to show them how because if you let some of the guys put it away by themselves, it'll be all over the floor and you can't get around it and it'll take you half an hour to get to the bathroom." Even so, crates of oranges and potatoes occupied the aisle in the center of the galley between cooking and dishwashing areas. There was just enough room to squeeze by. Now I understood why dining-car menus are limited to just a few entrees. There just isn't space to stow the supplies for more.

John held up four gallons of Heinz Barbecue Sauce and grimaced. "They should send us ketchup," he said contemptuously, " 'cause they don't know nothin' about barbecue sauce." He will, however, use the Heinz as a base for his own recipe.

"Michael Campbell, if you want to live, get those maps back aboard or I'll kill you!" snapped a woman's voice on the loudspeaker. Prudence, I decided, required keeping one's head down. I did not investigate.

At 1:45 P.M. the lights flickered out in the galley and all through the train. The *Zephyr*'s electrical cables had been disconnected from the "hotel power" mains in the yard so that the locomotives could be coupled onto the head end. The kitchen fell dark and gloomy except for battery-fed emergency bulbs and weak light from the galley door. "We're not supposed to work in the dark," said John, who kept on stuffing shelves in the shadows. "But what can we do? All this needs to be done and I got no time."

At 1:50 the train shuddered gently as the couplers locked again. Minutes later electricity flooded in from the locomotive generators, and light again bathed the galley.

"Carpenter to the dining car!" Here I should have gone up and inquired. Amtrak cars are constructed of stainless steel, plastic and synthetic carpeting; I can't think what object would have required the services of a tradesman in wood. Possibly somebody was being summoned by name, not craft.

At two o'clock the third cook still had not appeared, and Reggie loomed in the doorway. "Maybe I'll have to be the third cook," he said. John nodded, but he glowered to himself. "Chiefs want to come down here and tell me how to run my kitchen," he said after his superior disappeared upstairs. "I've been doing it all my life. They don't know nothing about it."

Upstairs another problem had cropped up. All the coffee the

commissary had given the dining car turned out to be decaffeinated. "Let's tell the passengers it's real coffee," a female waiter declared. "No, don't lie to these people," Lela said. "Admit it's decaf." The worst caffeine addicts, the waiter argued, could get their high-test in the lounge car, whose supplies are made up and delivered separately from those for the diner. Lela insisted otherwise. "I'll get a couple of cans from the station commissary when the train gets in," she told me, shaking her head. "It won't be enough to last the trip, but it's the best I can do. Some of these people . . ." She let the sentence trail away unfinished.

"Train Number Five departing for C.U.S.," a melodious voice murmured over the loudspeaker at 2:05 P.M. *"Have a good trip. We'll see you on the rebound."*

Slowly the *Zephyr* slid astern from the yards toward its departure berth in Chicago Union Station nearly a mile away. The last potato had been stowed, and the galley had taken on an air of scruffy neatness, like a freshly scrubbed, cowlicked small boy.

"Time to cook!" John said gaily. Immediately he poured five quarts of milk into a two-gallon pan on the steam table, opening and setting the tall containers on their sides almost faster than the eye could follow, letting the milk gurgle into the pan. John wastes no time, not even the few seconds it takes to empty a milk container. As the last trickles of milk dripped into the pan, John prised open a gallon of marinara sauce and poured it into a tall round stainless steel bowl. "For the lasagna," he said, adding spices and condiments so fast I had no time to note their labels. I did see, however, that the lasagna was Stouffer's Food Service brand in six-pound trays. John thrust two of the trays into the oven.

Whirling about, he picked up a steel pan of large baking potatoes, scrubbed each under running water and finger-sprinkled it with vegetable oil. Into the oven went the pan. "Forty-five minutes to an hour at three hundred seventy-five degrees," he said. "I'll cook the steaks, prime ribs and fish to order, but I'll start the chicken just before we leave."

Inside the terminal the slowly rolling *Zephyr* paused briefly—a "safety stop" while backing into a station is a federal regulation, thanks to one too many accidents in which a train overshot its mark and crashed through the bumping post at the end of the track—then inched the last fifty yards to a halt on Track 28 at the eastern edge of Chicago Union Station's brightly lighted south concourse. It was 2:15 P.M., one hour and twenty minutes before departure time.

TWO

At the very moment the *California Zephyr* tied up on Track 28, the inbound *Lake Shore Limited* arrived on neighboring Track 26 an hour late from New York and Boston, backing in as the *Zephyr* had done. Most incoming Amtrak trains reverse direction outside Union Station in order to keep the noisy locomotives, and the worst of their diesel exhaust, away from the concourse. Metra commuter trains back in also; they run in "push-pull" fashion, their locomotives always facing outward.

Attendants opened their cars' doors to a great hustle and bustle of incoming and departing Metra trains. Almost as soon as the *Lake Shore Limited* halted, John dashed over to it to dog-rob an extra coffee pot for his galley. It was 2:30, and upstairs the waiters busily set tables, filled salt and pepper shakers (always washed after each trip) and wrapped stainless steel cutlery in paper napkins. I followed Lela off the train and into the small, lively satellite commissary in the basement underneath the concourse. Besides the coffee, Lela needed eight more serving trays for the diner, plus a few last-minute items she'd forgotten to back-order, such as small packets of condiments.

A grizzly-haired, hard-hatted commissary worker leaped to do Lela's bidding. As he handed her the supplies like an eager puppy proffering a ball, Lela kissed him squarely, and moistly, on the mouth. "He hates me because I'm beautiful!" she announced as he blushed in confounded surprise. Every face in the place split in a grin.

Waving gaily, Lela swept out of the commissary and up the ramp into the concourse. At the ticket counter she picked up a large black sample case containing the meal checks and cash for the trip. As she returned to the train, I strode through the low-ceilinged passageway into the broad, high-vaulted waiting room and took a deep breath. The place never fails to stir my imagination.

For almost a century the phrase "going down to the depot" rang out throughout American life. Like cathedrals in the Middle Ages and piazzas in the Renaissance, railroad stations were great gathering places of people and goods. Lovers met "under the clock" and townsmen and women shopped in terminal shops and mingled in terminal restaurants while baggage handlers unloaded goods and newspapers in freight rooms. George H. Douglas observes in his superb 1992 book *All Aboard! The Railroad in American Life* that "many developments that have been said to be the product of the automobile were tried first by the railroad. The huge malls found almost everywhere today were in fact pioneered by the railroads back in the early years of the twentieth century. The great city terminals—South Station in Boston, Grand Central in New York— were malls even before the word 'mall' was brought into use."

The men who ran these malls, however, have no modern equivalent, though their titles and official duties survive. The station agent of the nineteenth century was the local representative of the railroad; he sold tickets, arranged freight shipments, sent messages over the telegraph and communicated with train crews. "In some communities," Douglas writes, "he became a figure of some note, a social eminence, even a father confessor. It was not unheard of that the station agent doubled in brass as barber, postmaster, express agent, real estate dealer, seed salesman, druggist, florist, cemetery manager, even dentist. In small-town America he was often the focal point of the social life in these places where the coming of the accommodation train was the only event that broke up tedious and sleepy afternoons. As such, he was the great hero of small boys and the interlocutor of roustabouts, idlers, roisterers, and crackerbarrel philosophers."

Their stations were not merely exchanges of commerce but also information. News arrived by train, most often in the form of metropolitan dailies but also in fresh gossip from debarking passengers. During the last quarter of the nineteenth century, telegraph offices brought news not only of train movements but also momentous events that had occurred scant hours before.

News was made, too, in both great urban stations and small-town depots. Presidential candidates' campaign trains rolled in on "whistle stops" to bolster the faithful and convert the skeptics. They still do it today, simply as a traditional lark and for a few seconds of sound-bite time for television news, but as late as 1948 the whistle-stop trip made a difference in a presidential campaign, helping the Democratic incumbent, Harry Truman, upset the polls and defeat Thomas E. Dewey.

A different sort of news came out of big-city terminals when each day reporters and lensmen met embarking and detraining celebrities for a quote and a photo: a senator departing for Washington on the Baltimore & Ohio's *Capitol Limited*, a Hollywood actress in mink debarking from the Santa Fe's *Super Chief*. This harmless fluff lasted through the 1950s and died with the luxury limiteds. In the late 1960s, when I was a copyreader for the old *Chicago Daily News*, the paper tried to revive the custom at the airport with a sleek blonde society reporter it called Sally O'Hare. The stunt was short-lived; by that time the reading public no longer cared about the comings and goings of celebrities, but what they did in bed and with whom. (Still the custom survives in the memories of a few publicists. Just the other day, as I write this, Melvin Belli's press agent tried to promote an impromptu press conference at Chicago

Union Station during the flamboyant criminal lawyer's three-hour layover between trains on his way from the West Coast to the East to deliver a speech. Nobody seemed interested.)

Stations also were a haven for derelicts and a magnet for crime, especially in the big cities. Footpads, cutpurses and pickpockets snaked through crowds and pederasts haunted lavatories. Today the homeless are still with us, especially in New York City's underground Penn Station, but pimps seeking to recruit fresh young women off the farm hang out in Greyhound and Trailways bus stations.

Many writers have praised the early American railroads for their democracy. From the beginning, they said, American passenger cars featured a single long compartment where all classes could mix, while Europeans preferred to separate the aristocratic from the commoners in small compartments seating half a dozen. American railway stations also were places where classes and races mixed; the depots, said the writers, were accessible to all levels of society.

That was true to a point, but there was also considerable myth in the assertion. Southern railroads herded blacks into bare Jim Crow cars and segregated station waiting rooms and drinking fountains. The big Northern railroads soon fielded spartan cars for smelly immigrants, and their terminals shepherded gangs of laborers and new arrivals from Ellis Island into shabby, flea-infested immigrant waiting rooms so that the prosperous would not have to mix with the poor. Gender also entered into the equation of separateness; some stations featured women's waiting rooms as well as men's smoking rooms so that the "fairer sex" need not endure the smoke and juice of tobacco addicts.

Whatever the democratic trappings of a station, with it the traveler from afar could size up at a glance the community in which he had just arrived. Its station—which ranged from a simple shelter to a grandiose temple—would give clues to the town's size, its affluence, the livelihoods and professions of its citizens, their standing in society, and especially their taste in architecture.

The first American railroad stations hardly merited a second look. They were converted wayside homes, hotels or inns onto which (if the tracks came close enough) long verandas were built to shelter travelers from the elements. The first purpose-built stations, ironwork-and-glass train sheds, were the unmemorable work of engineers, not architects. By the 1850s, however, architects began to realize that the railroad station, as well as the county courthouse, was a fitting subject for their talents as designers of public edifices. For city terminals many favored the Italianate style, with bell and clock towers. They dressed small wooden rural stations in Country Gothic and Gothic Revival styles, trying to make the most of a standard, inexpensive, cookie-cutter architecture.

In the days before sleeping cars became common, larger rural stations often did double duty as hotels. I spent much of my boyhood on my grandparents' farm near a famous relic of that age in Susquehanna, Pennsylvania. There the Erie Railroad's Civil War–era Starrucca House, a long, barnlike brick structure, served the old main line to Buffalo and Chicago. My grandfather often took me to visit it in the 1940s, when the Erie still used it. Now and then today I drop by to see that it still stands, partly restored and housing a restaurant, on what is now a secondary line lightly used by Conrail and the New York, Susquehanna & Western Railroad.

Susquehanna was once a brawny railroad town known the world over for its sprawling Erie locomotive shops as well as the great stone Starrucca Viaduct of 1848 just outside town, still carrying long and heavy freight trains after almost a century and a half. The little town is now remembered if at all as the birthplace of B. F. Skinner, the behavioral psychologist famous for running rats through mazes. In the 1970s and 1980s its most prominent citizen was the novelist John Gardner, who perished in a motorcycle accident on the highway high above the old Erie main line one rainy day in 1982.

It was during the late Victorian age and the Edwardian age, when capitalists did things on an obsessively heroic scale, that the grand railroad terminal became an architectural monument in America. Jeffrey Richards and John M. MacKenzie, keen observers of the British railway scene, described the terminals at their florid best when they wrote in matching prose that the stations—American and continental as well as British—were "great, echoing halls of glass and iron, colonnaded, canopied, buttressed and turreted, living temples to the worship of King Steam."

In London today, you can still see what the authors meant. The ornate St. Pancras and Victoria Stations still exist as they were built, hosting thousands of long-distance travelers and commuters every day. Daniel Burnham's colossal Union Station of Washington, D.C., not only still stands but, after long neglect, was refurbished and rebuilt by Amtrak in the 1980s so thoroughly that it is not only an architectural monument but also a modern multiple-use mall whose ancestors George Douglas perceived in the old stations. Cincinnati's long-shuttered Union Terminal, an endearing Art Deco pile of 1933 that from the front looks like an old table radio, also was recently rebuilt with Amtrak's help, reopening in 1992 as a natural history museum as well as a stop for Amtrak's Chicago-to-Washington *Cardinal.*

New York has not fared so well. The monumental 1913 Beaux Arts edifice called Grand Central Terminal has managed to elude the wrecker's ball, but it's now just a sally port for commuters from and to the north. Grand Central's 1910 sister, Pennsylvania Station, has been less lucky. Penn Station's old underground warren of tracks still serves Amtrak trains, but the magnificent Roman Revival structure above them was torn down in 1963 for the misnamed and misshapen Madison Square Garden building.

Part of the reason so many grand old terminals were lost in the 1960s is that affluent people with the power to save them had moved to the suburbs and cared little for the structures of the city. What the railroad companies' real estate analysts failed to understand in the 1970s was that this lack of fondness was beginning to extend to the workplace as well. Now much of the office space in the high-rise towers thrown up over the old stations lies vacant, victim of wholesale corporate defection to the far suburbs. At least Penn Station in death left one enduring legacy: Public anger over its demise gave rise to New York's landmarks law and the Landmarks Preservation Commission.

Another of Amtrak's smart decisions in the late 1980s and early 1990s was to participate in rebuilding some of these grand stations. Washington Union Station was the first to be refurbished, followed by others—most notably Cincinnati Union Terminal, Philadelphia's 30th Street Station and Chicago Union Station, with New York City's colonnaded Post Office across the street from Penn Station waiting in the wings to be converted into a palatial passenger depot. They were throwbacks to the old days when railroad stations were the architectural and social centers of the cities they served, and they attracted new riders in droves. The renovation and rebuilding did not cost Amtrak great sums; the railroad worked with private developers who installed shops and malls and absorbed most of the financial burden.

In Chicago, stations that were built to last centuries lingered only a little more than fifty years. In the heyday of passenger trains, the 1½ square miles of business district were surrounded by railroad tracks, freight houses and no fewer than six passenger stations. Today only half each of two—North Western Station and Union Station—remain as stations. The grand vaulted Roman-style gray Maine granite headhouse of the former was torn down early in the 1980s, leaving only the train shed to be fronted by a nondescript steel-and-glass skyscraper.

The oldest of the six main terminals, Dearborn Station just south of the Loop, still stands as an architectural monument, though its train shed and tracks were demolished long ago. Built in 1885 in High Victorian Gothic style, it looks like a Transylvanian castle. Originally it had a huge clock tower with a singularly ugly hood of a roof that looked like an enormous foreskin; the tower was clumsily circumcised by fire in 1922 and replaced with a smaller, squarish roof. Once called the Polk Street Station, it was home to Santa Fe, Erie, Wabash, Monon, Grand Trunk and Chicago & Eastern Illinois trains. When Chicagoans decided to honor their structures by naming them for north-south streets pointing to the Loop, the name was changed to Dearborn. It faded with the passenger railroads after 1960 and finally shut its doors in 1971.

The undistinguished 1902 La Salle Street Station, originally called the Van Buren Street Station, looked like an office building and was. For years its eleven stories housed the executive offices of the Rock Island and the regional offices of the New York Central and Nickel Plate Road.

Central Station on the city's front stoop, Grant Park, was never called that. Chicagoans knew the eccentric, mostly Romanesque structure of 1893 as Illinois Central Station, or, more familiarly, IC Station. Only long-distance riders used it; commuters arrived and departed at another station farther up Michigan Avenue. The great trains Central Station hosted were the Illinois Central's *Panama Limited* and *City of New Orleans*. Amtrak used the station for a year, but in 1972 managed to connect the IC tracks with those leading to Union Station, and Central closed the same year. It was demolished in 1974.

The jewel in Chicago's railroad crown was Grand Central Station, architecturally the most beautiful of the six sisters. Modest in size, the warm and graceful Norman fortress held only six tracks in its train shed as well as a five-story office building and a 247-foot-high campanile. Grand Central was built by the Wisconsin Central in 1890 and a few years later was sold to the Baltimore & Ohio, whose *Capitol Limited* called it home. It was torn down in 1971.

The architect Daniel Burnham, whose Union Station in Washington, D.C., set the standard for American terminals, wanted a true Chicago Union Station that would gather all Chicago's passenger trains under one roof, but the vast web of incoming tracks proved impossible to relocate. After his death his firm changed the original plans—which carried remarkable echoes of Penn Station, especially in the Roman Revival riverfront concourse building—to reflect the rapid rise in real estate values after 1910. A low office building was grafted atop the headhouse and its waiting room, like Penn Station's, modeled on the Baths of Caracalla.

Union Station today is a symbol of what has happened to latter-day American passenger railroading. In 1969, when everybody thought passenger trains were headed for the scrap heap, the station's owner railroads decided that only commuters would be riding trains in the 1970s and 1980s. Palatial accommodations therefore were no longer necessary. The concourse building was torn down and its air rights sold for a nondescript office tower.

The adjoining headhouse and its glorious barrel-vaulted waiting room survived. Its interior was and still is monumental in feeling. Everything is on a vast scale, including the twenty large Corinthian columns and the walls of Roman travertine. Great indoor space is ennobling; it gives people a sense of worth, the idea that humanity has value. That great space, however, is expensive to heat and maintain, and Amtrak wants eventually to tear down the headhouse and drive another steel-and-glass office tower high into the sky above the waiting room. The depression in land values and glut of office space that struck Chicago during the early 1990s, however, gave the headhouse a reprieve that may last years.

After the concourse building was demolished, its lower level became a low-ceilinged maze of dim chutes and dingy shops guiding rivers of lemmings from commuter trains to the headhouse and streets. In the late 1960s and early 1970s, I was one of those lemmings—a Burlington commuter from west suburban La Grange.

Amtrak fooled everybody by not only surviving but also prospering. By the late 1980s so many new passengers had come to Amtrak that its long-distance trains sold out during the summer and sleeping car space was difficult to get at any time of the year. So popular had the national carrier become that its federal operating subsidy steadily had dwindled from more than 58 percent of revenues in 1971 to 21 percent in 1992—the best ratio among the world's nationalized passenger railways.

To continue attracting trade, Amtrak needed to greet departing and arriving passengers with something better than a musty dungeon in Chicago, still the hub of American passenger-train transportation. In the mid-1980s Amtrak set out to rebuild the concourse interior; during the summer of 1991 the job finally was done. And for the most part it looks as if it was done right.

The lower level of the concourse seems almost as if it had been made over by a disciple of Raymond Loewy, the brilliant industrial designer of the 1920s and 1930s who favored the style of Art Deco, especially for his railroad work. The marble walls and wide terrazzo floors of the new mezzanine are an enormous improvement over the Skinnerian rat mazes of the seventies; Amtrak passengers and hurrying commuters are now separated, a blessing for everyone during rush hour. Brass railings, metal ceiling panels and shiny train gate soffits recall the 1930s, when passenger trains were still at their zenith. The whole reflects an appealing mix of old technology and new, just like Amtrak itself.

Flashing my ticket at the attendant, I entered Amtrak's first-class Metropolitan Lounge. I had never seen the lounge; it had just opened a few months before. Open to all holders of sleeping-car tickets, the lounge is warmly inviting, like the lobby of a modern two-star hotel that caters to middle-class guests and doesn't put on airs. Over marble and granite floors and subdued colorful carpeting sits an eclectic choice of overstuffed chairs and sofas, with a cheery gas fireplace on one cherry-paneled wall and a large TV set on another. Custom fixtures bathe the room in soft and indirect lighting. Multicolored video train boards announce arrivals and departures, while a bank of pay phones and a sideboard of free coffee and soft drinks complete the ensemble. (No free alcohol, however, as in airport first-class lounges. Amtrak has difficulties enough with boozy passengers and does not need to help them top off their tanks.)

For all the latter-day changes in railroad stations, they are still places where people come and people go. In his 1950 book *Steam Up*, Eric Treacy, an Anglican bishop who was a connoisseur of "station farewells," wrote:

> There are those who scorn any demonstration of affection in public. As the train leaves, with an unnatural casualness they will separate with never so much as a pressure of the hand; others there are who, oblivious of the world around them, stand gazing into each other's eyes, spending their last few moments clasped in each other's arms—matching a succession of last kisses—to separate with a look

of bewildered agony on their faces. Then there is that numerous class of people for whom 'seeing people off' is a bit of an outing, not one minute of which is to be lost. So they stand cheerfully by the carriage window revealing in loud voices the personal secrets of the wretched traveller, who winces as he realizes that he has to travel two hundred miles with a carriage full of strangers who know his family history, how prone he is to chills if he wears a damp vest, what he has to do when he arrives at his destination.

This was the railway station in England in the first half of the century; the scene in Chicago Union Station near the end of the second half of the century is hardly so melodramatic. Yet there are imaginative rewards for the traveler willing to study his fellow passengers. Unlike the antiseptically utilitarian O'Hare Airport terminals, temporary holding tanks for passengers who squirt in on one flight and squirt out on another twenty minutes later, Union Station still can display homely little dramas of humanity. While everyone in an airport waiting lounge tries not to notice one another, there is time and space in a railroad terminal to contemplate one's fellow passengers.

What are their stories? Has a weeping family reunited to bury a loved one? Why does this young girl seem so frightened as she kisses her sailor lover good-bye? The eye naturally goes to her tummy. Is that only a slight protuberance or is it a pregnancy? That stolid Hispanic family sitting unmoving amid a small mountain of suitcases, eyes focused on the distance: Is theirs a picture of south-of-the-border peasant endurance amid urban Anglo indifference and hostility? Probably not—if they're first-class passengers, they're most likely just bored Houstonians waiting for the *Texas Eagle* to depart later in the afternoon.

A young woman dressed for success in heels and a gray woolen suit tapped away at the keyboard of an IBM PS/2, hooked by telephone cable to the Prodigy telecommunications service. She was calling up the weather report for Minneapolis/St. Paul. Very likely a passenger on the *Empire Builder* to Minnesota, I thought. A lawyer, perhaps, or some other kind of businesswoman? On occasional tables all over the lounge, complimentary copies of both Chicago dailies, *USA Today, The New York Times, The Wall Street Journal* and *Investors Business Daily* lay in smart rows like regiments of salesmen. Evidently Amtrak is attempting to win the business traveler away from the airlines, at least for the short hauls to Milwaukee, Detroit and downstate Illinois.

At this hour, just before the *Empire Builder* and the *California Zephyr* were to depart, the lounge was packed standing-room-only—a phenomenon that gave me pause. If the place is full already, what happens a few years down the road if Amtrak continues to attract new passengers? At any rate, I saw only a few business suits. Nearly everyone dressed casually, many in jeans or lumpy sweats and some in après-ski attire, all belying the place's middle-class-hotel ambience. In the old days, travel was a rite, and Americans dressed up for it, men in coats and ties and women in skirts. That began to change when the airliner crammed passengers into tight rows of seats barely large enough for the average American posterior. Business travelers still have to put up with wrinkles, but the rest choose comfort.

Nevertheless, the first-class denizens seemed a noticeable cut above the hundreds of coach passengers, slouched on hard plastic seats over naked tile floors in their glass-walled departure lounge. The place was bright and clean, bare and practical, like a rural county airport. Some of the passengers looked like—and probably were—rough trade that customarily traveled by Harley-Davidson rather than train. Others affected varying degrees of punkitude, one young man's particular pride the spikiest green Mohawk this side of Trafalgar Square. Completing his ensemble was a heavily studded black leather motorcycle jacket. Close by, several chunky Mennonites sat all in a row like blue-denimed haystacks, determinedly ignoring the display of extremes in modern fashion. Most passengers, of course, dressed ordinarily, some in threadbare polyester and run-down heels, some in jackets and ties, but the great majority in casual middle-class attire. A big-city railroad passenger terminal reflects all American society, and in about the usual proportions.

. . .

A figure loomed close by. It was a stubbly, middle-aged white man in a shabby suit. "Can you help me out, sir?" he said. "I've lost my wallet and I've got to get to Detroit tonight."

Even after years of encounters with urban hustlers, I can't help taking people at face value—at least until they show their true colors. But I'm too smart to open my wallet to strangers in apparent distress. Taking the man by the elbow, I said, "Travelers Aid is over there," pointing him in its direction. "They'll help you."

"Not that!" he shouted. "Not *that!*" A cloud of garlicky alcohol billowed into my nostrils as his face contorted with a snarl. He turned on his heel and stalked away in as much of a huff as he could muster.

I smiled. He reminded me of the small black boys who used to pluck incoming white commuters of their spare change at Union Station by hoodwinking them with convincingly piteous, tear-stained stories of losing all their lunch money as well as bus fare and having to get home to help Mama. Some of them made small fortunes, working different tracks each day so that the same commuters wouldn't spot them. Nonetheless, I recall seeing the same one half a dozen times in a month before he disappeared, presumably having been rousted by a station cop.

But then I winced as another old memory of Union Station surfaced. I had just dismounted from my Burlington commuter train when someone tugged at my sleeve. It was a short balding man in his fifties, panting and sweating heavily. "Help me, sir," he said. "I'm . . ." I did not quite catch the rest; he was a moving target for a lip-reader as the crowd jostled and pressed against my back. The usual hustle, I thought, and not a very original one either. I irritatedly shook my head and strode on with the flow of commuters.

Just as I emerged into the waiting room, it came to me with a sudden chill what the man had said: "I'm having trouble with my heart."

In embarrassed dismay I turned and paddled my way back through the surf of travelers. What a son of a bitch the poor guy must think I am! I searched and searched in the swirling eddies of the crowd, but there was no sign of him. I hoped he had been able to find a willing Samaritan. Maybe he was already on his way to the hospital. Then I spotted him hunched in a phone booth, receiver to his ear.

I dashed over and rapped on the glass door. "I'm sorry," I tried to say. "I'm deaf and didn't understand. . . ."

He pushed open the booth door and waved me off. "Go away," he said.

"But I want to help," I said.

"I don't need your help!" he replied. "Go *away!*" He pulled the door closed and turned his back.

For the next year that I continued to commute from La Grange, I looked for him on the platforms and in the trains, wanting to explain what had happened, that it was all an honest mistake, that I was not the callous bastard he must have thought. But I never saw him again.

Maybe that's why I just can't give the quick brush-off to obvious hustlers even today. If there's a chance he's really in distress . . .

"May I have your attention please? Trains Number Five, Twenty-five and Thirty-five, the California Zephyr, *the* Desert Wind, *and the* Pioneer, *are preparing to board. Passengers please go to Gate C for boarding."*

A few minutes earlier the sleeper passengers had filed out through a door in the lounge to their cars, and now a flood of coach riders surged to the sliding glass doors of Gate C, guarded by a small but fearsome figure, a short, blue-uniformed black woman with a fierce expression and a sergeant's voice that needed no electronic amplification.

"We will board in small groups!" she boomed. "*Walk!* Do not run!" The passengers crowded closer, some pressing luggage carts into the backs of annoyed riders ahead of them. Nervous vibrations of expectation fluttered among the passengers, as if they were Indianapolis racing cars trembling with revving. Though the *Zephyr* is an all-reserved train, coach seating is catch-as-catch-can, and many passengers anxiously hoped for choice window seats. It was 3:10 P.M.

At the head of the line glittered a short, obese black man in a turn-of-the-century gray frock coat. Every one of his fingers was encrusted with bejeweled golden rings and his neck bent from the weight of a large diamond-studded ruby medallion on a thick gilt chain. At his elbow was an equally elephantine woman in bright orange dashiki and colorful kerchief. With them stood a tall, slim young white woman, also dashiki-clad. A minor African potentate with his wife and European secretary? I wondered. Or a flamboyant storefront minister with mate and mistress? Before I could inquire, the glass gate cracked open and they surged through, a redcap wheeling ahead the trio's small mountain of Louis Vuitton luggage. I never saw them again.

Nor would I locate aboard the train the tanned, wrinkled, late-middle-aged white cowgirl in tasseled Western boots in the crush just behind me. Peroxided and whipcord-lean in Levis so tight they looked as if they had been Sanforized on her, she also wore a snug red-and-white gingham blouse stunningly thrust out into Atlas-Centaur nose cones in Frederick's-of-Hollywood fashion. It was hard not to gape at her either, and the "American Gothic" farm couple next to her fought to keep their eyes straight ahead.

The glass doors swung open again, and the crowd trickled dutifully past the glowering little Cerberus. Once on the platform, a few passengers trotted and at least one ponytailed young man broke into a sprint. But he decelerated to a saunter at the small gauntlet of conductors standing by the last car. I followed slowly, the stream of passengers swirling and eddying about me, until I found my sleeper. Boarding it, I stood in the open vestibule and watched the last riders trickle aboard.

"Attention, please! Trains Five, Twenty-five and Thirty-five are about to depart for Denver and points west. All visitors please leave the train—now!"

Up ahead, the three silver-gray, 3,000-horsepower Electro-Motive F40 locomotives loomed motionless through the gloom of the train shed, nose to tail like elephants waiting for a rap from the mahout's baton. The exhausts of the lead engines burbled at an idle, drowned out by the chesty roar of the third, running at full revolutions to provide electrical power for the quickly stirring train.

"If you are a visitor on board, you have just become a passenger on board!"

Attendants hustled out the stragglers and mine motioned me to stand aside so that he could close the door of our car. A moment later, as I peered out the small vestibule window, baggage-car doors slammed shut and carts clanked away behind their tractors. On the platform near the middle of the train, the conductor peered at his timepiece. *"BoooaaARD!"* he sang in a rising inflection. At precisely 3:35 P.M., with a bark into his hand radio, he stepped up into his train "right on the advertised," as old railroaders used to say.

THREE

With two long hoots on his horn, the engineer notched forward the throttle. The locomotives surged into high revolutions, the banshee roar of their combined 9,000 horsepower rattling the dim train shed. Huge electric alternators, driven by diesel prime movers, rammed high-voltage direct current into whining traction motors on the locomotives' axles. Slowly, like massive dray horses into their traces, the three engines leaned into their load. The *California Zephyr* was on its way to Oakland, two-thirds of a continent distant.

Emerging from the train shed into daylight, the locomotives tiptoed gingerly through scores of switches, towing their long rope of cars southward across a broad sea of tracks. Past a huddle of darkened double-deck Metra commuter trains, past the huge Amtrak coach yards, past ready tracks of drowsing locomotives glided the *Zephyr*. At an ancient brick building emblazoned in badly faded letters, "BAKING POWDER 25 OUNCES FOR 25 CENTS," the train leaned west onto the Burlington Northern main line, gathered its skirts, and hustled into a lope.

Piles of ties and tracklaying equipment, an abandoned brewery and small yardfuls of freight cars receded in the *Zephyr*'s wake. Just three minutes after departure she reached a steady gallop of fifty miles per hour, and at Western Avenue flashed past a vast yard of train-borne trailers awaiting tractors to haul them away, then long ranks of empty automobile carriers. Every mile or so the train's wash dusted an abandoned, boarded-up signal tower, derelict of the computer age. At Harlem Avenue the inbound *Zephyr*, Number 6, burst past us, on time. A moment later we dashed by Cicero and a towheaded small boy at trackside, saluting with upraised middle finger. I have often wondered why suburban kids flip the bird at trains while country youngsters wave. . . .

"This is the chief of on-board services, Reggie Howard. You'll recognize me as the tall man in blue blazer and gray slacks. . . . " This is how life begins on a long-distance train—the chief's opening spiel on the PA system. Reggie continued, explaining in detail the locations of drinking-water fountains and restrooms and how they worked, that smoking was limited to sleeper rooms and the lower level of the lounge car, that passengers must wear shoes at all times, the dining-car seatings, happy hour in the lounge car, tonight's movie and a thousand and one other details.

The first few minutes of departure are my favorite time on a train. I'm not quite settled in, still eagerly anticipating the adventure of going somewhere, still learning my surroundings, which always seem fresh and new although I have occupied them scores of times. It is a time of expectant change.

These moments always remind me of a passage from one of T. S. Eliot's *Four Quartets*. In a poem called "The Dry Salvages" Eliot captures perfectly the passengers' heady sense of loosing the bonds of time as the train slowly accelerates away from the platform:

> *Their faces relax from grief into relief,*
> *To the sleepy rhythm of a hundred hours.*
> *Fare forward, travellers! not escaping from the past*
> *Into different lives, or into any future . . .*

Traveling by train does not, of course, alter one's ultimate fate, but in that enchanted time when the rails first converge in the distance behind the train, my life and its burdens also recede into the twilight, as I am carried off to uncharted territory.

My compartment, Room 14 on the lower level of Car 3530, was in the *Desert Wind* section of the combined train, and I would occupy it until Denver. I had been unable to book a ticket all the way through to Oakland in the *California Zephyr* section, which had been sold out from Chicago for months. Next morning, however, a Chicago-to-Denver passenger would vacate his *Zephyr* room, and I would move up a few cars to take it over for the rest of the journey.

At three feet, six inches wide by six feet, six inches long, Room 14 is an "economy" bedroom. It's about the size of a very tall pup tent, but more upscale. There are two facing seats, a narrow closet just large enough for a couple of jackets, and a picture window that runs the length of the room. These snug little earth-toned rooms are ample for singles but less so for a couple, especially if both members are corpulent. The seats unfold into a twenty-eight-inch-wide bed, and a twenty-four-inch-wide berth drops from the ceiling above the window. The lower bunk is quite comfortable, the upper rack best for small or skinny people. More than once I have slept above; so narrow is it that every time I turn over I take the sheets and blankets with me, baring my backside. More cleavage is displayed through those economy bedroom doors than onstage at an opera.

Four economy rooms share the lower level of a Superliner sleeper, with a large "family" compartment occupying one end and a commodious bedroom for a wheelchair user and companion at the other end. In between are four small lavatories and (in some newly rebuilt sleepers) a shower room. On the upper level, ten economy rooms run halfway down the car, five to either side of the aisle; five large deluxe bedrooms with private shower-toilets occupy the other half.

Just as I was beginning to feel settled in, an angry hubbub echoed down the stairwell. I climbed up to investigate. A gesticulating knot of a dozen passengers surrounded the conductor. They were vacationing Germans, and they were angry only as vacationing Germans with their noses out of joint can be. The attendant looked weary, as if the trip had ended almost before it began.

The Germans, he said, had been told by their travel agent in Stuttgart that they were booked into deluxe bedrooms with all the amenities, but their tickets entitled them only to economy bedrooms. "Ain't no way to start a trip," moaned the attendant, who saw half his tips disappearing. "Ninety-nine percent of our accommodations problems are caused by travel agents who don't know anything about Amtrak."

Shrugging sympathetically, I returned to the lower level. As I reached my compartment the door to the handicapped bedroom opened, and a tall, stunningly attractive woman emerged. She smiled at my shy consternation. Even in what must have been her mid-fifties she was head-turningly beautiful. She was dressed in expensively simple good taste, understated gold and diamond jewelry at neck and wrists. She was cordial yet uneffusive, clearly a woman comfortable in any milieu in which she might find herself.

" 'Allo," she said, lightly placing her hand on my arm and reducing me to jelly. She was a Québecoise now living in San Francisco, whose husband—a handsome but vacant-looking gray-haired man visible on his seat over her shoulder—was recovering from a recent stroke, which had all but paralyzed his left side. He did not require a wheelchair, she said, but some of the sleeper stairways had handrails on only one side—as did ours. Though he could manage going up (she bearing nearly all his weight from below) because the handrail was on his good side, he could not come down. Therefore he would have to remain in the room for the entire trip, she said, adding that, like me, she and her husband would change sleepers (with assistance, of course) at Denver. "I hope the constant coming and going of ze attendant will not be a bother." Shaking my head far more than necessary, I assured her it would not.

At that moment a sandy-bearded man in his forties who was a

ringer for Sir Francis Drake loomed in the corridor. "Tickets, please," he said pleasantly, punch at the ready.

In the days before Amtrak, and through many of its early years, the conductor was the undisputed king of the train, responsible for everything aboard, including the service. His authority evolved slowly. During the 1830s and 1840s he was little more than an usher. "The conductor, or check-taker, or guard, or whatever he may be, wears no uniform," Dickens observed in *American Notes.* "He walks up and down the car, and in and out of it, as his fancy dictates, leans against the door with his hands in his pockets and stares at you, if you chance to be a stranger; or enters into the conversation with the passengers about him."

By the Civil War, however, the conductor had adopted formal dress, including a stovepipe hat. He now was a man of parts, able to project dignity, aplomb and absolute authority. In the 1880s he took on all the majesty of a master mariner. Indeed, passengers often called the imperious man in the gold-buttoned blue-serge suit "Captain."

Almost always the conductor had worked his way up from an extraordinarily perilous job. During the nineteenth century, freight-train brakemen had to stagger to and fro from lurching boxcars, wrestling massive brake wheels open and closed. Frequently they slipped on icy roofwalks and hurtled to injury or death. The early cars were coupled together only by simple links and pins, and it was the brakeman's job to stand between cars being pushed together by a locomotive, dropping pin into link at the last second. Mishaps were frequent and fatal. Brakemen therefore tended to be a cranky, misanthropic bunch, and when they finally worked their way into the blue uniform it was hard to blame them for being more often grouchy and brusque than kindly and avuncular.

Complaints about conductors are hardly new. In *Across the Plains* Robert Louis Stevenson told of an encounter aboard an emigrant train bound for California in 1879: "I asked a conductor one day at what time the train would stop for dinner; as he made no answer I repeated the question, with a like result; a third time I returned to the charge, and then Jack-in-office looked me coolly in the face for several seconds and turned ostentatiously away. I believe he was half ashamed of his brutality; for when another person made the same inquiry, although he still refused the information, he conde- scended to answer, and even to justify his reticence in a voice loud enough for me to hear. It was, he said, his principle not to tell people where they were to dine, for one answer led to many other questions, as what o'clock it was? or, how soon should we be there? and he could not afford to be eternally worried."

Sadly, conductors like that still can be found on Amtrak. Not, however, Mike Kemp, a familiar face on the *Zephyr*. He is no shirty "Jack-in-office," but a genial, relaxed man. His official title, "as- sistant conductor," is the genderless Amtrak term for brakeman, or "trainman" on some old passenger railroads. (Amtrak firemen are called "assistant engineers.")

I never get much chance to talk to Mike. With as many as five hundred tickets out of Chicago to lift, manifests to prepare for the next crew, difficult passengers to soothe and rambunctious chil- dren to corral during a 2¾-hour stint on the *Zephyr*, Mike and his crew (his boss was upstairs trying to placate the angry Germans) always seem too busy for more than a perfunctory chat. They live near the first *Zephyr* crew change point at Galesburg in western Illinois, and early every morning they take charge of Number 346, the eastbound *Illinois Zephyr*. This short-haul train from West Quincy, Missouri, arrives in Chicago just before noon. After a rest the crew works the *California Zephyr* back to Galesburg, stepping down at suppertime.

Over several trips I've pieced together a few facts about Mike. After two hitches in Vietnam as a Navy Seabee, Mike joined the Burlington in 1971 as a brakeman. He has been an Amtraker since 1987, when the passenger road decided to hire its own operating crews—engineers and conductors—rather than employ those of the freight railroads over which its trains run. That decision has had two important effects. One is that working for the same boss often (but not always) engenders better relations between the service crews—the car attendants, waiters, stewards and train chiefs, who remain aboard the train for its entire run—and the operating crews.

A related consequence is regular hours for the operating crews, which puts them in a better humor even though Amtrak pays less than the freight roads. Freight crews are on call at all hours of the day and night, never knowing when they might have to drop everything and go to work. "Whenever they decide to run a train, they call you," Mike said. "You may work one day or you may find out when the day is over you aren't going to work that day, and you work a lot in the middle of the night. Now I know exactly when I'm going to go to work and come home, and my family thinks that's the best thing that ever happened."

Since 1983, when Amtrak began employing on-board service chiefs, command has been divided between chiefs and conductors. Chiefs, as their title indicates, are accountable for the service and the conductors for mechanical operations. On paper the conductor is still number one aboard his train, but, Mike said, "it's much easier just to work together than with an attitude of 'I'm in charge of you' or 'You're in charge of me.' "

There are other compensations in working passenger instead of freight trains. Human cargo is always more interesting than inanimate goods. In the autumn of 1990, Mike said, he punched the tickets of nine Soviet veterans of the Afghan war. They had been invited by an American veterans organization to visit the Vietnam War Memorial in Washington, and hoped to find inspiration for their own memorial.

"It was like stepping back twenty years, almost like watching movies of the Vietnam era," Mike said. Like their American counterparts, the Soviet veterans were bitter toward a government they felt had betrayed them. They wanted to engrave the names of their fallen on the Afghan memorial, but the Kremlin either could not or would not provide them with the casualty records. The depth of their disenchantment surprised Mike, who is no stranger to indifferent officialdom. "When I told them I'd been to Vietnam, they just took me in like I was one of them," he said with deep emotion. "They gave me a little Soviet flag pin, and I gave them a United Transportation Union pin and a California Zephyr pin in return. When I finally got off the train at Galesburg, they raised a salute to me—a closed fist."

Later on, Mike said, he encountered a happier sort of Russian, "a little old lady who just tickled me, she was so sweet." At the time, Amtrak provided each sleeper passenger upon departure a package of snacks, including a split of California wine. With characteristic Russian generosity upon meeting a congenial stranger, the woman wanted to shower Mike with gifts from the package. "I had to explain to her that I couldn't take the wine—it's against the rules. Then she wanted to give me her potato chips and her crackers and everything, and I kept trying to tell her I appreciate it, but it's hers. She wrote down my kids' names and later sent them postcards from Leningrad. And when I got out of there I checked my pockets, and there were potato chips in one and pretzels in another. I don't know how she did it."

Mike said he wishes he had more time to talk with passengers— he considers "doing PR" part of his job. "I missed an opportunity the other day. There was another little old lady who got on the train that I would have loved to talk with. We were within half a minute of departure, and her daughter was with me standing by the last car saying, 'My mother's coming, my mother's coming.' But Amtrak won't allow us to wait for late passengers if we can't see them.

"Just at the last moment I saw this lady running through the concourse and out on the platform. It wasn't a little-old-person trot but a full run. She was picking them up and laying them down. And she got on the train and we were gone. I went back to her room and said, 'I'm glad you made it. You'd better sit down and catch your breath.' She said, 'No, no, I'm fine. I'm going to be seventy tomorrow.' And she goes on and on, happy as can be. How remarkable that a lady that age could come out of a dead run like she did, just bubbling and happy!

"I got too busy and never did get to talk to her. She was going to be a candidate for me and my partner Bob's 'Solid Gold-Colored Paper Clip Award' that we give out once in a while to special passengers. It's just kind of lighthearted, a little card that Bob's wife had printed up for us. We've got 'em in England and France and Russia and Australia and Belgium."

And on the bulletin board above my desk. It's a jumbo-sized, golden-hued steel paper clip over a calling card emblazoned with the Amtrak logo and reading, "This card verifies that the bearer has indeed received the highly coveted Solid Gold-Colored Paper Clip Award given only to those individuals deemed worthy of the honor."

Mike checked his watch—a Pulsar electronic wristwatch, not the conductor's massive golden pocket timepiece of old. Accurate timekeeping still is the rule on railroads. Before each run Amtrak crews synchronize their watches (always railroad-approved analog timepieces with white face, black numerals and sweep second hand) at the standard clock in each crew base, which daily is set to the official time calculated by cesium atomic clocks at the U.S. Naval Observatory in Washington and the Bureau of Standards and Technology in Boulder, Colorado.

In exactly twelve minutes, Mike said, the *Zephyr* was to arrive at Naperville, where an ailing elderly man would board the train for Omaha. "He asked for lower level seating in a coach next to an electrical outlet so he can plug in his breathing equipment, and we have to be sure to save that seat for him." With a smile and a casual salute Mike disappeared upstairs, heading toward the rear coaches.

The *Zephyr* now rocketed at an effortless sixty miles per hour past La Grange, fifteen miles out from Chicago, and I decided to return to the diner to catch up with John and Lela. Mounting the stairs, I walked through the sleeper toward the front of the train and emerged in the second Los Angeles coach. An interesting tableau presented itself: a harassed-looking conductor and a stocky, brush-cut fellow in a business suit squatted in the aisle. They were whispering with a blowsy-haired, rheumy-eyed woman slouched in her seat, clutching an unlighted cigarette in one hand and a book of matches in the other. As I approached, the reek of stale alcohol assaulted my nostrils.

"I'm sorry, ma'am, but you can smoke *only* on the lower level of the lounge car," said the man in the suit. His tone was low and soothing, and he smiled gently. "Otherwise the smoke would bother all the other passengers here, and we wouldn't want that, would we?"

"I'm going from Chicago to San Franshisco," said the woman, slurring slightly. "I only have ten dollars."

"Okay," said the man. "Don't worry."

"It would help if I could smoke."

"I can do a couple of things for you," said the man. "The first thing is that we can miscellaneous-bill you for your meals while you're on board."

"You can do that?"

"Yes, we can. We'll keep a running tab and mail you the bill."

"My Social Shecurity check comes in to Alameda, California, on the fourth."

"That's fine," he said. "I'll introduce you to the dining car steward."

"Cigarettes, too?"

"Cigarettes? You've still got ten dollars. I can't miscellaneous-bill you for that. However—"

"Coffee?"

"Coffee you can get in the lower lounge car."

"Food?"

"Now the food you can eat in the dining car and that's two cars forward."

"You mean the shnack bar?"

"No, that's the dining car."

"I can eat in the *dining car*?"

"Yes. Real good food. Now smoking—you have to smoke in the lounge car."

"Where is that?"

"That would be your third car forward."

"I got run over by a truck five years ago. My feet, they told me I'd never walk again, but I walked."

"One other item, ma'am," interjected the conductor, trying to maintain a patient expression but losing the battle. "In order to get you to San Francisco we'll have to eventually put you in another car three cars forward. We can either do that in Naperville at the next stop or in Denver tomorrow morning."

"Okay."

"Whatever's easier on you," the conductor said.

"I'll be in Denver?" she said.

"You'll be there tomorrow morning for about an hour."

"How long will I be there?"

"An hour," said the man in the suit.

"He's in the brokerage business, he's a nephew of mine," said the woman, her voice rising. "And then I wouldn't have to ride on a tab?" The woman did not explain who "he" was.

"If you'd like to ride from here to Denver that's no problem," he replied, still in the soothing voice and with the gentle smile.

"Excuse me for shouting, I don't think she knows I'm on vacation, she's trying to—" she said.

"I will talk to the dining car steward. What is your name, ma'am?"

"Mildred McCaskey."

"Mildred McCaskey?" the man said, writing in a notebook.

"Exchange widow. Sixteen years ago I regained my virginity."

"Okay. I'll tell the steward you'll be in for dinner."

"You're about the age of my middle child. I have a forty-four-year old, a thirty-year-old, a thirty-nine-year-old and a twenty-nine-year-old. How many children do I even have?"

"No, no," said the man, whose smile was still gentle and friendly, although I thought I saw his eyelid twitch.

"She's gorgeous. I hate her. She's getting married in September. The race will be over."

"What we can do, like I said, is—"

"You're Irish?"

"Very. I'll tell the steward you're coming. We'll get your address and—"

"That's why I'm going to California. My rich baby daughter, she, seven years ago, gets out of college, she doesn't know I'm taking it over again."

"Well, that's okay," said the man, rising to his feet. "We just want you to enjoy yourself. Like I say, we'll do anything we can to help you out."

"Can I ask you a question off the subject?"

"Sure," said the man with a small sigh.

"Chicago is a bigger station than Grand Central in New York. There's not a wooden bench left in Grand Central, 'cause of the homeless, excuse the privilege. They sleep there."

"Sure."

"They've boarded up the whole Grand Central waiting room. They're making a shopping mall out of it. You've got more benches than the Smithsonian, but you don't have any homeless in Chicago."

"Sure, we've got a few."

"Where do you keep them in the daytime?"

"I guess they just wander around in the streets."

"You feed them?"

"There are different programs."

"How many do you got?"

"I couldn't tell you."

"You're not homeless, but you will be," she said.

"I'm sure I will be," he said.

"I hope you say your prayers? Save your money? I get a pension check which just covers my trip to San Francisco and my dear little twenty-nine-year-old baby daughter, who's the only one like me in the whole bloody Republican conservative rich family, lent me eighty-five dollars for food. Which thirty dollars I ate on the way here and the other thirty dollars I gave for this ticket and the other ten dollars I spent on beer and cigarettes and I got to get from San Francisco to Alameda, California, over the Golden Gate Bridge and that's a long walk for my feet. And a hurricane or a tornado or an earthquake will happen, I'm sure. I have to eat."

"Well, I'll take care of you in the diner," said the man, who refrained from pointing out that it was the Oakland Bay Bridge she meant, and that in any case Alameda was next door to Oakland; she wouldn't even have to take the bus across the bay to San Francisco. "I'll tell the steward. They'll be starting dinner at five o'clock."

"Are these new cars?" she said.

"In the last ten years, yes."

"Ten years!" she said, wiggling the seat reclining control. "Then why is this broken?"

"That's not broken."

"I tried it. It doesn't stay up."

"You're right," said the man. "That one doesn't work."

"I know all about mechanics," she said. "My car's always in the shop."

"At least you don't have to hang from the ceiling," he said.

"I've done that, too," she said.

In the lounge car I sat down next to the man in the suit and complimented him on his world-class patience. He was Don Cushine, train manager of the *Zephyr*, riding today on an inspection trip. I asked how the drama had begun.

The woman had boarded half stewed, Don said, and had wanted to light up in her coach. Reminded by the conductor that the lower level of the lounge car was the only place she could smoke, she'd put up a drunken fuss. The conductors had considered putting her off at the first stop, Naperville, so that she wouldn't disturb the rest of the passengers. "People like her calm down for a while and get out of hand again," Don said. "But she seems a little confused. I told the steward to take care of her, and make sure she has no alcohol for the rest of the trip."

Don is the kind of up-and-coming young manager all business enterprises seek: personable, educated and ambitious, yet sensitive to human vagaries, perhaps because of his early experience in the trenches of heavy manual labor. A powerfully built fellow of thirty-five in the final days of his bachelorhood, he is a rugby addict and plays in international competition with Chicago's Lincoln Park club. Indeed, rugby indirectly led to his career with Amtrak. During the late seventies, when Don graduated from Brockport State University near Rochester, New York, a fellow college rugger enthusiast told Don that Amtrak was hiring workers to rebuild an abandoned twelve-mile stretch of track near Albany in order to knock forty-five minutes to an hour off the time of its Chicago-to-Boston trains. "I said, 'Gee, I just went to college. I don't know if I really want to swing a hammer for the rest of my life.' " But Don took the job. "Amtrak wanted to keep the costs low," he said, "so we used old thirty-nine-foot sections of rail, old tie plates, old joint bars, and an old World War II Army crane to put the rails down. We used new ties and spikes but did everything by hand. We did it under budget and we did it under time."

Track work, Don added, is dangerous, especially done the old way, with a spike maul like the one John Henry swung in the old ballad. "A master spike driver can place a dime on top of a spike and flatten it unrecognizably in one blow," Don said. Inexperience, however, is perilous. Once Don took a mighty swing and struck his spike just a tad off center, the maul kicking upward a large piece of stone ballast that shattered his safety goggles. One doesn't wear that equipment just because a fussy federal agency demands it.

When the project was done, Don was laid off, as he had expected. He didn't mind; he had been a marketing major and, after traveling over the winter, wanted to land a business job. In the spring, however, his savings had been depleted. When Amtrak sent out a call for experienced trackmen for the Northeast Corridor outside New Brunswick, New Jersey, Don signed on.

Don and his 120 track-gang mates lived in old boxcars but ate well; a chef cooked all their meals. "With modern equipment we tore out old rail beds and built new ones. I was a scrap car operator. Its conveyor belt fed old spikes and anchors into a couple of bins that I dumped every half mile or so. After a summer I realized this was not where I wanted to head, so I put in for a transfer to Passenger Services."

He found a job in the Albany commissary, then over the next four years he "basically did all the station jobs—tickets, baggage, everything. Albany was a big station but not New York or Washington." All this time Don sought to wedge a foot in the management door. "It had always been 'We like your credentials, we know you like to work, but we have no openings at this time.' Then in 1983 the train chiefs program began, and suddenly there were an instant 150 to 200 openings across the country. I became a *California Zephyr* chief out of Chicago in June 1983 and became train manager on January 1, 1987. I just love the *Zephyr*. It's my baby."

Does Don miss the traveling? "The nice part about being a train manager is that I still have to travel. I'll do surprise inspections. Sometimes I'll jump on in Chicago, as I did today. Sometimes I'll fly to a destination and hop on unannounced. I'll jump on one train and the next day jump on another going the other direction. I ride three or four times every month." Don, however, is not a railfan. "People call us closet buffs, but I see too much of it every day to want to do it for a hobby."

Gazing out the window of the lounge car as the train slowed for the 4:10 P.M. stop at Naperville, twenty-eight miles out, I was reminded of a bit of history that querulous, confused and drunken passengers like Mildred McCaskey likely would rather not know about. Certainly Amtrak would never think of putting the episode into its *Route Guide to the California Zephyr*, a leaflet that coach attendants place into the kangaroo pocket behind each seat before a trip.

It was almost exactly one o'clock in the afternoon on April 25, 1946, when a predecessor of the *Zephyr* called the *Advance Flyer*, westbound for Omaha and Lincoln, Nebraska, braked to an unscheduled halt at Naperville. A brakeman thought he had seen an object, perhaps a brake shoe, fly out from underneath the train, and had signaled the engineer to stop.

The *Advance Flyer*, with thirteen cars and 150 passengers, was the advance section of the Burlington's famous transcontinental express, the Oakland-bound *Exposition Flyer*, with eleven cars and 175 passengers. It was common during the heyday of passenger trains to run separate sections of the same name train a few minutes apart. The separate, shorter trains were easier to handle, especially at station stops, than enormously long stretches of passenger and mail cars. Both sections of the *Flyer* had left Chicago at 12:35 P.M. on separate tracks, but after a few miles merged on a single center track with the *Advance Flyer* in the lead, three minutes ahead of the following train. At 12:57 the *Advance Flyer* had raced through Downers Grove sixty seconds late, running at eighty miles per hour.

As the *Advance Flyer* drew to a stop, the Burlington's automatic traffic control system snapped into operation. A yellow light calling for caution blinked on well ahead of the *Exposition Flyer* a mile and a quarter east of Naperville. A red light ordering a mandatory stop flashed on a quarter of a mile behind the halted train. As the *Advance Flyer*'s engineer and conductor alighted from their train, looking for a damaged or overheated axle journal box, the rear brakeman ran back down the tracks for eight hundred feet with a large red flag, waving it back and forth as the rules required, as a fail-safe backup to the signal lights. To the brakeman's horror, he saw in the distance the *Exposition Flyer* roaring on, its speed undiminished.

The nation's press had a field day, even the sober *New York Times*. For more than a century terrible details of train wrecks had captivated American newspaper readers, and this one provided vivid nuggets of gore. "It came fast," the *Times* quoted a twenty-six-year-old wounded Marine it said was standing on the rear platform of the *Advance Flyer*. "I watched it horrified. The train came on, bigger and bigger. I saw a man climbing down out of the engine cab, and start down the ladder, that's all I saw. The next second it hit." Whether that Marine could have survived an eighty-miles-per-hour impact on the rear platform is doubtful—he most likely would have been crushed like a bug—but that's what the *Times* account said.

It is certain, however, that the man who jumped from the *Exposition Flyer*'s cab an instant before the crash was the fireman, and he was killed. The sixty-eight-year-old engineer, William W. Blaine, stayed at the throttle "as his big train raced on," the *Times* continued. "Then it struck. Its flat, silver nose plowed into the rear standard steel coach of the *Advance Flyer* as though it were a cigar box. For a second it appeared to pose in the air, tear through the roof, then plunge down with terrific force. It continued on through three-quarters of the length of the coach, ripping its top, spreading its sides and killing or maiming most of its occupants.

"The titanic crash shook the two trains, but almost all damage was confined to the *Advance Flyer*. The diner, just ahead of the telescoped coach, buckled under the impact, and was torn into a heap of shredded steel and debris. In all, six coaches were overturned on the *Advance Flyer*, and five on the *Exposition Flyer*."

Nearly all the forty-five dead were in the *Advance Flyer*'s rearmost coach and diner, and most of the one hundred injured were passengers in the two or three coaches just ahead. Aboard the *Exposition Flyer*, just half a dozen passengers were hurt.

In its late afternoon editions, the *Chicago Daily News* pulled out all the descriptive stops. "Bodies are lying all along the right of way," it quoted an eyewitness as saying. "Babies were thrown through windows. It was horrible . . . horrible." Nearly ten thousand spectators crowded around the wreck, the *Daily News* added, and their three thousand automobiles created an enormous gaper's block.

Help was swift in coming, however. Some eight hundred employees of the Kroehler furniture manufacturing company by the side of the tracks stopped work and ran out to help. Fifty students from North Central College volunteered to serve as litter bearers. "In minutes doctors, nurses and ambulances were racing to the scene from Aurora, Hinsdale, Downers Grove, Naperville and other communities," reported the *Times*. "Rescue lines were formed. Labor crews with acetylene torches started burning through twisted metal train plates to reach the injured and dead.

"The warehouse of the Kroehler Company was converted into a temporary hospital. . . . Three priests passed among the stricken and administered last sacraments of the Catholic Church."

Time magazine carried the most voyeuristic detail of all: "Alfred Wiley was at work in a diesel locomotive plant when he heard the fearful news. Frantically he borrowed a car, raced twenty-eight miles to Naperville. First he went to the bloody emergency stations and a hospital teeming with injured. They weren't there. Then he went to Naperville's three mortuaries. Nothing at the first or second. At the third he found the bodies of his wife and two children."

Miraculously, barely before the cloud of dust thrown up by the impact had settled, engineer Blaine crawled without help through the window of his cab, picked his way through the debris and staggered into the emergency hospital. Why did he fail to stop his train despite the signal lights, clearly visible and functioning properly? Burlington officials later duplicated the events leading to the accident, sending a test train past the signals. At the yellow light, traveling at the *Exposition Flyer*'s estimated eighty-six miles per hour, the engineer stopped the test train more than half a mile short of the crash point. Because engineers often "rode" yellow lights in order to keep to their schedules, the test engineer on the next trial run kept up speed until he reached the red light, then set full emergency brakes. With brake shoes smoking, the train had slowed to twenty miles per hour—a speed that would greatly have reduced the disaster—by the time it reached the crash point, and it stopped 393 feet beyond.

Blaine told the board of inquiry that he had hit the brakes at the first signal, and some of the crew on the *Exposition Flyer* testified that they had felt a slight but insignificant decrease in speed just before the crash. Blaine, who never gave a satisfactory explanation to the board, later was charged with manslaughter but never was tried, perhaps because of his advanced age.

That was on the editorial minds of two Chicago papers, the *Tribune* and the *Daily News*, both of which blamed union seniority rules that put old men at the throttles of high-speed trains. The *Daily News* editorialized: "A radical change in custom . . . would seem to be in order. . . . Experience, seniority and faithful service should be rewarded but not at the expense of public safety."

The argument could also be made that Murphy's Law was bound to catch up with the perilous practice of running two trains three minutes apart at eighty miles per hour on the same track. Nonetheless, accidents involving the operation of multiple sections of a limited express were few, thanks to careful signaling and human alertness. Today Amtrak does not have enough cars to run more than one section of a train, although it could easily fill two and perhaps three *California Zephyrs* during the holidays. Still the practice survives, in different fashion. Like railroad dispatchers, air traffic controllers shepherd 727s and DC-10s through the airlanes to the runways of O'Hare and LaGuardia scarcely sixty seconds apart. It's a profession for young people with quick reflexes.

It's still true that speed of response undiminished by age is important for the safe operation of trains. An Amtrak engineer told me about an incident that could have killed him and many of his passengers had he not reacted quickly to an unexpected peril.

Wally Prince, a tall, burly man in his early fifties with brown hair combed forward into Prince Valiant bangs, is a veteran who early in his career fired the original *California Zephyr* for the Chicago, Burlington & Quincy. He has been a railroader for thirty-two years, twenty-five of them as an engineer, working out of Galesburg, Illinois.

"We got as much responsibility as an airplane pilot, but we don't get paid nowhere near what they get," Wally said. "This train's got five hundred people on it, and we're on it for eight hours going seventy-nine miles an hour. Crews used to have like one-hundred-mile runs. Now we're running almost four hundred miles. If the old-timers knew what we're doing now, running a train seventy-nine miles an hour for four hundred miles, they wouldn't believe it."

One day Wally took an eastbound *Zephyr* out of Lincoln, Nebraska, and performed a running test of the air brakes, mandatory after a crew change. Air pressure keeps the brakes open; releasing the pressure applies the brakes. "They worked fine," Wally said, "and I took the train about twenty-four miles to a point where I had to slow from seventy-nine to thirty miles an hour to go through a turnout, or switch. I 'set the air' on the train. Nothing happens. So I set more air. Nothing happens. So I throw the whole train into emergency." That means dumping all air pressure; the effect is "like slamming on the brakes of your car and just standing on them. Nothing happens. We kept picking up speed.

"So I quickly grabbed the radio and asked the conductor, 'Is the train in emergency?' He said, 'No.' I yelled, 'Put it in emergency!' He did, and we stopped just in time. Had I not thought quick enough, we would have turned over when we hit the turnout and the fireman and I probably would have got killed. In fact, we'd have rolled half that train over and killed some passengers."

After the train stopped, Wally climbed from the cab, walked back down his train and discovered that one of the valves between the cars that controls the brake air pressure had vibrated shut, preventing the brakes from being applied in the locomotive, although they could be operated from back in the train. "When we got to Omaha I sent the fireman back to check the valve, and it was starting to vibrate shut again. So we got some wire and tied it open."

Wally believes that if the train had derailed and rolled over, the valve that had vibrated shut would have been jarred open again in the wreck, disguising the malfunction. "And I would probably have been blamed for not paying attention to my job," he said wearily. "See, it's easy to criticize somebody after they're dead."

As with airline crashes, Wally's experience emphasizes that disasters can be caused not only by human error but also by malfunctioning machinery—and averted by quick thinking based on long experience. Because railroading is an old and commonplace technology, it's easy to forget that those who sit in the engineer's seat still hold their passengers' lives in the palms of their hands.

. . .

As the *Zephyr* pulled away from Naperville, my historical reverie dissipated as Lela's crisp, melodious voice awakened the PA system.

"This is Lela Janushkowsky, your dining-car steward. The train chief and I will be coming through the cars taking reservations for dinner in the dining car. The first seating will be at five o'clock. The next seating will be at six-fifteen, then seven forty-five, then last call. Tonight's entrees are as follows: New York strip steak, oven baked chicken. . . ."

Scarcely had the PA speakers cooled down when John's voice crackled, *"This is the chef. That's not oven baked chicken we're having. It's* barbecued *chicken!"*

"The smart chef *never* has oven-baked chicken the first night," John explained when I caught up with him in the galley. "If you serve barbecued chicken the second night, everybody thinks it's leftovers from the first night and you can't sell it. So I always barbecues my chicken the first night."

Laura Andrews, John's third cook, finally had arrived at 2:45 P.M., shortly after I had gone into the Union Station concourse with Lela. A slim, pony-tailed young woman with just six months on the railroad ("I got tired of having a regular job," she told me), she worked from the Chicago "extra board," on call all hours of the day or night for a run anywhere in the country. She had been called just three hours before. John immediately put her to work washing and preparing the chickens—four large trayfuls, each holding twenty-four two-piece servings—while he fixed the rice side dish to serve with the chicken. Some Amtrak chefs use Uncle Ben's Spanish Rice straight from the box, but John prefers to make a pilaf with the Uncle Ben's as a base, adding chopped tomatoes, vegetables and his own seasoning.

Without stopping to pause John poured frozen baby carrots, clunk-clunk-clunkety-clunk, into a large pan on the steam table, following it with "au jus" for the prime rib in another container. Dissatisfied with the young third cook's handiwork, he re-prepared the chicken by wrapping wing and drumstick breasts into what he called a "figure 8," tucking leg under wing in what looked like a wrestler's hold. "I do this so when I take out the cooked chicken with my fork, they won't flop out into two pieces. Makes things go faster."

Next John sprinkled vegetable oil on the chicken, then seasoned it with cracked black pepper and "my special mix"—salt, pepper, garlic, onion powder and celery salt in a large shaker. As he confided the ingredients of the mix in a low voice, the third cook drifted by with another pan of chicken and John fell theatrically silent. Trade secrets are trade secrets, his tight smile seemed to say. Again he sprinkled oil on the chicken, and into the oven went the trays. "Three hundred fifty degrees for forty-five minutes," he said.

John wore an apron of thick doubled toweling and a chef's hat, having hung up the baseball cap when he began cooking. Now that the heat from the ovens began to warm the galley, John worked in a T-shirt, donning his tunic only when he went upstairs to meet his public.

Now Altagracia chopped mushrooms and onions and Laura cut tomatoes. John stopped by Laura's table to demonstrate exactly how he wanted them done—to me his handiwork looked exactly like Laura's, but then I'm no chef—and returned to the steam table to begin preparing his New York strip steaks, some of which he pre-grills lightly before the first seating, finishing them to order. Opening two cans of mushrooms, he poured out the juice and with a sharp paring knife sculpted the mushrooms into delicate fans. "It's not required, but it looks better on the steaks," he said. He did the same with whole radishes, carving them into florets for garnish on the catfish.

Glancing at his watch, John said, "I don't usually make mashed potatoes this early, but in a little while we'll hit some rough track, and if I don't make 'em now they'll slop all over the steam table." Pouring a generous slug of milk into a container of powdered potatoes, he whipped the mixture briskly with a whisk, then dumped it into a double pan "so they don't cook too fast." All the while he paused now and then to stir the carrots. John worked almost too quickly for the eye to catch everything he did.

John then folded Altagracia's chopped mushrooms into the

marinara sauce, and slid a plate of her chopped onions into the microwave. "Microwave elements all shot out," he said as the onions took longer to heat than he expected. "Because I'm making a pilaf with that Spanish rice, I'll use the seasoning packets that came with it for a mix to roll the catfish in." Now for his *pièce de résistance,* a dill sauce for the catfish. Using low-calorie ranch dressing for a base, he added a splash of low-calorie Italian dressing, sprinkling the mixture with garlic and onion powders, dill weed and mustard.

Lela stepped downstairs and announced that lots of room was available for all seatings, surprising with such a heavy passenger load. "Word of mouth," John said confidently, in the eternal chef's claim. "They'll come." As diners return to the cars after the first seating, he added, they'll sing his praises to passengers who otherwise would opt for a sandwich in the lounge car.

John set to his barbecue sauce. Using the bland Heinz sauce as a foundation, he built upon it a superstructure of large dashes of Worcestershire sauce, generous pinches of celery salt, garlic salt, onion salt, several squirts of Tabasco sauce, great splashes of mustard, maple syrup intended for pancakes and French toast, and the juice of several lemons. After mixing it all thoroughly in a large stainless steel bowl, John set it aside and changed the cassette on his boom box. He kept the music low, swaying now and then and snapping his fingers to the beat, always in motion, never stopping to rest.

Whang! Whang! The dining car suddenly jolted from side to side, nearly pitching me off my feet. The car rocked briefly and settled down once again to a gentle rumble as the train reached smoother track. "See what I mean?" John said. "The mashed potatoes woulda been all over us if I'd been fixing them when we hit that spot."

John removed his baked potatoes from the oven and piled them behind the grill, where they would remain hot. "I'll save me a pan of firm ones for home fries at breakfast tomorrow," he said. "*Much* better than those canned spuds. I leave mine at the commissary. I bake whole potatoes halfway, and the next morning I dice them up and I make pan-fried potatoes. I use green peppers and season them down."

Doesn't Amtrak care that he's using fresh potatoes instead of the canned stuff?

"No. It's cheaper to use fresh spuds. Some guys in the commissary don't like your being too independent, but the chiefs always tell them to give me what I need."

Is he ever refused?

"They tried to in Oakland. They had a note up there in the commissary that said, 'No backorders to enter the trains.' So I took the note off and I went upstairs to the boss and said, 'Could I get a copy of this, please?' I put the copy in my pocket and went to the train, and the steward came aboard and said, 'Oh, the commissary chief says she made a mistake and you can have anything you want.' You have to use intimidation sometimes."

Altagracia began zebra-peeling, then slicing cucumbers and green bell peppers for the salads, Laura washing and tearing lettuce. ("A good chef wants his lettuce torn, never cut," John said.) Altagracia, I notice, has been working with John in the oven half of the car, Laura in the dishwasher/refrigerator half on the other side of the central vestibule.

At 4:40 P.M. John scrubbed his grill with vegetable oil and scraped it clean with a fragment of box cardboard. Laura sliced pies and carefully placed the slices on edge in foam bowls. A few moments later John removed the two pans of lasagna from the oven. One pan, not quite done, went back in; John nestled the other into the steam table. He tested the chicken, still in the oven. One of the most common complaints about Amtrak dining-car meals is dried-out chicken. Experienced riders often order chicken only at the first seating, before it's had time to dehydrate on the steam table. How does John solve that problem? "I keep the chicken in the oven where it'll stay moist," he said.

Twice during the last half hour Reggie dropped by to check on preparations and twice John complained about the dirty galley. "I want it written up in the trip report," he said emphatically. The chief nodded, making a note.

At 4:55 the salads were done, the desserts ready, the side dishes—rice, mashed potatoes, carrots, broccoli—ready to serve. Pre-grilled steaks and prime rib still in individual plastic wrappings lay stacked next to the grill. "Most of the first seating will be from the sleepers," John said. "Because their meals are complimentary they'll order the expensive stuff, the fourteen-dollar prime rib and steaks, rather than chicken and fish. But when word of mouth gets around, the fish will go at the later seatings."

I began to understand some of the problems of dining-car cookery. An Amtrak Superliner diner contains seventy-two seats, four of which are reserved for the crew, leaving sixty-eight for the passengers. Of a full 500-passenger load out of Chicago on the *Zephyr*, as many as 250 riders may want dinner in the diner. That means four seatings in four hours. It's imperative to get the dishes on the table as soon as possible after the passengers place their orders. That's why it's necessary to prepare ahead as much as possible, minimizing the time-consuming cooking to order.

I headed upstairs to the dining level for the 5:00 P.M. seating. Lela put me at a table with another singleton—a cheerful law student from Rio de Janeiro on vacation—and a young couple from Australia who had squirreled away their salaries for two years to see the world. ("Mum and Dad thought we were saving for a house. Were they ever surprised!")

Lela helped a blind passenger with a seeing-eye dog into a booth. The dog, a large black Lab, lay out of sight under the table. The opposite seats were taken by two other blind passengers, companions of the first. The waiter, clearly experienced in dealing with unsighted customers, announced the position of each dish on the table as he served it. "Now your salad is in front of you," he said, "and your water is on the right." He then read the menu aloud, marking the customers' choices on the meal checks.

"If your destination is Princeton," bellowed the conductor on the PA, *"this is your chance!"*

Lela brought our meal checks just as the dining car halted directly across from the little station at Princeton in west central Illinois, 104 miles from Chicago, almost ten minutes before the scheduled 5:20 P.M. departure. I asked Alfredo what he'd recommend. "The fish or the chicken," he said forthrightly. "Not the steak, I'm afraid. The meat they delivered today is a little tough." I'd planned on the catfish anyway. When it came less than ten minutes later, Alfredo twirled the plate so that the entree lay closest to me, a graceful restaurant-style touch. That helped put out of mind the picnicky foam plastic dishes.

All the same, what was on the plate looked attractive. The catfish lay bifurcated by a delicate stripe of dill sauce, a generous helping of pilaf to one side. On the other side John had laid a garnish of orange slice, tomato slice, cucumber slice and that lovely radish flower, and a large sprig of broccoli. The fish was extraordinarily delectable, with a delicate taste beautifully complemented by the dill sauce. Only the broccoli seemed wanting; it was tough and stringy, not of good quality to begin with. Add two rolls with butter, a vegetable salad with French dressing, and tea—and the tab to a coach passenger would have been eleven dollars (my sleeper ticket included all meals for the trip). Few other eleven-dollar meals I have had matched that one.

In the galley between seatings there was a lull, rare for the *Zephyr*'s first night out. Over a cigarette by the dishwashing machine—"the designated smoking area"—John said, "We'll serve breakfast at six tomorrow so we can get everybody fed before Denver. Other days we'll start at six-thirty." He tapped his wristwatch, which bore on its dial a likeness of Santa Claus. "Passenger gave it to me," said John.

Don't passengers ever tip John in cash?

"Yes, forty or fifty dollars a trip, and I use the money to buy spices and stuff I need. That way it's no money out of my own pocket."

Does anyone ever send food back? I asked.

"Oh, yes, every night we'll have a couple of passengers that for some reason or other may not like their meal. There may be four people at a table. This one has fish, this one has chicken, this one has steak. This one has lasagna and may have seen how good the fish looked, heard how great it tasted. She's going to find something wrong with the lasagna so she can get the fish. If she sends it back, I just make whatever she wants. Try to keep them happy, you know."

At 6:20 P.M., the meal checks again flooded down a glass-fronted chute to the galley from the dining level above. Altagracia read them aloud. With great economy of movement John arranged a plate with garnish and a spoonful of pilaf, then bedded a catfish fillet. With a careful flourish he poured a stripe of dill sauce across the catfish and handed the plate to Altagracia. Next he arranged a chicken plate, but when he forked a wrapped wing and leg out of the pan, the "figure-8" combination flopped open into two loose pieces. "Makes a liar of me," John said with an embarrassed laugh. As he slid a well-done steak onto still another plate, fanning mushrooms on the meat, a misdirected squirt of juice splattered his trousers. "I get a seventy-five-dollar allowance every six months from Amtrak for uniforms," he said, "but it costs me seventy-five dollars a week just to get them cleaned." He popped open a baked potato. Altagracia added the vegetables, Laura garnished the whole with parsley and sent it up the dumbwaiter with the catfish plate. Everyone worked in constant, synchronized motion.

At 6:25 Lela appeared. "More kids than we thought," she said. John turned to the freezer for a double handful of children's dinners, slipping them into the microwave to thaw. The train slowed for its station stop at Galesburg, and I took my leave.

At the last seating, it turned out, almost everybody had the catfish. Word of mouth.

FOUR

Like an impatient rooster stealing a march on dawn, the *California Zephyr*'s horn blared its arrival at Galesburg early, thanks to its heavily padded schedule. Every experienced air traveler grumbles about barefaced airline claims that a flight has left on time if it pulls away from the gate at the appointed hour, even though it might sulk on the runway for thirty minutes waiting to take off. Amtrak and its host railroads work the same scam, pumping air into long-distance schedules in order to post better on-time numbers.

Just look at a timetable and check the elapsed time between a train's point of origin and its first stop. Now compare that with the time between the same stations for a train going in the opposite direction: the twenty-eight miles from Chicago to Naperville takes thirty-five honest minutes, but Naperville to Chicago is carded at a languid eighty-one minutes. Often, if it's not delayed, the eastbound *Zephyr* ties up in Chicago Union Station at 3:55 P.M., twenty minutes before official arrival, even after a time-consuming "wye" move, in which the train curves south away from the station, then backs north into it on another track.

As a result of this padding, an Amtrak train often rolls into an out-of-the-way station well ahead of time, idling there as many as ten minutes until the appointed departure hour. Many engineers and conductors snort contemptuously about timetable stuffing, declaring they could run the trains to a tighter schedule if the dispatchers gave them half a chance. In the 1950s and 1960s the Burlington's *Zephyr* engineers often made up lost time by opening their throttles to more than one hundred miles per hour on straight and level track, speeds that struck some riders as skirting the outer edge of safety. "Just take me places fast enough to get there," a shaken newspaper columnist of the 1950s named Bob Considine wrote after an Oakland-to-Chicago dash, "and slow enough to keep from wondering if I will."

Today the top speed allowed most of Amtrak's Western trains is a stately seventy-nine miles per hour, no more, for safety reasons. In any case, Amtrak management argues that allowing host railroads a little leeway in the schedules encourages them to collect incentive cash for bringing the passenger trains home on time. (That's quite all right with me. Just give me modern plumbing, a decent dinner and a little light to read by, and make sure the *Zephyr* traverses the best scenery during daylight. If I worried about the clock, I'd fly.)

At eighteen cars the train was so long, and the Galesburg station platform so short, that the *Zephyr* stopped twice to unload and load passengers from front and rear. During most of the year Galesburg, 162 miles from Chicago, is not a major off-on stop, just a crew change point. In winter, however, it is a favored port of embarkation for ski groups from all over western Illinois. Tonight only two passengers detrained, but sixty skiers headed for Winter Park and Aspen crowded into one of the Los Angeles cars, a coach-baggage with a cargo room in place of the usual lower-level seats. Squeezing aboard all their unwieldy skis, bagged in saggy nylon condoms, took many minutes.

I used the lull to dash over and examine the 1930s-era Chicago,

Burlington & Quincy steam locomotive, Railway Post Office car and caboose preserved behind a wire fence close by the station. Under the black-and-silver engine lay four pilot wheels up front, six massive driving wheels in the middle and four trailing wheels supporting the firebox and cab. Rail buffs would call the locomotive a "4-6-4" or "Hudson type." Though years of exposure to the elements probably had rusted solid its innards, the engine looked ready to steam away with the *Exposition Flyer*. Almost certainly the locomotive had hauled the *Flyer* before the coming of the *California Zephyr* and the end of steam on the Burlington in the mid-1950s. Hundreds like her lie preserved in parklike settings in small towns along the main lines of America. No more vivid and colorful symbol recalls the opening of the American West than does the steam locomotive.

During Chicago's early boom as a rail hub, locomotives popped up on the prairie west of the city with the enthusiasm of black bears in a newly discovered berry patch. The great Western railroads were aborning, much as their Eastern counterparts had—by the creation of loosely connected short lines, then wholesale merger. Like tendrils of frost creeping across a windowpane, they grew in slow and unorganized fashion.

In 1849 the citizens of Aurora, forty miles west of Chicago, built a twelve-mile rail line eastward to the one-year-old Galena & Chicago Union Railroad (now the Chicago & North Western). By 1853 the Chicago & Aurora had added thirty-seven more miles southwest to Mendota. The next year, another company built the Central Military Tract Railroad from Mendota seventy-nine additional miles westward to Galesburg. In 1855 still another railroad struck westward from Galesburg forty-one miles to East Burlington on the Mississippi. In 1864 the Chicago & Aurora lost its trackage rights into Chicago on the Galena & Chicago Union, and had to build its own thirty-six-mile line into the city.

It wasn't easy. A huge swamp between the towns of Hinsdale and Western Springs had to be bridged. In those days a traveler could go from one town to the other by boat, and in the winter skate over an icy marsh. The railroad had to dump thousands of carloads of rock and earth into the bog before it could lay rail. Today Interstate 294, the Tri-State Tollway around Chicago, cuts through the center of the old swamp; not a sign of the marsh remains.

While all this was going on, settlers on the west bank of the Mississippi had built the Burlington & Missouri River Railroad from Burlington, Iowa, across the state to Pacific Junction on the east bank of the Missouri River. A few years later, other little railroad companies in Nebraska built west and east from their central towns, hooking up with one another and eventually disappearing into the maw of the railroad that had begun in Aurora and was now called the Chicago, Burlington & Quincy.

Once they had secured their footing, the Western railroads never would have been able to push westward without land grants—the outright, nearly string-free gifts the federal government made of 131 million acres of vacant lands between 1850 and 1871. In turn, the railroads financed their construction by selling settlers small pieces of their land grants along rights-of-way.

Land! Today it means to the average American a little square in a suburban checkerboard, furnished with house, two-car garage and backyard deck. A century and a half ago, however, land was one of democracy's basic elements, a powerful symbol of freedom and prosperity. Urged on by a snow of handbills and full-page advertisements in Eastern newspapers, hundreds of thousands of Americans departed teeming cities and stagnant small towns and sought their fortunes on this wonderful cheap land, some bought from the railroads and some obtained free just for the homesteading. It seemed as if all one needed to carve out a piece of the American Dream was a horse, a plow, and unlimited self-reliance. (It is not being churlish but simply historically precise to point out that this "self-reliance" was subsidized in part by the government in the form of those land grants.)

All the railroads needed to do to repay the government was to haul federal traffic at half the regular rate. It was one of the great deals of American history: The railroads won free rights-of-way and land that financed their expansion. By 1946, when the arrangement ended, the railroads had paid back the government about nine times the original value of the land grants. Thanks in great part to the land grants, by the Civil War so much rail had been laid that total mileage in the United States was nearly equal to that in the rest of the world, and when hostilities ended in 1865, the rush west began again.

I merged (westward, as it happened) into the flow of passengers heading after dinner to the lounge car of the *Zephyr*. A double-decker like the sleeping car, it contains a lower serving level and a single long room topside. The upstairs' narrow aisle is lined with two-person bench seats facing outward through windows that reach from knee height upward over the curve of the roof, giving a huge field of view to the outside. Amtrak's marketing department aptly calls the car a "Sightseer Lounge." It's the closest thing to a Vista-Dome car on Amtrak's Western routes (old dome cars of the 1950s still run on some of the Eastern trains), although there's no view directly forward or to the rear, thanks to the double-height cars coupled to both ends, blocking the sight lines.

On the first evening after departure the lounge car always rever-berates with tentative, polite cheeriness as passengers shyly begin to take each other's measure. Their ice-breaking conversation al-most always concerns why they're taking the train. Many don't want their fellow passengers to think they're either too poor or too afraid to fly; they're quick to volunteer reasons for their presence.

Half a dozen gray-haired men in the center of the lounge car wore gold-braided Navy baseball caps emblazoned "USS ATTU, CVE-102." Miller Lites in grizzled fists, they beerily revealed to one and all that they were shipmates from an old World War II escort carrier named for the obscure Aleutian island that was the site of an inconsequential battle between Japan and the United States during the same conflict. They were going home to the West Coast after a reunion in Chicago, to which they had flown from San Francisco; the ride back was part of the air-train tour package.

Hearing them, a young mother with a six-year-old daughter announced that they were Navy, too. They had been living on a small island off Sardinia in the Mediterranean for two years, and had recently returned with the victors from Operation Desert Storm. They had been visiting relatives in Ohio and now were going home to their seaman husband and father in Tacoma, by train just so the little girl could "have an old-fashioned adventure." The island, said the mother, possibly was the most isolated American military outpost in the world—so isolated that they had never felt any threat from terrorists or other anti-American elements. But when Desert Shield turned into Desert Storm, her husband and his shipmates disappeared for three weeks with their submarine tender, and she and the other spouses left behind were consumed with worry. She was glad to be home. "You just can't believe the difference between there and here," she said.

Of course fear of flying does push many long-distance riders aboard the train. Occasionally I tell them about poor William Ellery Leonard, a now obscure poet of the first half of the twentieth century who taught at the University of Wisconsin. For decades he never set foot outside the city limits of Madison because train travel terrified him. It was as if he worshiped at the altar of a fearsome, fire-breathing iron deity, propitiating it by staying home. He titled his psychoanalytic autobiography *The Locomotive God.*

There seemed to be a bit of Leonard in a small, bearded man in a Greek fisherman's cap, who spoke in that odd, whiny accent which makes questions of statements. "I take the train because I'm a pilot?" he said. "I own a small plane? As long as I'm in the left seat flying the plane, I'm fine. But I can't stand to fly with a pilot I don't know? He might kill us all." I peered at him, thinking this a not-so-subtle leg-pull. The man was serious.

"*I* am not afraid to fly," said a pleasant, chunky woman in her forties. She was riding the train for the second time that year to Sacramento to visit relatives. For years, she said, she had taken the *Zephyr.* "I'm a nurse," she said, "and I work with mentally handicapped children. It's a stressful job, and I'm on call for twenty-four hours a day. When I'm away, I just prefer the train. It's my relaxation."

Next to her on the bench sat a willowy Chicago-Oakland rider about fifty years old. The two women had just met. "I thought I'd try it just once," said the second woman, "and I don't like it. I have a bad back and I'm going to have to sit up all night for two nights in coach. I would have taken a sleeper but I tried to get one two weeks ago, and they were all sold out. Can you believe it? Amtrak sleepers sold out?" She made a contemptuous *moue*.

Several passengers smiled indulgently. That's a complaint often heard aboard long-distance Amtrak trains, usually from older riders who haven't taken a train since the run-down sixties or the ramshackle early seventies, when sleeping cars ran almost empty. Today, often on most Amtrak routes and always on the western runs, sleeping cars are sold out three months ahead of departure. Seasoned riders know, however, that it's often possible to book space a day or two ahead, because Amtrak requires that sleeper rooms be canceled no fewer than forty-eight hours before departure time if a ticket is to be refunded. Each morning at 4:00 Eastern Time, Amtrak's reservations computer opens up all surrendered space on train manifests. Those who call by 4:05 A.M. often get lucky. More than once I have.

One of two thirtysomething men spoke up. "I don't fly," he said, "not because I'm scared, but because I *love* trains." Chubby, balding, toothbrush-mustachioed, with lots of chins and an amiable Ipana smile, Tom Hankins was a salesman of incidentals—potato chips, cigarettes—to gas stations, and was bound for a filling-station industry convention in Las Vegas. After five years of taking the train from Syracuse, New York, to conventions all over hell and gone, his assistant refused to ride the rails anymore. He *hates* trains. So does Tom's present companion, Matt Skonieczny, tall, skinny, broad-shouldered, with a scrubby mustache and sleepy eyes.

"Can't stand 'em!" said Matt with only a touch of irony. "I have to sleep in the top bunk, and it's *way* too short." Nevertheless, Tom, a boyhood chum, not only is paying all his expenses but had bribed Matt's wife with five hundred dollars in shopping-spree money so his friend could go on the journey. (Matt had been married two years and this was his first trip away from his wife.) To help persuade Matt to go, Tom had bought a portable videocassette recorder with built-in screen and had stocked his suitcase with fifteen video movies. Unhappily, though they'd tried it out before leaving, the VCR won't work on the train. The high amperage of such devices simply trips the circuit breakers protecting the 115-volt electric-shaver outlets in sleeping compartments.

Tom and Matt had taken the *Lake Shore Limited* from Syracuse to Chicago. The crew, they confided, was very unpleasant. "They didn't like each other, and they didn't like the passengers," Tom said. "But the crew on the *Zephyr*—they're wonderful! I've never met so many friendly people."

This was an unsolicited comment I have heard many times: Amtrak crew on Eastern trains sometimes seem sullen and churlish, while those on Western runs on the whole are cordial and neighborly. Why should this be so? One passenger theorized that New York City–based crews simply reflect the town's famous urban hostility. Another suggested that part of the problem may lie with the passengers; Easterners can be surly and demanding, and rudeness simply begets rudeness.

"Amtrak employees on those runs have to develop an aggressive attitude," a train chief once told me. "If they don't, the passengers will eat them alive." Another factor, she said, was the difference between the grungy forty-year-old cars in the East—rebuilt "Heritage Fleet" hand-me-downs from the old passenger railroads—and the much newer Superliners in the West. "In the West, the scenery distracts the passengers," she said, "so they're not so demanding on the employees and they don't notice the little mechanical problems so much."

Some older passengers who rode the trains in the 1950s and 1960s say they recall that even then, Western train crew members were friendlier and more relaxed than those in the East. What's more, they say, their parents told them the same thing about the 1920s and 1930s. That's evidence of a long-standing attitudinal divide between East and West, at least on the railroads.

• • •

Outside, grain elevators gleamed in the evening sun as we approached Iowa, racing past seas of freshly turned cornstalk stubble. I was glad to see that Reggie hadn't yet begun screening the evening's video movie. Partly because of the defensive snobbery of my declining profession as a book review editor in a postliterate age, I'd rather see people reading at quiet moments aboard civilized conveyances such as trains, not staring blankly at a video screen. On the other hand, airline passengers expect in-flight movies on long trips, and Amtrak simply follows suit. (And I must admit that as a deaf person I can't enjoy the on-board movies. Amtrak video players aren't hooked to closed-captioning decoders.)

To be sure, a few passengers always will clutch books—"all book lovers, I think, like to ride on trains," Catherine Drinker Bowen observed thirty years ago in *Adventures of a Biographer*—but not all train lovers like to read books. Of those who do, the vast majority tends to be female and fans of LaVyrle Spencer and Jude Deveraux rather than Margaret Atwood and Toni Morrison. (Those with their noses buried in Kafka or Kierkegaard almost always are college students under pain of assignment.) A great many long-distance train riders seem to be small-town or rural Midwesterners and Westerners and blue-collar suburbanites—the kind loftily called "middle Americans" by those a worried rung higher on the social ladder and "real people" by those untroubled by the status scramble.

Once in a while I will happen upon someone reading a British mystery, an addiction of mine and always a good conversation opener. Tonight I spotted a tall, burly, bearded, bespectacled man in his late forties. He was Bob Locher, a vacationing businessman from the Chicago suburb of Deerfield, Illinois, and he was reading a Dorothy Sayers mystery, *The Nine Tailors*, between bursts of energetic debate over commercialism in the national park system with a young Sierra Club type across the aisle.

I see you're a Lord Peter Wimsey fan, I said. Did Sayers ever send her hero chasing after a mystery on a train, the way Agatha Christie did hers? "No, Sayers never really did a train whodunit," he said. "Anyway, Wimsey always takes an active role in the course of events, even affecting them, rather than being the passive observer Agatha favored in her sleuths."

Bob had brought a clutch of mysteries, intending to inhale them one after the other in his Oakland sleeper room. Trains, we agreed, provide perhaps the world's most relaxing ambience for the devoted reader, especially a sleeper compartment. There is no distraction from other passengers. Having finished a chapter, readers can look up, rest their eyes on the passing countryside for a bit, and once again lose themselves in the interior existence their books provide. Now and then they can stretch their legs with a trip to the lounge car for a snack, and return at their leisure.

All that is true, I said, but at certain times on the *California Zephyr*, the passing scenery will just be too insistently spectacular for even veteran riders to ignore. Just wait until the next afternoon, I said, when the train's going through the Rockies, and I'll bet cash money Bob won't find a soul buried in a book. There are other impossibly distracting stretches—the third morning's long pull across the Nevada desert and that afternoon's mounting of the Sierra in particular. With those sentiments I surprised myself. I don't often sound like a travel brochure. All the same, it's true. More than one *Zephyr* passenger has confessed to reading again and again the same opening paragraph of Chapter One as startling vistas passed above and below the train.

"It's the Mississippi!" someone sang as the *Zephyr* nosed out onto a long steel bridge over the wide river, flowing slowly southward under the moonlight. The lights of Burlington (Mile 205) winked at the train from the Iowa shore, and in a few minutes we glided to a stop at the depot. Again the *Zephyr* was running hot, and again the train tarried, burning off empty minutes before the advertised 7:07 P.M. departure.

"Tonight's movie in the lounge car begins in ten minutes," said Reggie on the PA. *"It will be* Backdraft, *with Kurt Russell and William Baldwin."*

"At least it's not *Robin Hood,*" said a portly man in red suspenders and St. Louis Cardinals cap. "I've been riding this train between Galesburg and Omaha a lot this year, and the only movie they show anymore is *Robin Hood.* I can't abide the sight of Kevin Costner." The movies are PG-rated airline videos, salty language and sexy scenes edited into blandness.

A few minutes later, as the downtown buildings of Burlington slowly slipped past and an actor's face faded in on the video screen, I took my leave and stepped downstairs to the lower level of the lounge car, a tight space with the dimensions and layout of a World War II submarine wardroom. Half the long room, filled with a quartet of tables, was the train's only designated smoking area. The other half contained two booths emblazoned "NO SMOKING" and the lead service attendant's bar. Noel Prell, the attendant, squinted through the fumes, looking for all the world like a bored Bogart behind the bar.

Despite an electronic air scrubber laboring hard at its job, cigarette smoke choked the room. This is no place for those who value their healthy lungs, but in the off-season it's the only source on the train for à la carte coffee and beer, sandwiches and munchies, and nonsmokers had to brave the fumes for refreshment. (During the crowded summers a second attendant mans a tiny booth on the upper level for the faint of heart and frail of lung.) Is Noel a smoker, like so many Amtrak crew? "Don't need to be," he said. "Down here I breathe the equivalent of eighty packs a day anyway."

A former Louisiana oil-field roustabout, this lounge-car attendant is an eighteen-year veteran of the trains. Like several other Amtrakers, Noel lives in New Orleans and commutes north to his job in Chicago aboard the *City of New Orleans.* Pushing beer and chips may not sound like a demanding job, but it's a grueling one, because he's on his feet for six consecutive thirteen-to-eighteen-hour days. Why does he do it? Because he gets nine days off between runs. It's like alternating short weeks of slave labor with long ones of vacation.

The only thing about his profession he cannot stand, he said, is the smoking in the lounge car, which has "made the job a living hell." Superliner lounge cars were not built as smokers, but given the railroad's constant equipment shortage, they're all that's available. Designating a ten-by-twenty-foot space in the lower lounge as the sole area for smokers from five and sometimes six packed coaches is mindful of an old World War II term Kurt Vonnegut has kept alive in his novels—a "blivit," the misbegotten result of a bureaucratic attempt to "stuff ten pounds of shit into a five-pound bag."

Naturally smokers crowded out of the tiny designated area try to light up in the forbidden serving portion of the lower lounge level, and Noel must remonstrate with them, even if the smoke from the designated area is already so thick it's like telling a toddler in the middle of a forest fire not to play with matches. "It turns into a battle, a battle every trip, and it gets to be really tedious," he said. "I tell the passengers from the very beginning of the trip that I'm a mindless flunky, that I don't make the rules but I do have to enforce them, and if they have a problem with that to write to Washington." Sometimes Noel just overlooks the spillover smoking. "I'm not supposed to, but I'm too busy behind the counter to be a smoke policeman the whole trip. I just don't have the time to deal with it." (Noel's wish would soon come true: In 1993, weary of passenger complaints about secondhand smoke, Amtrak banned smoking entirely on short-haul trains, and on the long-hauls the railroad banished smokers to the lower level of a coach toward the rear.)

The mix of alcohol and tobacco sometimes gives the lounge all the ambience of a biker bar where drunken fistfights break out and the police come to haul the unruly to the local hoosegow. As the night wears on, a favorite drinker's game is to see how many people can be stuffed into the restroom. Ten is the record, one attendant told me, but they were all skinny teenagers.

Smoke-choked as a downtown poolroom it may have been, but at this early evening hour the *California Zephyr's* lower lounge offered all the sleepy atmosphere of the coffee shop in a small-town Holiday Inn. True, the tail of a tattooed dragon peeked promisingly from the deep cleavage of a potato-faced white biker in a dirty black tank top. But she stood sullenly alone, taking deep drags on her cigarette in the corner of the room near the toilet. She pointedly ignored an empty booth across from an ample, gray-haired woman who at first glance looked like Mrs. Midwest House-wife, African-American Division. On her breast was a tag inscribed "GOLDEN AGE CLUB." Sitting next to her was a young white man in a Wesleyan University sweatshirt. "May I sit down?" I asked. "Sure, darlin'," she said with a smile under sparkling eyes.

My usual question about Trains, Planes and Automobiles brought from her the arch rejoinder, "I usually take the bus 'cause it's faster than the train." Before I could reply, the young man spoke up. "Are there a lot of you in the Golden Age Club?" he asked the woman. "Yes," she said, "we're a women's club from the Pittsburgh area, and we're twenty-nine of us going to the mountains for a week."

By and by it emerged that she was an academic librarian at California College, a small institution near Pittsburgh, and the young man revealed that he had worked part-time not only in his home town public library in Farmington, Connecticut, but also in the library at Wesleyan, from which he had graduated the previous June. I listened interestedly as the two unlikely new friends—middle-aged black woman and young white man—exchanged amused tales about tiresome patrons, from youngsters who wanted the librarians to do their homework for them to oldsters who demanded they compute their taxes. They laughed over a favorite retort of librarians to panicky students who have left important papers until the last minute and can't find sources checked out long before by more enterprising scholars: "A lack of planning on *your* part does not constitute an emergency on *my* part!"

Neither smiled when she observed that even university librarians are taken for granted by those they serve. "Instructors with master's degrees assume we don't know much about anything," she said, "and we've got *doctorates*." Both her M.L.S. and her Ph.D., she added in answer to my question, were from the University of Pittsburgh.

Through the haze of smoke I saw a lean and ill-dressed couple at a booth nearby. He wore grease-stained denims; his long, lank hair peeked out from under a crumpled baseball cap. His finger-nails were black. She was painfully thin, even anorexic, her chest hollow where it should have been protuberant. AIDS? No; her skin was too clear, her eyes too bright and alert. (I never discovered the reason for her emaciation.) In her arms she cradled a baby no older than nine months. Suddenly she gestured to her companion, and he responded in kind, without moving his lips. They were deaf, and they were conversing in American Sign Language. A nearby passenger said something aloud to them, and they shook their heads, pointing to their ears. At their table they sat in an invisible cocoon of gentle regard for each other, walled off from others by an accident of language and culture, either oblivious to or ignor-ing the few wrongheadedly pitying glances that came their way. Their aloofness seemed neither studied nor self-absorbed, simply accepting and enduring.

I felt a kindred tug—I have experienced the same isolation from hearing society—but I cannot speak the rich language of sign, having been brought up oral. I wanted to talk to these young people, to find out who they were and where they were going, what special problems they faced on the train, and if they hadn't heard of the Surgeon General and the smoky perils to which they were exposing their infant. But I couldn't. I had pencil and paper, but to speak to them in that fashion, I thought, might be patronizing. There is a wide gulf between the signing deaf and the speaking deaf, and it's not easily bridged by mere good intentions. Many of those who have been brought up in a sign-language culture regard the speaking deaf as irrelevancies at best and traitors at worst.

There are two ways to root oneself in society. The first is to carve out one's own place in the scheme of things. The other is to learn and appreciate one's cultural heritage. I had done the former; presumably they had chosen the latter. Our deafness gave us little in common. Besides, my intentions were suspect. Would I ap-proach a hearing couple to warn them of the dangers of tobacco smoke? No, of course not. I'd mind my own business. And so, suddenly shy, I hid in my own shroud of silence.

A no-longer-young woman sat in a booth across the aisle from mine. Though a wedding band gleamed on her left hand, her eyes sparkled flirtatiously as she chatted up the man sitting next to her. Clearly this was not a married couple; the mutual liveliness of their conversation belied domesticity.

I grinned to myself. The lower level of a Superliner lounge car, legend has it, is the nearest thing to the Casbah on Amtrak. It's supposed to be the transcontinental equivalent of a downtown singles bar where young romances take root, where traveling sales-men prey on innocent farmer's daughters and where middle-aged wives on separate vacations seduce young bachelors. Car attend-ants cluck amusedly about the course of lust, often fueled by booze, aboard the train. More than one has confided, "They say good-bye in tears to their husbands and wives on the platform, clutching each other as if they can't bear to be apart, and ten minutes later they're tomcattin' in the lounge, wedding rings in their pockets."

Women as well as men, and not just because American society today allows females the right of predatorhood. They—not the men—initiate most of the encounters, a female assistant conduc-tor insisted during one *Zephyr* run. "As soon as it gets dark, they get involved," she said. Women feel much safer aboard a train than they do in a bar, she added. It's not merely that there's nowhere for a hit-and-run artist to escape; the crew is there to protect the women from unwanted consequences. "What can happen to you? People are all around you. You're in control. On the train women are always in control of the situation, which is so rare for them."

Perhaps that is why women always seem to be at the center of the attendants' stories of comic moments in the lounge car. One never tires of telling how a woman in her eighties, well oiled after a long and quiet evening soaking up screwdrivers, suddenly stood up in the lower lounge and screamed, "I want a man! I want a man! They told me I could buy a man aboard this train!" Another time, the same attendant swore, a young woman emerged stark naked from the lower lounge washroom very late one night, after the bar had closed, and announced brightly, "I'm here to take care of business!"

Most sexual encounters on the train, I suspect, consist of little more than hours of heavy flirtation full of lubricious innuendo, for pickup sex among strangers is no longer so common in the age of AIDS. It is true, however, that some lounge-car relationships are quickly consummated elsewhere on the train, especially in the sleeping cars. If a man (or a woman) picks up someone in the lounge car and the pair repair to a sleeper for the night, conductors and attendants will not stand in their way, provided one of them has paid for the compartment. Sleeper space is sold by room, not by berth; whether one, two or three people occupy a single compartment, the price is the same. So long as each rider has paid the fare of passage and the room supplement has been taken care of, who cares what goes on within?

All the same, said a veteran sleeper attendant, amorous couples "come looking for an empty room, and you can't monitor everything all the time. Somebody will slip in. I've busted many people taking an empty room." Like many a veteran attendant, he has a standard method for dealing with such passengers without sending them away angry. Frustrated, maybe, but not furious. "The first thing I tell them is, 'Now, would you sneak into a room at the Holiday Inn without paying because it was empty?' And they say all innocent-like, 'Oh, we didn't know, we didn't know we weren't supposed to.' I just say, 'Come on, don't play me for a fool. I'm a young man too. I like to do the same things you're doing, but I just don't do them that way. You disrespected me. You're insulting my intelligence. Now, come on and leave.' That usually works."

Conductors and attendants are quick to intervene if a lusty pair is heedless of privacy. Each Superliner sleeper compartment fronts onto the aisle with large glass windows and doors covered by curtains not always drawn completely in the couples' eagerness to get down to business. "You wouldn't believe the nonchalance of some of these people!" attendants often say. Casual as they may be about the morality of consenting adults, they're fiercely protective of the sensibilities of the other passengers. To Amtrak crew, sex is not a spectator sport.

"In particular you've got to watch these young couples in the coaches who ask for extra blankets," one confided to me. "People go by up and down the aisle all the time and they're gonna be offended if there's obvious goings-on." Very late at night, when the entire train is sleeping except for the conductors huddled around their table far up in the dorm-coach, youngsters for whom nocturnal groping is too tame will tiptoe down to the lower level of their coaches and disport themselves inside the tiny bathrooms. To do so requires an athleticism sometimes defeating to those for whom the bloom of youth has disappeared. A favorite place of assignation therefore is the much larger handicapped bathroom—much to the irritation of wheelchair passengers who need to relieve themselves in the middle of the night and find the door locked, lascivious noises emerging from behind.

A choice love nest, I discovered quite by accident, is the shower room new to some recently rebuilt sleepers. Arising in my economy compartment at dawn one morning, I decided to grab a shower before the rest of the car woke up, and tiptoed down to the lower level. Just as I reached for the knob on the shower room door, it swung open upon a sweating young man hurriedly buckling his belt. Close behind him, blushing, his inamorata shrugged into her bra. "Excuse me," I said in an embarrassment that matched theirs, and departed. When I returned ten minutes later, they were gone. Twice more that trip I encountered them in their coach, and each time the young man winked and grinned when our eyes met. His girlfriend simply gazed out the window, smiling.

Not long afterward, I described this encounter to Glen Sullivan, a former West Coast conductor who until recently was a regular on both the *Zephyr* and the *Coast Starlight*, the overnight train between Los Angeles and Seattle. He laughed, waving his hand in dismissal. "That's nothing," he said. "The *Zephyr* is really a very staid train, a *family* train. Now there's more screwing on the *Starlight* than you can shake a stick at. You wouldn't believe it. I'm not kidding you.

I've seen passengers engaged in oral sex right in their seats!" He shook his head.

Twice he has found "two people stark naked, I mean *stark naked*," in baggage rooms. On the first occasion, the *Starlight* had stopped one evening at Sacramento, and Sullivan was offloading passengers from a Superliner coach with a large baggage room on the lower level, separated from the vestibule by a sliding door with a large window. As he helped passengers down onto the stepbox, he said, "I hear this familiar murmur. People are saying, as they always do when they get off, 'Where's my bag, Martha?' and 'Joe, you seen the grip?' But there's a funny *gasping* in the middle of the murmuring. I didn't think about it at first, but after we got the detraining passengers off and we're getting the new ones on, the gasping starts up again. I realize that there's something going on here, and look through that window to the baggage room. There they are, completely nude, just having a ball in front of everybody. They were just totally oblivious to what's going on the other side of the door. And I said, 'Oh, my God!'

"After we hustled everybody upstairs, I went back downstairs and opened the door and said, 'C'mon, folks. You know everyone's been watching you!' The girl said, real enthusiastically and with a big smile, '*Yeah.*' So I said, 'Are you going to be long?' She said, 'All night.' I said, 'Oh, Jesus.' I went and got one of our plastic trash can liners and taped it over the window on the inside. I don't care what people do so long as nobody sees them. And they said, 'Thank you very much.' Nice folks," he added with heavy irony.

On the second occasion, Glen said, he watched as a man and a woman in their early twenties spent the daylight hours getting acquainted in the lounge car, lubricating their relationship with more than a few drinks. As night fell, Glen noticed that the pair had disappeared, but thought nothing of it until he went forward on an errand to the baggage car at the head of the train. "There's not supposed to be anybody up there," he said. "All these signs on the doors say, 'Authorized Personnel Only.' "

And he opened the baggage-car door upon two very unauthorized persons, the couple missing from the lounge car. "Here they've got suitcases all spread out on the floor, and here they were on top of them, just going at it. I said, 'Uh, excuse me, I'm sorry, I didn't mean to interrupt.' And as I was going out the door I turned back and said, 'By the way, when you folks are finished, would you kindly put things back where you found them and get out of here, because you're not supposed to be here?' And they said, 'Oh, okay. No big thing.' "

The root of the problem, Glen said, is alcohol. "The whole trip's thirty-six hours long. When they get on the train in L.A. at nine o'clock in the morning, they're saying, 'Oh, boy! Choo-choo ride! We're going to see some beautiful scenery.' But when the sun goes down, everything starts to happen. They've been drinking all day, and they know they're on public transportation. By then they've got this attitude of 'I'm going to sue the hell out of you if you look at me cross-eyed.' They figure they can get away with just about anything. If they get abusive and threatening, we *will* throw them off the train. But sex—who does it harm, anyway, so long as they're discreet about it?"

Glen Sullivan's stories may reflect a laid-back California indulgence toward sex on the train, but one tale I heard in several manifestations—each attendant who told it claimed its events happened in his very own sleeper—carries a pointed moral. In Colorado one fine evening, according to the story, a gentleman who had booked a *Zephyr* sleeper compartment met a lady from a *Desert Wind* coach in the lounge car. After a few libations the fellow suggested that they repair to his room to get further acquainted, and so they did, for the better part of the night. At dawn the lady rose, pleasantly sated, and padded back through the snoring train to her coach. As she traversed the dining car, occupied only by waiters setting up for breakfast, she suddenly spotted daylight through the window of the far door. She had failed to remember that at Salt Lake City five hours before, the *Desert Wind* had split from the *Zephyr*, and all her baggage and belongings were rolling unaccompanied hundreds of miles southwest toward Los Angeles.

"My God!" the waiters heard her wail. "What am I going to tell my husband?"

. . .

None of this is to imply that the *California Zephyr* is merely a rolling den of lust. Singles bar on wheels it often is, but the passenger train can also be a meeting place of the most charming respectability— and happenstance. As that assistant conductor said, women feel safe in the lounge car. So do shy men. Over the endless miles ahead, in fact, both sexes tend to let down their guard, allowing themselves to be caught up in the relaxed feeling of a resort community on rails. In a place like this, sincerity begets sincerity, and lasting connections often are made.

On many trips I've watched as single people, young, middle-aged and old, connected in linkages that may be only temporary or that may last a lifetime. In a small way, I think, I may have encouraged one such pairing. The story is so "Love Boat"–hokey I am embarrassed to relate it, but it happened, and here it is:

At dinner late one evening as the train rolled across Iowa, I sat across from what appeared to be a couple in their late twenties. They were, after all, of the same age and of opposite genders, and they both carried sleeping-car meal vouchers. As the waiter took our orders, they were discussing the relative merits of upper and lower berths in the economy compartments.

"And which of you has to take the top bunk?" I broke in heartily. To the young woman I said, "Does he make you sleep topside, or do you put your foot down and demand the lower berth?"

Simultaneously and quickly they replied, "Oh, no, we're not together! We only just met." He was a transportation lawyer from New York on a rail inspection mission for a client, and she a theatrical actress on her way home to San Francisco. They just happened to occupy economy bedrooms across from each other in the Oakland sleeper, they said, and quite by accident they'd been seated together in the diner. It was plain by their brisk matter-of-factness that neither had the slightest attraction for the other.

Later, after the two took their separate leaves, I said to the fellow in the seat next to me, "Put my foot in it, didn't I, assuming they were an item? I'm always saying things like that without thinking!"

"Aw, don't worry. Honest mistake," he replied. With a wink, he added, "Maybe you put an idea in their heads."

I thought no more about them until two days later, when I debarked from the Amtrak bus that had brought San Francisco–bound passengers from Oakland to the Transbay Terminal. I'd just taken a *Chronicle* from an honor box when I felt a tap on the shoulder. It was the man who had sat next to me at dinner. "Look," he said with a small smile, pointing at a couple in a passionate clinch at the cab stand. It was—you guessed it—the lawyer and the actress.

Lela Janushkowsky once told me a story that is a further emblem of train-borne serendipity. One evening on the *Zephyr*, the diner had a very tight early seating. "We had too many parties of three," Lela recalled, "so when a couple came in I had no place to sit them together. So I asked for a volunteer from a threesome to join the swingin' singles table. An older man volunteered. He was in a seniors group going to Vegas. He had lost his wife and was still in mourning—he hadn't been out of the house in a year. I sat him down with a lady from Kentucky going to Truckee. They *communicated*. They fell in love right at that table! The next morning when I came through the coaches to the diner, he was sitting with her with his arm around her shoulder. They had their last meal together, and then their trains split at Salt Lake City. He was begging her to come with him, but she was visiting her children in Truckee.

"She was sitting alone in the coach the next morning. She said, 'Thank you, thank you so much for introducing me to that man.' He was going to come chop wood for her in Kentucky, and she had a little boat, and he said he loved to fish. He promised to visit her the next month when he could get away."

Lela does not know the end of the story, but she is certain at least part of it ended happily. "People in his tour said to me, 'This is a miracle! We're his neighbors, and we had to force him out of his house to go on this trip, because he was so devastated when his wife died. His life was empty. But here he meets a nice woman.' It made me feel very, very warm," Lela said, hugging herself.

. . .

Upstairs, *Backdraft* at last had ended. The two dead Chicago firemen had been buried, the grieving widow had been handed the folded flag that had graced her husband's coffin, and the passengers were stumbling teary-eyed to their coaches. Downstairs I had barely noticed the train's brief stops during the evening in Mount Pleasant (Mile 233) and Ottumwa (Mile 280), and upstairs the lounge was nearly empty as the train departed Osceola (Mile 360) on time at 9:47 P.M.

Outside the lounge car night had fallen and the small towns and farms of central Iowa had faded into the gloom. Arising to return to my sleeper I saw, through the windows of the upper level of the lounge car, three figures by a streetlight at the edge of a lonely field, bent over a harrow coupled to a big John Deere. One, white-haired and stooped but still powerfully built, wielded a pry bar. The second, perhaps thirty years younger, stood tall and straight. The third, a teen-aged girl, squatted by the axle, wrench in hand.

No doubt here were three generations of Iowa farmers still working the spread the old man's great-grandfather had carved out of the raw prairie more than a century ago, after the train had carried him from somewhere in the East to settle the property he had bought from the railroad. Here, I thought, was the perfect picture of an unbroken line of sturdy Emersonian self-reliance—three unfettered individuals on their own land, answerable to no one but themselves, a symbol that still signifies to many people what it means to be American.

The way these farmers and their ancestors lived are both root and product of the nation's frontier character, sometimes in contradictory ways. People everywhere need meaning in their lives. They need a grail that transcends the self, an ideal that joins them to their fellow humans. Independent the pioneers may have considered themselves, but they also wanted to impose collective order on their surroundings, order that not only fed their spirit and helped them survive but also increased their profits.

That is why Plains farms and towns are laid out in such tidy rectangular fashion: to produce and ship to market agricultural

goods as efficiently as possible. This tendency to right-angled or-
derliness also helps explain why those who dwell on the plains
seem so stodgy and conservative to those who live in the cities. In
the heart of every footloose individualist is a paradoxical yearning
for purposeful cooperation with his neighbors—for community.

Most of those gazing out from the windows of the lounge car of
the *Zephyr* that evening probably were unaware that that square-
edged frontier icon is fast disappearing. The family farm of the
Great Plains is drying up, as the younger generation who left after
high school and college for office jobs increasingly become unwill-
ing to return to the economically precarious existence of farming.
Without anyone to take over the reins, older farmers have no
choice except to sell to larger farmers—in many cases enormous
agribusiness concerns—or to sell their irrigation rights and allow
their farmland to return to its natural arid state.

The nation doesn't care. It simply needs fewer farmers to produce the same agricultural bounty it has always enjoyed. But by
letting our farmers go, we are also losing our small towns. The
communities that depend on trade with farmers are evaporating.
For every half-dozen farmers who sell out, a Plains community
loses a store. Sam Walton and his ubiquitous Wal-Marts, selling
goods of all kinds at deep discounts, may have contributed to the
death of downtowns everywhere, but they haven't been the only
agent of mortality.

All over the Great Plains during the last half-century, many
counties have lost 50 percent of their population. Some are now as
sparsely inhabited as they were when they were still frontier lands.
A few radical thinkers claim that it is not only economic pressure
that is chasing the descendants of the frontiersmen from the
Plains, but also the nature of the land itself.

Frank and Deborah Popper, planning professors at Rutgers University, believe that trying to farm the Great Plains in the first place
was a colossal mistake. The arid plains' thin topsoil, they say, has
always been better suited for nomadic animals than for wheat or
corn. It was foolish, they said, to try "to force waterless, treeless
steppes to behave like Ohio."

The Poppers came up with an idea so novel, so controversial, so outrageous that a few hundred thousand Iowans, Nebraskans, Coloradans, Kansans and Dakotans wouldn't mind seeing them tarred and feathered and run on a rail clear out of the Plains. The Poppers proposed the creation of a giant nature preserve, a "Buffalo Commons" extending from north Texas to Canada and from the Mississippi to the Front Range of the Rockies. They would let this immense land mass—one-fifth of the United States—revert to its original state, an endless sea of tall grass and buffalo.

At a series of town meetings in the late 1980s, the Poppers hoped to persuade the farmers that the smart thing to do was follow the exodus. They also wanted the farmers to repudiate the efforts of their ancestors, to admit that they had been wrong all along in trying to settle the Plains. In places like McCook, Nebraska (where the *Zephyr* stops in the small hours of the morning), outraged audiences of farmers and ranchers and merchants shouted "I ain't selling!" and "Give Manhattan back to the Indians!" while deputy sheriffs' hands hovered over their revolvers. As a mission of persuasion, the Poppers' effort was a debacle.

The essential problem was that the Poppers—as impractical and naïve a couple of Eastern academic carpetbaggers as ever lived— hadn't the slightest idea of the terrible taboo they were violating in challenging the farmers' deep emotional roots. "The Plains are full of forbidden ideas," wrote Anne Matthews in her book on the Poppers, *Where the Buffalo Roam*, "as in 'thou shalt not think about the bad years. . . . Thou shalt pretend the crisis is not there.' "

Of course the crisis is there, Matthews concluded, but the future of the Great Plains is more likely to contain high-tech office parks than buffalo. In many places farm belts are becoming "urban archipelagoes," islands of home telemarketing and computer programming. Some surviving towns are taking on all the character of retirement villages, thanks to affordable properties that attract older urbanites who want to spend their last years in the peace and quiet of the countryside. Other towns have become targets of preservationist-entrepreneurs seeking to transform them into historic bedroom communities.

All these places attract dreamers from the cities, dreamers in whom the westering spirit lives on, however transformed it may be by modern circumstance. The frontier ideal of the lonely hero may be largely myth, but it is a myth of powerful appeal. Americans are both rooted and restless, linked to their ancestors not only by the love of land but also the need for new horizons.

As I reached the lower level of my sleeper, I spotted a rumpled room-service tray just inside the open door of Room 12, the econ-omy room directly in front of mine. Next to it was a thick leg, encased like a crude kielbasa in a wrinkled support stocking. The miasma of stale cigarette smoke hung heavy in the air. The woman in Room 12 was frog-heavy, with wattles and chins. She smoked like a foundry, cigarette after cigarette dangling from her maw. And with her compartment door open, so the rest of us in the car could enjoy it. Although Amtrak permits smoking in bedrooms—once I heard a sleeper passenger say he travels by train between Chicago and the West Coast because he can't bear to be four hours in the air without a cigarette—few smokers think to keep their compart-ment doors shut.

Muttering to myself, I turned into my room. The attendant already had made it up for the night; the bed was down, the covers carefully turned back, a foil-wrapped mint on the pillow. Ah, I thought, this guy cares about the details. Most nights on a train I never see those mints; when I inquire, a "shortage in the commis-sary" is the convenient answer. Whatever the truth, this attendant knows it's the little things that please a passenger, and I'll bet his tips are generous. I thought about the angry Germans upstairs. I hoped their experience in John's diner tonight would mollify them into magnanimity with their purses.

For an hour I read a Rumpole of the Bailey paperback novel. It was getting on toward midnight when I doused the light and pulled the curtain to watch the bridge lights as the train crossed the Missouri River into Nebraska. Poor Nebraska! A state so unin-vitingly flat and featureless (except for grain elevators every twenty miles) that the only passenger train left in the state sneaks through during the small hours of night. Only during the summer, when both westbound and eastbound *Zephyrs* slip out either end of the state just after dawn, can a rider catch a glimpse of Nebraska by daylight. Even then there is not much to see, unless one is a connoisseur of agricultural land. Only the tankers and reconnaissance planes landing at and taking off from Offutt Air Force Base, headquarters of the once-feared Strategic Air Command, offer a respite from the monotony.

As the train slowed for its scheduled 12:12 A.M. arrival at Omaha (Mile 501), I began to drowse. Now I had to decide whether to lock my compartment door. It latches only from the inside; a locked sleeper room cannot be opened from the outside, except by crow-barring the door off its tracks. Because I'm deaf, I can't tell if there's a knock at the door, and hate to lock myself away from quick rescue if there should be an emergency. One night years ago on the *Broadway Limited* from Chicago to New York, I left my roomette door unlocked. A nocturnal intruder awakened me, leaning into the room with a perverted hand where it shouldn't have been. I reacted too slowly to give chase, and the fellow escaped.

It would, I thought, be simple and inexpensive for Amtrak to place a battery-operated flashing device inside a room when requested by a deaf passenger. I could then latch myself in safely for the night, yet be assured that a hard rap on the door would trigger the flasher, awakening me instantly. Someday, perhaps. Meanwhile, as the lights of the Omaha station platform flooded the room a good fifteen minutes before the scheduled arrival time, I pulled down the shade and snapped off the light.

And locked the door.

FIVE

T he minute hand on my watch had crept just past 5:30 when I arose in a sour humor. Twice during the night the tobacco freak next door had stirred for a cigarette, first at 1:30 and again at 4:00, and had shared the experience with me, her smoke seeping under partitions and through cracks. I was not grateful. On other trips I have slept soundly through Iowa and Nebraska as the *Zephyr* glided over smooth, jointless welded track, barely stirring at the clatter of wheels over switches and crossovers, and slumbering through the crew change point at Lincoln (1:39 A.M., Mile 555) and three other Nebraska station stops at Hastings (3:22 A.M., Mile 652), Holdrege (4:15 A.M., Mile 706), and McCook (5:25 A.M., Mile 784).

I suffer not only from the reformed smoker's guilty hatred of other people's cigarette fumes but also from a nameless horological malady: Wherever I am in the world, no matter how late I have been up the night before, I awaken every morning between five and six. At some point during that hour my eyes slam open like barn doors before spooked horses, and will not close again for sleep, no

matter how weary I may be. At home I can use the early hours
before going off to work to pick up my electronic mail from Com-
puServe and Prodigy, and see who's phoned in messages during
the night on my other computer, on which I run bulletin-board
software. Right now, however, the nearest telephone jack is reced-
ing aft at sixty miles an hour, making telecommunications useless.
I envied the ingenious fellow I had seen on a previous trip who
plugged his laptop computer into a portable cellular phone, en-
abling him to pluck the latest stock quotes from the Dow Jones
electronic news service every time the *Zephyr* dashed through a
community large enough for a cellular relay station.

I did not swear overmuch. Soon the aroma of fresh coffee—a
first-class perk in the sleepers—at the attendant's station upstairs
would rouse others, and by then I'd be shaved and dressed and
ready for the breakfast rush. I knew that John Davis would be up
at five, to get ready to start serving early, at six, to feed as many
passengers as possible before the train's scheduled arrival in Denver at 8:40 A.M. There the *Pioneer* would be cut off from the *Zephyr*
and *Desert Wind* immediately, and its passengers wouldn't get a late
breakfast in the Seattle-bound diner waiting to be coupled onto
Number 25.

Automatically I glanced at the crack under my compartment door.
No daily paper, another first-class perk, yet had been slid under the
door; not until Denver in midmorning would baggage handlers
throw aboard stacks of the *Denver Post* if we were lucky, the toy
newspaper *USA Today* if we were unlucky. Reading the newspapers
to be found along the run of the *California Zephyr* can be a grand
experience for the traveler who is a news junkie. I vastly prefer the
local papers, even the fusty *Omaha World-Herald* on the eastbound
run; at the very least, local dailies offer an individuality, a sense of
place you just can't get in *USA Today*.

I always marvel, for example, at the things Herb Caen gets away
with in his insouciant column in the *San Francisco Chronicle*. On the
train leaving Oakland one morning during primary election season, I opened the paper and learned that a Chinese-American

named Hsieh—pronounced "Shaw"—was among the motley crowd running for mayor of San Francisco. No other metro daily in the United States would have let a columnist sneak into print "I don't give a hsit if Hsieh wins." That made me whoop aloud, but the San Franciscan in the next seat just chuckled. It was a perfect example of the liberal nonchalance that marks the Bay Area's sense of humor—a humor that often teeters on the edge of taste.

In the more than a quarter of a century I've been a newspaperman, the business—and the profession—has changed deeply, perhaps more in my time than in the century and a half since the iron horse began to carry it westward. Before then Americans thirsted for news, because it took so long to arrive by stagecoach and riverboat. Many days, even weeks, passed before accounts of great events could arrive. In such isolation we wanted our news as thorough and detailed as possible, even when the railroads began bringing bundles of newspapers from the great cities. Who knew if further details would arrive aboard the next train?

Today, of course, television news arrives in our living rooms the instant it happens. News is cheap—it's even free—but together with newspapers and magazines there's more of it than we can handle. Now that we have all the news we want, we're overloaded. It's easier to allow the quick images of the ten o'clock news to inform us, and for that reason we're letting our newspaper subscriptions lapse. If we still read newspapers, we read them for the same reason we watch television: to be entertained.

True, the country still fields great, influential newspapers such as *The New York Times, The Washington Post* and the *Los Angeles Times,* all run by families with a sense of noblesse oblige. The vast majority, however, are owned by absentee corporate chains to whom the bottom line is paramount. Rather than encourage hard-hitting investigative articles and strongly opinionated editorials that might drive away their remaining readers and advertisers, market-driven owners play it safe for the sake of circulation and revenue.

The smaller country dailies and weeklies, often discarded on seats in the *Zephyr*'s lounge car and sometimes available in station honor boxes, don't rock the boat, either. Today they tend to be little more than shoppers designed to maximize ad income for the chains that own them. Their editors—hired carpetbaggers, not homeboys intimate with their surroundings—assemble their news reports in formula fashion with grayly written wire-service copy, canned features, church reports and items from neighborhood "correspondents" whose idea of news is that "Einar Gunderson and his wife, Tillie, and 12-year-old daughter, Inga, from Fayetteville, Ark., are visiting the Erho Kekkonens this week."

On the other hand (any discussion of American institutions is full of "on the other hands"), nowhere else in the United States can we find a complete week's worth of local court decisions and police reports except in those little newspapers. Even if we do not know the names or all the details, the anonymous facts start the imagination stewing. "A Spirit Lake woman reported at 12:49 A.M. that her best friend's boyfriend had assaulted her. No charges were filed." And: "A subject reported at 9:51 P.M. that his girlfriend had taken two handguns from his residence. He did not want to press charges."

Someone who reads every Monday morning in his major metropolitan daily that thirty-eight murders were committed in his city over the weekend can't help smiling when learning that there are still communities in America with so little crime that a weekly can carry the news that "Norman Apfel of Wooded Acres reported at 7:48 A.M. that someone had damaged the pole which supports his mailbox." Or that "when a patrol officer checked out screaming he heard on Westview Street Oct. 4 at 12:26 A.M., it turned out to be sons upset with what their mother had cooked for dinner."

In those papers we can learn which of our neighbors was "assessed" ten dollars for letting his dog "commit a nuisance" in the next-door backyard, or sentenced to a month's "supervision" for public intoxication. Often lifted verbatim from the police blotter, complete with the cops' colorful "apprehendeds" and "perpetrators," this is great stuff, news that means something to the people who take these papers. These, after all, are the people they grew up with, not the celebrities whose lives they know only from *Cosmopolitan* or the Colombian drug lords whose faces they know only from

CNN. What's more, their actions and the consequences thereof are authentic, not gossip and rumor. Everyone thrills secretly to the just misfortune of people they know. The Germans have a great word for that emotion—*Schadenfreude*. This is the kind of news our ancestors thrived on 150 years ago.

The more sparsely populated the countryside, the more often sex offenses seem to arise in the columns. Is there, for instance, some sort of relationship between geographic isolation and statutory rape? Some of this stuff is so weird that it seems a candidate for a new edition of Krafft-Ebing's *Psychopathia Sexualis*. I wish I could remember the name of the Colorado weekly I once found in the lounge car whose police column reported that a funeral-home worker had surprised a prowler in an act of necrophilia. The perpetrator escaped, the paragraph reported tersely, and police were seeking the man on a charge of illegal entry.

Without a newspaper to occupy me, I stowed the bedding and had plenty of room to dress. Of course, one can call the attendant to remake the compartment while one is at breakfast, but when the bunks are down one must dress in a tiny space less than two feet square. For a middle-aged singleton that's clumsy enough; for a couple it's impossible without careful negotiations.

A gray-haired woman across the aisle had been up awhile, in the fashion of elderly light sleepers. "It's a *beautiful* morning!" she said as I slid back the door of my compartment. "Look!" I peered out her window onto the high plains, sparkling in the rising sun. Close by, a rancher tossed hay bales off the back of his pickup to his hungry Herefords. A red-tailed hawk swooped down after a panicked rodent in a bare tractor furrow. It was so windy that when the train slowed to a crawl on a siding to let a freight go by on the main line, I could feel the gusts buffet the high cars. I smiled and turned down the corridor to the bathrooms. There's always something about waking up to a fine day aboard a train that stirs the spirits. Hers, anyway.

In the nearest bathroom, I noticed that it was still clean, the mirror and washbasin spotless. No doubt the sleeper attendant believed in keeping on top of things, but perhaps, I thought, he had had a little help from fastidious passengers. If there is any reliable measurement of American success at following an honor system, it is the daily response to the sign affixed in each Amtrak bathroom, whether coach or sleeper: "IT ISN'T POSSIBLE FOR US TO CLEAN AFTER EACH USE. PLEASE BE THOUGHTFUL OF THE NEXT PASSEN-GER." As one might expect, consideration tends to decline with the passengers' economic status; sleeper bathrooms are much tidier than coach toilets. Exceptions abound, however. A sleeper may contain a spoiled rich jerk who never once in his life picked up after himself, and a coach may contain indigents who never have lost dignity and respect for others.

This is not a piddling subject. For both passengers and crew, toilets are almost invariably the most-complained-about aspect of American train travel. Especially in the East, what passenger on an overloaded train has not suffered filthy, stinking, plugged-up johns, cursing attendants for not being quicker with the plunger and Lysol? For their part, crews characterize Americans as so slov-enly that it's impossible for a car attendant to keep up with their debris. More than one train chief has told me horror stories of passengers taking revenge for unavoidable delays by jamming blankets and pillows into the toilets.

When Amtrakers tell "war stories" of trips that turn them prematurely gray, those involving toilets always head the list. Reg-gie Howard's meanest headache occurred during one winter trip when the *Zephyr* arrived in Oakland sixteen hours late with one operating toilet for more than two hundred passengers. The line for it extended many cars through the train. "People were banging on the door," Reggie said. " 'When you going to get out? I'm in pain!' they'd say. 'Can't you just wait?' the person inside would scream. You almost know you're going to have a trip like that when the temperatures fall below zero. You'll be sixteen hours late one way, eight hours late back. Once you get off the train, you want to kiss the ground."

Similarly, Don Cushine's favorite train-from-hell tale involves toilets and weather, and it occurred on Christmas Eve in 1983, when he was a young train chief. It was his first Christmas away from his family in Albany, he said, "and I wasn't looking forward to that. But it was part of the job and I was going to make the best of it.

"When the *Zephyr* left Chicago, it was seventy degrees below zero by the windchill, and most of the toilets on the train were frozen shut even before we pulled out of the station. And we had more than five hundred passengers aboard. Two hours into the trip the only toilets that worked were the two in the dorm car."

On Western trains, the dorm-coach is usually not a Superliner, but a Hi-Level, a thirty-five-year-old double-decker relic from the Santa Fe's *El Capitan*, which plied between Los Angeles and Chicago in the late 1950s and early 1960s. Today, their fluted sides stained, pocked and dented, and their roof line several inches lower than that of the Superliners, the Hi-Levels look distantly related to them, like a scruffy uncle at your sister's garden party.

Amtrak loosely based its Superliner design on the Hi-Levels, but the one thing it could not improve upon was the old cars' toilet technology. Hi-Level plumbing is utterly simple: just wide, straight pipes that dump directly onto the tracks. Superliner toilet systems, by contrast, are high-tech marvels. They feature thirty-gallon holding tanks and a mechanical digestive system that liquefies waste and ejects it onto the tracks in a fine mist, leaving no unsightly residue. In arctic weather, however, the Superliner apparatus freezes solid, and even in balmy temperatures it is easily choked into a coma by small objects such as sanitary napkins and toy cars. "They've tried everything," Don said. "They've tried a short pipe. They've tried a long pipe. They've tried a funnel pipe. Everything they come up with, there's always something that seems to plug it up."

America may have put a man on the moon, but it can't design a train toilet that works all the time. And it can't go back to the old straight pipes, thanks to the anger of two men innocently fishing under a railroad bridge near Jacksonville one day in May 1989, when a train passing overhead let fly. Amtrak was convicted in a Florida court of commercial dumping, a felony. This was absurd.

Flushing toilets onto the track, a practice as old as railroading itself, is hardly a threat to either public health or the environment. Graveled roadbeds are perfect septic fields; on rights-of-way far out in the country, the waste is quickly biodegraded by sun and weather. Crews can easily lock the bathrooms off limits when trains are in stations or traveling over environmentally sensitive areas, such as reservoir embankments. And there just isn't much waste anymore. In 1929 there were more than 20,000 intercity passenger trains to dump their loads on the tracks; in 1989, only 110. The controversy clearly has been a tempest in a chamberpot.

Amtrak did win its Florida appeal, but the country's politicians, ever on the hunt for an easy way to wrap themselves in environmental concern, smelled a good thing in the noisome controversy. Congress decreed that by November 15, 1996, all Amtrak trains must keep a tight sphincter. Toilet waste was to be retained in holding tanks and pumped out at major station stops.

Of some 1,400 passenger cars on the Amtrak roster at the beginning of 1991, only a third, all short-haul cars of newer design, already possessed retention systems. Another third, the old cars Amtrak inherited on start-up in 1971, were headed for the scrap pile. Retrofitting the remaining third, including the Superliners, was to be an $85-million capital-spending headache.

Don's Christmas migraine, however, went far beyond toilets and winter weather. Amtrak had expected a light holiday load, and rostered just two waiters and two cooks for the trip, instead of the usual three and three. The train, however, was nearly full, forcing Don to double as a cook and waiter. "We fed anywhere from two hundred fifty to three hundred people at each meal," he said. "We were using coach attendants as waiters."

The second night out Don cut his foot in a trap door, opening a deep gash in the skin over the Achilles tendon just above the back of his shoe. Because the crew was so understaffed, he could not take himself out of the line of fire. "I just put gauze pads on the cut, changing them every couple of hours, and kept working."

Nearly toiletless, delayed by severe cold and its service chief gimpy, the *Zephyr* limped past San Francisco Bay toward Oakland fourteen hours late. The night before, the diner was down to its last supplies. It had to serve a free meal, Don said, "and all we had left for the last ten or fifteen people were grilled cheese sandwiches. Everybody had expected to be home by five P.M. Christmas Eve. It was now dawn on Christmas Day, and they were not happy campers. They were ready to string me up because I was the chief and it was of course my fault."

In desperation, as the *Zephyr* approached Oakland, Don wearily changed into the Santa suit with which he had planned to surprise youngsters Christmas Eve, and entered the lounge car. When they beheld the bedraggled, limping Santa, the passengers relented, resigning themselves to their fate, some even becoming jovial, and disbanded the lynching party.

At 7:00 A.M. the *Zephyr* finally reached Oakland, its exhausted crew unconscious over the tables in the diner. "We had had only two hours of sleep," Don said, "and when they were pulling the train from the station into the yards they woke us up to get ready to come right back to Chicago." Number 5 was now Number 6 eastbound, and it was to leave Oakland at 10:40 A.M.

"From Chicago to Oakland we had handled a total of twenty-three hundred people," Don said. "Five hundred getting on, four hundred getting off, another four hundred getting on. At that point I told the crew, 'Don't worry, it's Christmas Day, it should be a light trip going back.'"

And because it was Christmas Day, just one food purveyor remained open in Oakland. "I went out and bought five chickens and some hamburgers for the crew. That was our Christmas dinner. And we ended up nine hours late coming home."

My ablutions at last performed, I stepped upstairs at 6:00 A.M. for a cup of coffee from the attendant's bar. Two of the Germans had beat me there, and they were, fortunately, in ruddy good cheer. "Stuttgart, ja, ja," was all I could make of their proffered conversation, which may have been in English but which was all but impossible for me to lip-read. There, however, was no *kaffee*. There was no urn. There was no attendant. Where could he be? This was the

California Zephyr, whose crews are supposed to be impeccable! Then I looked again at my watch and felt extraordinarily foolish. Shortly after McCook, the last stop in Nebraska, we had crossed from the Central Time Zone into Colorado and Mountain Time, and lost an hour on the clock. It was now five in the morning, not six, and there'd be another hour before coffee was on, let alone breakfast. Damn.

My circadian rhythm had run afoul of Standard Time, the invention that made sense of the mess that was American timekeeping before the Civil War. It was as if the country was an enormous watchmaker's shop operated by a quirky jeweler, the hands of each of tens of thousands of clocks on display set to a different time of day or night. Each railroad used the local sun time of its major city if it was a short road, or that of several cities if a longer road. Sun time varied by about one minute for every thirteen miles due west.

"The Baltimore & Ohio used Baltimore time for trains running out of that city, Columbus time for operations in Ohio, and Vincennes time for everything west of Cincinnati," wrote John F. Stover in his history of the early days of American railroads, *Iron Road to the West.* "There naturally was a crazy-quilt variation of dozens of local sun times across the country. In 1857 *Dinsmore's American Railroad Guide* showed that when it was noon in Washington, D.C., it was 12:24 P.M. in Boston, 12:12 in New York, 12:02 in Baltimore, 11:48 A.M. in Pittsburgh, 11:53 in Buffalo, 11:31 in Cincinnati and 11:07 in Saint Louis. Some cities served by more than a single railroad actually had several different times. The Buffalo station had three clocks, one for the New York Central, a second for the Lake Shore & Michigan Southern, and a third set to local sun time."

Reconciling railroad timetables to one another required a mathematician's nimbleness of mind. Wisconsin alone enjoyed thirty-eight different times, and piecing together a train trip from one end of the state to the other was like trying to assemble a steam locomotive from the parts of several different builders. The British had the same problem, and so did the French, and most of all the Italians, whose impossibly eccentric mode of measuring time was to count forward twenty-four hours from the varying time of vespers all over the country. Early on the British decided to convert the time at the Greenwich observatory near London to local times for the purpose of railway time sheets. By 1852, when the telegraph had spread throughout Britain, most communities had adopted a standard "railway time" based on Greenwich Mean Time. All Britain officially adopted GMT in 1880.

The United States, however, was much too wide for a single time zone as in Britain. An eccentric but very bright educator, Professor C. F. Dowd of the Temple Grove Seminary for Young Ladies at Saratoga Springs, New York, calculated that the United States boasted, if that is the word, a total of eight thousand separate times. He proposed that the United States be divided into four time zones, and that they be linked to the Greenwich meridian.

At first the railroads ignored the idea—it was suspect simply because it was intended to make things easier for the passengers, not the railroads—but by 1883 they, too, had had enough of the confusion. On November 18, at precisely noon at the U.S. Naval Observatory in Washington, the railroads established a General Time Convention based on Dowd's proposal that put into effect, for rail industry use, four standard time zones that spanned the whole nation. In one of those endless Victorian sentences that would never stop rocking if you bumped it at one end, *The New York Times* rhapsodized:

> When the time-ball on top of the Western Union Building of this City falls at noon to-morrow, the clocks at McAdam Junction, where Maine joins New-Brunswick; at Windsor, Ontario, directly opposite Detroit, Mich., and a hundred miles farther west, at Algoma, Canada, on the St. Mary's River, which connects Lake Huron with Lake Superior and is the boundary line between the United States and Canada; one-half the clocks in Pittsburgh, those used by the railroads entering the city from the east; the clocks regulating all roads running into Buffalo from every direction except those along the southern shore of Lake Erie, and generally those east of a somewhat irregular line running from north to south about 82½ degrees west from Greenwich, as far south as the South Carolina Railroad from

Charleston west to Augusta, Ga., will all strike noon, if they are regulated to the new standard, at the same instant of time.

So powerful had the railroads become in everyday life that just about every American followed their lead, setting their clocks and watches by "railroad time." Those stubbornly independent State-of-Mainers who lived in Bangor would have no truck with the notion that the railroads could tell them what to do; no one, they said, possessed the moral power "to change one of the immutable laws of God." Congress was just as mulish. It wasn't until 1918 that Capitol Hill, then as now slow on the uptake, officially adopted Standard Time.

Americans still live who remember the high level of on-time service Standard Time allowed the railroads to provide in their golden decades between 1900 and 1940. So important was split-second timing that an entire nation no longer arranged its days by the crowing of a rooster and the setting of the sun. As early as 1848 Henry Thoreau wrote, as a train passed Walden Pond,

> I watch the passage of the morning cars with the same feeling that I do the rising of the sun, which is hardly more regular. . . . The startings and arrivals of the cars are now the epochs in the village day. They come and go with such regularity and precision, and their whistle can be heard so far, that the farmers set their clocks by them, and thus one well-conducted institution regulates a whole country. Have not men improved somewhat in punctuality since the railroad was invented? Do they not talk and think faster in the depot than they did in the stage-office?

The conductor with official pocket watch in hand became the most familiar symbol of the new reliance on time. Engineers performed foolhardy deeds to make up time when their trains were late, and when their recklessness killed them as it did an Illinois Central engineer named Casey Jones, it was celebrated in song.

As a result of the new emphasis on time, railroads helped accelerate history. Americans could hurry and do new things. We learned to measure the distance between two cities not in miles, but the time required to bridge it. By rail time, Chicago was twenty hours from New York, not some nine hundred miles. Today, by jetliner time, it's less than two hours.

At precisely 5:11 A.M. Mountain Time I thought briefly of exercising journalist's privilege and cadging a splash from the coffee urn John Davis keeps perking for the crew in the galley, but decided against it. How would I explain the presence of a steaming cup of coffee in my hand to other desperate caffeine addicts among passengers who happened to be up and around at this hour? To stave off the pangs I decided to "walk the train," the rail-borne equivalent of circling the decks of a cruise ship for exercise, and started forward.

The first Los Angeles coach looked as if it had been raided by terrorists, mowing everyone down with automatic fire during the night. Bodies sprawled across seats and in the aisle in every conceivable position, mouths agape, limbs and heads flung helter-skelter over armrests and seat backs. One hefty woman lay prone on a blanket spread on the floor beneath two seats, a fraction of an inch separating the back of her head from the bottom of the forward seat. A young man lay supine on the floor, nose barely clearing the seat in front and his legs thrown atop his own seat.

Couples huddled spoon fashion under blankets both parallel to the aisle and across two seats. The legs of one pair were entwined in what appeared to be a complicated Hindu sexual position. Still another couple slouched deeply in their seats, legs thrown up over the seat backs ahead. The sight made my sacroiliac ache. One figure slept swathed head to toe in a white sheet, looking for all the world like a corpse stiffening in a shroud. The scene, however, did not look entirely like a killing field. In several charming tableaux babies slept atop their fathers' bellies, snuggled between their parents, or snoozed on the floor between pillows in impromptu cribs. It all was a remarkable demonstration of the human body's desperate search for comfort during that long-distance American ordeal called Sitting Up All Night in Coach.

The second coach stank of stale farts, bodily crevices and morning breath, a cloying floral air "freshener" failing to mask the effluvium. It is almost a rule that one car on every train will smell either from passengers' poor personal hygiene or from plugged-up toilets. I managed to hold my breath long enough to retain my appetite as I ran the gauntlet past sleeping figures and burst into the dining car, taking a deep breath.

Striding through the empty lounge car and into the Oakland section of the train, I soon arrived in the dormitory car, and found Don Cushine beginning the train chief's morning patrol, freeing Reggie Howard to help John Davis get ready to feed the unexpect-edly heavy load of 480 passengers entering Denver. First Don tweaked a testing beep from the smoke alarm in the center of the car. Alarms have been installed in all of Amtrak's dormitory cars since 1988, when a sleeping crewman died of smoke inhalation after fire broke out in a *Zephyr* dorm car near Hastings, Nebraska.

"I knew Cesar Arguelles," said Don sadly. "I was vacationing in Europe when it happened. I got the call the following day in my hotel room, the very beginning of my vacation. My whole life I'd planned on taking this long trip to Europe and enjoying myself, and Cesar was on my mind the whole time. He was a true gentle-man, seventy years old, a food specialist in the kitchen."

No smoke alarms had been installed in sleeping cars, because most commercial devices are as sensitive to cigarette fumes as I am and would howl awake the entire car every time someone stirred for a smoke. Nonetheless, Don said, Amtrak's mechanical department was testing newer alarms, trying to find one that'd do the job. The railroad, however, wasn't overly worried about the lack of alarms in sleepers and coaches. At all hours someone's always up and around in those cars. In the 1988 fire, the conductor and his crew had been back in the coaches, getting ready for a station stop, while all ten service crew members in the dorm car were sound asleep.

With me at his heels, Don walked back through each car, stop-ping on the lower level to check the Map 21-A to see if the attend-ant had "written up" any defects. "If a toilet has been written up as bad and then fixed," Don said, "I'll flush it to make sure it's working. Every time the train gets to Oakland they'll take this top sheet out and send it to Philadelphia to be entered into a computer. Each car has a history of what's been written up, what the recurrent problems are."

On some cars certain problems crop up so often that the crew declares them "possessed." One *Zephyr* sleeper, a chief said, "would get hot, then cold, then hot, then cold—and we never touched it. When they got the news to me that it was hot I'd start back to take care of it, but it had begun to cool down by itself and by the time I got there it was always cold. A woman said, 'But it was hot twenty minutes ago—it was *hot!*' Sometimes you get so frustrated with these things you have to make a joke about it. I tell people, 'It's not just a ride, it's an adventure. You paid for that adventure, and I'm giving it to you.' "

I followed Don on his dawn patrol back through the train. In the second coach, the reek of last night's liquor on the breath of a snoring male passenger greeted us from at least fifteen feet away. "He's still asleep right now," said the attendant, accentuating the obvious. The passenger, as do so many, had brought aboard his private stock—a confiscatory offense in the coaches—and drunk himself into a stupor. He had been otherwise well behaved, the attendant said, and was not put off the train. "He left his bag in the lounge with some pints of vodka. We threw the vodka away, and the other items we've got set aside for him for when he wakes up." Don nodded wearily. Par for the course.

As we entered the lounge car, the chief caught Don's eye. "Yeah, Reggie?"

"We're having trouble again with Mildred," Reggie said.

"Mildred?" I asked.

"Yeah, you remember the lady from yesterday, the one who got her virginity back."

"Ah."

"When I went through her car this morning, she had her bra off, and was about to take off the rest of her gown right in the middle of the car to get dressed. When she saw me she stopped. I told the attendant to make sure that she wasn't drinking or anything like that. She doesn't have any money, remember?"

"Yup."

"Every now and then we get a few like her, talking about owning condos and—aaah, last night when we got to Lincoln, she was just lost."

"She was lost *long* before Lincoln," Don said.

"She started arguing and gabbing," Reggie said. "We've told her if there's one more time, just one more, we're putting her off the train."

"Is there any name, any code term, Amtrak people give to such alcoholic troublemakers?" I asked.

"None that are printable," Reggie said.

During the time I had spent walking the train with Don, the diner had opened for business. I stopped by to find it packed. Reggie was holding court in the lounge car, passing out numbers for breakfast. It'd be at least half an hour before mine came up, he said, so I returned to the lounge car for that elusive first cup of coffee for the day. Alas, it was not to be, not just yet. I was still in line threading down to the lower level for Noel Prell's coffee urn when the *Zephyr* coasted to a halt at Fort Morgan (Mile 960), the first Colorado stop, at a little past 6:30. An assistant conductor shouldered his way through the crowd. "Clear the lounge car," he said quietly but insistently. "Smoke's coming from the battery compartment."

The chief nodded calmly and stood up. "Please return to your coaches and sleepers," he called to the crowd. "We're having trouble with the lounge car and we need to fix it." The passengers did not panic, but a few growled. Some of the *Pioneer*'s passengers weren't going to get a bite to eat before Denver. "I bet they just burned the toast!" snapped an irritated older woman. Nonetheless everyone departed the car almost immediately.

As the train stopped, what must have been the entire Fort Morgan Volunteer Fire Department arrived in force—two pumpers, an emergency van and a chief's car. As I watched from the open window of the vestibule of my sleeper, a firefighter wrested open the door to the battery compartment and heavy gray smoke billowed out. In a few minutes some two dozen railroad, fire and police officials milled about outside. Two firefighters donned rubber suits, masks and air tanks, placed a ladder against the car and climbed into the battery compartment with long iron tongs. "The batteries have melted down!" one shouted. In a moment all power throughout the train was shut off, and the firefighters lifted out ten smoking batteries with the tongs and deposited them gingerly on the roadbed next to the train.

"If you are a smoker, please go back in your seat and do not collect in the vestibules to smoke!"

"They're just emergency batteries," said an assistant conductor, opening the door of Car 3530 and climbing back aboard the train. "The water level in them was low, and they just melted down. Nothing to worry about. They're just auxiliaries, backups in case both the main generator in the locomotive and the auxiliary generator in the car go out at the same time. We'll be able to use the lounge car all the way."

"No, ma'am, the train is not *on fire!"* crackled the voice of a coach attendant who had left her microphone open. *"This is* not *an emergency. Now* please *put out that cigarette and return to your seat. No smoking in the vestibules!"*

Half an hour after the little drama had begun, power was restored. The lights all through the train, including the lounge car, flickered back on. Service resumed and things settled back down to their normal crowded confusion. To my surprise my number was called for breakfast just as the train pulled away from the batteries smoldering by the track in Fort Morgan, only ten minutes behind the scheduled departure at 6:58 A.M. "We'll still arrive in Denver early," said the assistant conductor as I left for the dining car.

Lela stood in the center of the dining car with the cheery imperiousness of a racehorse broker, waving one couple to a table behind her and the next pair to a table in front, seemingly selecting them for some invisible bloodline. Vivacious even at that early hour, she greeted her charges with merry sunshine. Asked if there was a difference between first-class and coach food, she said with a wink, "If you're in coach, we feel sorry for you and give you larger portions!" As she seated each passenger, she asked, "Chair or bed?" At the puzzled expressions of some, she added, "Coach or sleeper?" Then she placed in front of each the suitable meal check. If a passenger hesitated before saying "Sleeper," she asked to see the first-class voucher. When one such young man shrugged, she said with a you-can't-fool-me smile, "Coach!"

The dining car of a train, Lela likes to say, is unique in American society. "It's the only place I've seen where everybody from every little pigeonhole in society can sit together at a table and talk. Rednecks, hippies, yuppies, old people, young people. A whole community comes together on the train."

She said she tries to encourage this sense of community by seating different kinds of people at the same table. "That's a real art, I think. I try to seat couples with other couples, singles with other singles, but I try to combine people who look as if they can connect, who can relate. They're not necessarily the same type. It's more interesting for them if they're not."

Every now and then, Lela said, she encounters antisocial passengers, those driven into a blue funk when seated with strangers. Many of these are shy couples who have never "left the farm," who have lived such isolated lives that they fail to develop sufficient social skills to deal with people unlike them. I have met a few of them. More than once my deaf person's breathy monotone and imprecise diction has spooked a rural couple into staring in terrified silence out the window. Far more often, however, my deafness whets the interest of my tablemates, who treat it as just another train-borne curiosity to investigate and even enjoy.

Some first-class riders assume their free meal tickets entitle them to private tables in the diner, but a train as busy as the *Zephyr* doesn't permit such a luxury. "Last trip I had this one little old lady from back East who seemed very nervous," Lela said. "She was in the sleeping car, and she would rush in and gobble her food down without two words to anybody. At the last lunch before Chicago I had to seat her with two very nice English people, who always had so much to say to everybody and were so friendly. I felt bad that I ended their trip on such a flat note."

Of course, Lela said, she has made many other memorable mistakes in seatings. "I once sat a nice looking single guy, and here comes this attractive, well-dressed woman about the same age. I sat her with him. It turned out that her looks were the most normal thing about her. She sat down and proceeded to lick all the salad dressings out of the little plastic cups we serve them in." Lela demonstrated baroquely, playing the dotty grande dame slurping from a champagne glass. "She picked up each one, opened it and drank every salad dressing there. He got a little nervous, because he didn't know what she was going to do next."

Some apparent disasters turn out to be thumping successes, such as the time a transvestite from San Francisco swept into the dining car. "One evening this very peculiar person comes in, a man dressed as a woman, but a very ugly woman. He's wearing a hat, like Dustin Hoffman in *Tootsie*. He was very dramatic, but nice, not obnoxious. I seated him in an empty booth and said to myself, 'Oh, God, how am I going to match this one up?' I mean, she—he—was *one of a kind.*

"It was a busy evening, and when my back was turned while I seated other people, a waiter put a couple with him. They were newlyweds, and they were just frozen stiff when they saw what was sitting across from them. They were probably just fresh off the farm and had never seen anybody like that in their lives. I could tell that this wasn't going to work. So I went over to the couple and said, 'Excuse me. That couple over there has asked if you would sit with them.' The girl knew right away what I was doing, but the husband was a bit of a dummy—he said, 'What couple, where?' And she said, 'Never mind, honey. They're back there. C'mon.' And they left.

"So I've got this guy sitting by himself right now, and he's pleasant, not a bad fellow, just very peculiar looking. All the other tables had filled up and I knew I would have to find a unique person to put with him. In walked this nice man who has been drinking ever since he left Chicago, and he was hungry. He's had enough booze and now he wants to eat. I said, 'Sir, the only seat I have left in the diner is with a Tootsie.' And he said, 'I don't care where I sit. Just let me have a steak now.' I said, 'Okay, have a seat.'

And to make a long story short, they sat and talked the *whole evening*."

The next morning, when the second man came in for breakfast, Lela thanked him for being understanding. "He said, 'I didn't know what you were telling me until I saw him. All I wanted you to say was "Yes, you can eat now." Yeah, I've never seen anything like him in my life. But he turned out to be a very interesting guy.' "

The story doesn't end there, Lela said. A week later, on her next run, "here is this man who ate with Tootsie. He says, 'I've got the funniest story for you.' He was visiting his mother in Emeryville, a tiny town between Berkeley and Oakland where he grew up, and he was schmoozing with his childhood buddies, macho guys, in a small bank. And who walks in but this Tootsie who had sat across the table from him? Talk about a small world. They recognized each other. The man said, 'I wanted to crawl into a hole, but I had to say hello, and I shook his hand. My friends gave me a very hard time.' I see that gentleman often. He lives in Chicago, and he rides the *Zephyr* a lot, and we always have a laugh."

It was not, unfortunately, a morning for me to have a laugh, for the seating of congenial dining-table companions indeed is an inexact art. I was happy to see one of my tablemates, the pleasant young Wesleyan graduate I had encountered the night before in the lounge car. The second I hadn't met. She was an Auntie Mame close to sixty, her flamboyantly wild red hair setting off a voluminous purple muumuu. As she sat down, she looked about theatrically, as if hoping people would notice her. A faded actress, perhaps?

"When you see a corral full of cows," she announced grandly, "we're almost to Denver."

We had been passing corrals full of cows every five miles since dawn, and the dark rooster's comb of the Front Range of the Rockies was just beginning to loom in the west, more than an hour and a half away. All the same, Auntie Mame seemed like a promising table companion, one whose colorful conversation could make the miles speed by. The fourth, however, was someone we three would just as soon never again meet.

By breakfast of the second day aboard a long-distance train, that sense of community of which Lela spoke is indeed beginning to coalesce. People who never saw each other before have become fast friends, at least for the rest of the trip, greeting each other familiarly in the dining car. By cocktail hour familiarity will turn into chumminess. Of course there is always a fly or two in this ointment; on every trip there is at least one impossible drunk, like Mildred of the detachable virginity. Worse, there may be a bullshit artist, a garrulous and tiresome pathological liar who inflicts himself on everyone.

This morning he sat across from me, a short rat-faced man in need of a shave. He announced as soon as he arrived that he was a Broadway producer. "How does one become a Broadway producer?" asked the young man from Wesleyan by way of polite conversation. "It's who you know," said the rat-faced man. "It's who you know." That was his favorite refrain. He shared neither backstage lore nor secrets about the mounting of musical comedies, but tried mightily to give the impression that he knew everyone of importance in the theatrical field and elsewhere, including the proprietor of a popular pizzeria in Middletown, Connecticut, home of Wesleyan University. "What was the name of that place?" he asked, and when the young man told him, he replied, "Oh, yes, I know the fellow who owns it." Then, astonishing in his transparence, he snapped his fingers and said, "What was his name? It was on the tip of my tongue. You know?" The young man looked across the table at me with a raised eyebrow.

At various times during breakfast the rat-faced man confided that he had recently traveled to South America for the State Department and was aboard an airplane that aborted its takeoff at Buenos Aires a hairbreadth before disaster. When Lela arrived to collect the meal checks, it turned out that the rat-faced man was riding in coach. Some big-shot Broadway impresario, I muttered to myself. And when it became apparent to the rat-faced man that the young man sitting next to him was a first-class passenger, the former said, obviously impressed, "Oh, you're in a sleeping car!" The young man replied pointedly, "It's who you know." Apparently missing the thrust of this sally, the rat-faced man nodded gravely. "Yes, it's who you know," he echoed. By now everyone else at the table regarded him as someone they would rather not know.

I spent the rest of the breakfast hour fiercely ignoring the rat-faced man and trying to eavesdrop on the diners near my table. Two women occupied one side of the table across the aisle. One was an elderly black woman, a social worker from Ohio headed for Las Vegas on her annual visit to the gaming tables. The second was a tall, weather-beaten white woman in her late fifties, returning to Boulder from visiting her children somewhere in the East. "I wanted to ride the train while there was still a train to ride," she said, apparently unaware of Amtrak's increasing success over the past decade, but that was the only ignorance she displayed. The facts slowly emerged: Intellectual and multilingual, she had lived in Europe and Asia while her husband built up an import-export business. He had, she said, sold his business and retired at age fifty-five. Bored, he went back to work and retired again at sixty-five. Now he was studying for a doctorate in economics at the University of Colorado.

Her small talk with the social worker touched thoughtfully on poverty, illiteracy, the plight of poor children, abortion, sexual harassment and Justice Clarence Thomas.

"I've felt from the beginning that he wasn't the strongest candidate for the Supreme Court," said the social worker, but before I could discover why, our breakfasts arrived, a little late because of early-morning confusion with another table's meal checks. (I had John Davis's "special pancakes," just to keep him honest. He boasts that he always runs out of pancake batter well before Denver, that at every breakfast at least one passenger sends down compliments and asks for his recipe. It was an unimpeachable claim: The pancakes were light, fluffy and with a thin, distinctive taste of vanilla. Yes, he does share the recipe. He is not as secretive a chef as he pretends to be.)

At the table behind my tablemates sat a shy young woman in sweats and a beret, so bereft of makeup that at first I thought she was a teenage boy. She hid behind a paperback novel rather than speak to her tablemates, a man and a woman who apparently were also singles. They, too, seemed to be loath to engage in conversation with strangers, staring past each other, out the window and into the next car, avoiding eye contact. Possibly, I thought, they had only recently boarded the *Zephyr*, and were still suffering the shy wariness of the brand-new passenger, waiting for a friendly approach from veteran riders. Out of their silence, however, they sang cheerily, "Don't worry!" when the waiter apologized twice for the inconvenience with the meal checks. She responded in kind, with frequent coffee refills for us all that soon had me afloat.

The next table demonstrated the First Law of Baseball Caps: Rural males never take them off, even for meals. Four hefty men in denim occupied the table. Two were middle-aged and wore their caps (one John Deere, one DeKalb Hybrids) in the usual mode of their generation, bills forward. The other two, apparently their teenage sons, wore their caps (both St. Louis Cardinals) in the usual mode of *their* generation, bills backward. There clearly was meaning in the difference, but that early in the morning I couldn't develop the idea past a simple observation.

Farther down, a three-year-old girl jumped down from her seat on the aisle and dashed up and down while her mother breakfasted next to the window. With a gentle smile Lela suggested to the mother that her child might like to sit by the window and look out on the passing world, that it was dangerous for the toddler to be in a busy aisle. There was no bite to Lela's voice; it was relaxed, cheerful and matter-of-fact. The mother did not take offense. As if she considered it simply an excellent idea that had never occurred to her, she swept up the child and put her next to the window, out of harm's way.

After breakfast I decided to move my two bags through the train from the Los Angeles section to the luggage rack in the Oakland sleeper to avoid the confusion and crush of the hour's layover in Denver. As I traversed the second Oakland coach on the way to the sleeper, I passed by the rat-faced "Broadway producer" in his seat on the aisle. He wore a dingy T-shirt, its tail hanging out of his trousers. Potato chip wrappers and disheveled newspapers surrounded him. He nattered rapidly at a gray-haired man who leaned away up against the window, gazing out at the countryside in helpless consternation. Poor devil, I thought, and I didn't mean the rat-faced man.

Fortunately the rolling community aboard a train is ever-changing, constantly turning over as people board and debark. Perhaps only about fifty passengers each trip will travel all the way from Chicago to Oakland; as many as two thousand will come and go, like transients in the night. In a real sense it's a microcosm of American rootlessness. We always seem to be from someplace else. Eventually we do arrive somewhere that looks good enough to suit us for the rest of our lives, and there we drive our roots. For one reason or another, however, our children blow elsewhere, like leaves. It's another tradition of the frontier.

Naturally this constant turnover can limit the depth of friendships we might make on the train as well as wherever else we hang our hats, but it also offers a constant replenishment of new faces and new opportunities. And, I fervently hoped, it increased the odds that the rat-faced man would disappear at Denver. As it turned out, he did.

"May I have your attention, please? We are approaching Denver, and all bathrooms are now being locked until the train leaves Denver at nine-forty. Attendants, inhibit your systems!"

Inhibit your systems? Passengers looked at each other blankly. What did that mean? "It's just Amtrakese for shutting down the plumbing," said a knowledgeable rider. It was now 8:20 A.M., and even with the fifteen-minute loss at Fort Morgan, the *Zephyr* was rolling past the Burlington Northern locomotive ready tracks in Denver, a sure sign that the station was only fifteen minutes away. All east-west trains must back into the historic station, built in the early twentieth century and aligned north to south with the traffic, which paralleled the Rocky Mountains. Slowly the train arched north until the last car cleared the switches, then stopped. And waited. And waited. Outside, bustling switchers kicked around boxcars and long freight trains arrived and departed. But the *Zephyr* remained still.

"Mechanical rider to the last car! Mechanical rider to the last car!" called an irritated voice on the PA.

"What went wrong?" I asked an assistant conductor when I arrived in the Oakland sleeper, just as the train finally began to move backward. "Why did it take so long to start backing?"

He chuckled wryly. "It was the mechanical rider, the fix-it guy who travels with the train. Last night he used duct tape to seal the outside door in the last car, the Seattle coach, because the wind was whistling through and keeping a passenger awake. The conductor, who has to stand in the open door with his radio to tell the engineer when to stop backing in, didn't know the door was taped and couldn't get it open. It's a little dark back there and he couldn't see the tape. One of those little damned things."

All the same the *Zephyr* berthed at Denver Union Station, 1,037 miles from Chicago, at 8:43 A.M.—just three minutes late. By Amtrak's book and that of any reasonable person, On Time.

SIX

O n Time, but without panache. The *California Zephyr* calls at Denver not as a train should—gliding in head high like the silvery diva she is, with fanfare from the locomotive horns—but in the manner of a bashful stripper who backs onstage, timidly wiggling her rump. With a soft bump and grind the train jolted back and forth for a few moments, the crew making sure the waiting Seattle diner had been coupled securely to the end of the train. On departure the *Zephyr* and *Desert Wind* would unhook from the *Pioneer*, whose locomotive, waiting alone on a ready track, would then back down to its charges and take them away.

"We'll be here for only about twenty minutes," the attendant said in the meantime. "Don't go far, and be ready to get back aboard fast." I smiled. He was dissembling in true mother-hen attendant fashion, worried about leaving behind his passengers. We'd stop in Denver a full hour.

Another familiar *Zephyr* scenario began to unfold. The young man ahead of me in the vestibule—the Wesleyan student—danced lightly from toe to toe. "Too much coffee?" I asked. He clearly was feeling the effect of the plumbing shutdown throughout the train, and scores of passengers must have been doing the Mile High Two-Step until they could storm the station. Unfortunately, the men's room in Denver Union Station contains only two urinals and three stalls. The lines are endless, and the agony is even worse for those aboard the evening's eastbound *Zephyr,* many of whose beer-drinking passengers grow painfully awash during the forty-five minutes between toilet shutdown and train stop.

My own bladder began to throb. The Oakland sleeper was near the head of the long train, the gate to the waiting room near the end. We'd be tail-end Charlies for the men's and women's. "I know how you feel," I told the young man. He winked and said, "Follow me," as the door finally opened. A large parking lot greeted us. Instead of trailing the snail-slow, suitcase-laden crowd down the endless platform, the young man—clearly a veteran at this sort of thing—led me at a brisk trot across the lot and around the front of the station, whose doors we burst through almost before the first passengers had entered on the opposite side. An empty men's room greeted us. *Wheeeeeeeeeew.*

Denver Union Station is a classic midsize Western railroad depot, well kept but smelling of musty age and utilitarian seedi-ness. Its high-vaulted waiting room seemed cavernous and nearly empty despite the milling of some one hundred passengers, almost all in ski togs, near the conductor's table for car assignments and boarding passes. In an hour the station would be all but dead, the only signs of life dust motes dancing in sunbeams. Only in the evening would it awaken, when the eastbound *Pioneer* arrived from Seattle, followed shortly afterward by the combined *Zephyr* and *Desert Wind* from Salt Lake City. (On weekends from January through early April there's a bit more activity when the *Rio Grande Ski Train* to Winter Park departs Denver at 7:15 A.M. and returns at 6:00 P.M.)

Meanwhile, car knockers crouched by each car, rapping its un-dercarriage with hammers, listening for healthy pings and un-healthy clunks, making sure all was well with the running gear.

Crews unloaded trash and replenished consumables: fuel and water for the locomotives and cars; beer, soda and ice for the lounge car. With a loud *pow!* as the air hoses parted, the engines and the first mail car separated from the train, heading for the post office just below the station. There the mail car would be spotted for unloading during the morning, loading during the afternoon and pickup by the eastbound *Zephyr* in the evening.

Mail? On *Amtrak?* Yes, indeed. Amtrak trains carry mail these days, almost entirely second class but occasionally first class between end-point cities served by its long-distance trains. In recent years Amtrak, seeking new ways of diminishing its red ink, has aggressively wrestled with trucking companies and the airlines for mail business. It has succeeded to the point that its old baggage cars no longer suffice to carry the mail; it has had to build a fleet of long, square-edged cars called "Amboxes." Three of them left Chicago at the head of the *Zephyr*, two would go on to Oakland.

They're the only visible reminders of the long trains that used to carry passengers and mail or, especially at night, nothing but the mail. One of the least-known items of American history is that by themselves the railroads created cheap, fast, high-volume mail service. Before they came along, the mail was carried by stage-coach, riverboat and square-rigger around Cape Horn. Wherever passenger trains went, the mail could go. In 1838 Congress declared every railroad in the United States a "post-route," and by the 1880s every major railroad fielded overnight expresses, each of them often called the *Fast Mail,* between major cities—long trains of mail cars. (In mid-1992 Amtrak's train Number 13 between Springfield, Massachusetts, and Washington stopped carrying passengers, becoming an all-mail train. Its name? The *Fast Mail,* of course.)

So important did the mail expresses become to the railroads that orders went out to make sure their engineers saw nothing but green lights before them. At stations along the way, special stanchions held mail bags to be picked up on the fly. Soon the *Fast Mails* were the flagships of the railroads that carried them. Later someone happened upon the seemingly obvious idea that human beings were worth rushing from point to point as quickly as the mail, and fast *passenger* expresses were born.

Though their main purpose was to speed the mails by sorting letters in transit rather than letting them lie around the post office, Railway Post Office cars were full-fledged, full-service outposts of the U.S. Mail, complete with their own postmarks. You could happen upon a passenger train on a siding in the middle of the most inaccessible nowhere, rap on the RPO car door and demand to buy a stamp and mail a letter. The men inside had to sell you one, take the envelope and speed it on to its destination. It was the law.

RPO men called themselves the "Railway Mule Service," and they had one of the toughest, yet least celebrated, jobs on the railroad. They'd stand on their feet in an RPO car bucketing at eighty-five miles per hour through the night, trying to keep their balance while flipping letters into an array of unmarked pigeon-holes that ran most of the length of the car. They sorted the mail not only by state, county and town—this was before ZIP codes—but sometimes by street and house number. They had to build accurate mental maps of the delivery routes in every city and town along their runs. They had to know postal laws and regulations as well. Each year for the first ten years of his employment, an RPO clerk had to pass a grueling examination.

Catching the mail on the fly was both perilous and difficult. During steam-locomotive days RPO men wore handkerchiefs around their mouths and goggles on their faces; anyone who had to go to the hospital with a cinder in his eye missed a day's pay. Operating the mail sack catcher took long experience; it wasn't just that the RPO man had to swing it down to snatch the heavy canvas mailbag hanging between the arms of the station stanchion. He had to know exactly when and where his target lay. Sometimes the only point of reference he had was the dim shape of a barn in the moonlight, and he had to count the number of seconds between landmark and stanchion. Too soon and he might catch the side of a wooden boxcar on the next track in a shower of sharp splinters.

Too late and he might miss entirely—delaying the mail. That was unforgivable in a day when the public had full confidence that a letter posted in the box on the corner would be delivered when the U.S. Mail promised.

In other ways RPO service could be a dangerous trade. The mail cars usually rode at the front of passenger trains, more vulnerable in wrecks and to holdup artists such as the James brothers and Butch Cassidy and the Sundance Kid. As late as 1940, a New York Central train heading out of New York City was held up near a bridge over the Harlem River between the Bronx and Manhattan. The robbers, packing tommy guns, grabbed two sacks of mail and fled into the night. However, they missed the registered mail containing Federal Reserve banknotes, escaping instead with newspapers and parcel post.

The old *California Zephyr* never carried the mail. As a tourist train, designed to see the prettiest part of the country during the daylight hours, it was poorly scheduled for postal service, leaving Chicago and Oakland before the day's mail was sorted and arriving in those cities after the delivery time. The mail went by the much faster Overland Route on the Southern Pacific, Union Pacific and Chicago & North Western until the middle 1960s, when the Post Office decided the nation's flagging passenger trains no longer were reliable carriers of the mail, and began sending it by plane and truck instead. It's probably unfair to declare that the U.S. Mail lost its on-time reliability because it no longer went by train—but it's hard not to believe it, either.

While the mail car was being spotted at the Denver post office, most of the passengers had detrained, even those going on to the mountains and points west. Some left the station and hiked around the neighborhood, an old warehouse area recently gentrified with shops, art galleries and restaurants. It is easy to grow logy and overstuffed on a transcontinental rail ride, and there would be no other opportunity for brisk exercise until the next servicing stops after midnight at Salt Lake City and the next morning at Sparks, Nevada.

Spotting a *New York Times* honor box in front of the station, I marched over, bought the last remaining copy, took the *Denver Post* and *Rocky Mountain News* from adjoining boxes, and set off on a brisk circumnavigation of the block, stopping now and again to peer inside galleries and stained-glass emporiums. Other passengers remained inside to buy snacks and reading material at the gift shop and mill about Grandpa's Depot, a corner of the station devoted to railroadiana.

On my way back I stopped in at Grandpa's and perused the old dining-car crockery and cutlery, timetables, switchmen's lamps and advertising posters, some with eye-popping price tags. They jostled for attention on shelves with Amtrak sweatshirts and engineer's caps. It takes only a few years to transform yesterday's kitsch into today's Americana, I thought ruefully as I handed over fifteen dollars for a stained, dog-eared *Condensed Profile of the D. & R.G.W.R.R. System,* a 1967 manual outlining track elevations throughout the Denver & Rio Grande Western Railroad. It was, of course, all but useless to me—but, in the classic tourist impulse, I wanted something to show just for having been there.

Near departure time I decided to return to the train by walking up the platform with everyone else. On the way Don Cushine stopped me. "I was planning to go on with you," the train manager said sweatily, "but I just got word that tonight's eastbound *Zephyr* has lost power in the diner. The chief's called ahead for hamburgers to be delivered to the train for lunch, but what's he going to do for tonight and tomorrow? I'll have to help handle this." Better you than me, I thought, envisioning his having to placate hundreds of disappointed dining-car patrons with bags of Big Macs and Kentucky Fried Chicken. We shook hands, and Don disappeared into the stationmaster's office.

Back aboard the Oakland sleeper I quickly stowed my coat and bags without waiting for the attendant to drop by, introduce himself and explain the operation of the room. That could wait. As soon as they can, knowledgeable *Zephyr* riders claim seats in the lounge car before the train departs Denver, for it'll be standing-room-only all the way through the spectacular scenery from the foothills to Winter

Park. In the lounge car I found a spot in the middle on the better side—the right side facing toward the locomotives. That's where the most gorgeous vistas lie during the first two hours of the run into the Rockies. Happily, despite the long night's journey the windows were still quite clean. Snow or rain would have spotted and streaked them. Amtrak keeps a mobile car washer at Denver that cleans one side of the train as it backs in and the other side as it pulls out, but it's used only from late spring to early fall.

My watch ticked to 9:40 A.M. As the passengers sighed in anticipation, the *Zephyr* began to creep forward. "We're on time!" someone crowed.

"There's a passenger on this train that should be in the Seattle section!" the conductor barked. *"Please respond!"*

Almost immediately the train halted, and thirty seconds later resumed its forward progress, the stray *Pioneer* passenger presumably having been shooed back to the proper train. Now a quiet hubbub bubbled through the lounge car as the train arched in a tight curve northward on the Denver & Rio Grande Western Railroad—or, to be strictly accurate, the Southern Pacific. In 1988 the owners of the 2,200-mile-long Rio Grande bought the 13,000-mile Southern Pacific and, in the fashion of such mergers, the name of the larger corporate entity swallowed that of the smaller. Nonetheless, locomotives on the Southern Pacific's Rio Grande Division are still painted for the old railroad, and everybody will call the historic line from Denver to Salt Lake City the "Rio Grande" for a long time to come.

The *California Zephyr* follows not the route of the first transcontinental railroad, the Union Pacific line from Omaha across upper Nebraska through Wyoming and Utah, but that of a comparative Johnny-come-lately. What it lacks in historical primacy, however, the Rio Grande makes up for in staggering beauty, and it has a pungent historical flavor of its own.

After the Civil War Coloradans had lobbied mightily for the transcontinental breakthrough to be built through their state, but the Union Pacific opted for the much easier route through the low

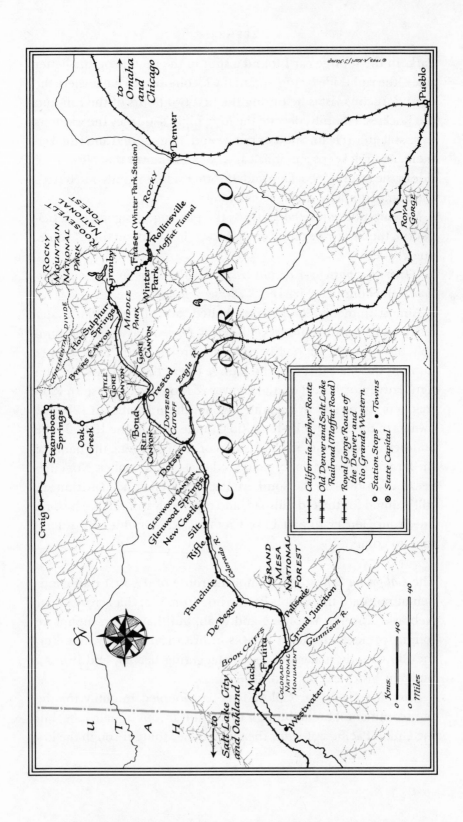

© 1993 A. Karl / J. Kemp

to Omaha and Chicago

Pueblo

ROYAL GORGE

Denver

Rollinsville
Moffat Tunnel

Fraser (Winter Park Station)

ROCKY

ROCKY MOUNTAIN NATIONAL PARK

ROOSEVELT NATIONAL FOREST

Granby

Winter Park

MIDDLE PARK

Hot Sulphur Springs

BYERS CANYON

CONTINENTAL DIVIDE

GORE CANYON

LITTLE GORE CANYON

Orestod

Dotsero Cutoff

Eagle R.

C O L O R A D O

Steamboat Springs

Oak Creek

BOND RED CANYON

Craig

Dotsero

GLENWOOD CANYON
Glenwood Springs

New Castle

Silt

Rifle

Colorado R.

Parachute

De Beque

GRAND MESA NATIONAL FOREST

Palisade

Grand Junction

Gunnison R.

BOOK CLIFFS

Fruita

Mack

COLORADO NATIONAL MONUMENT

Westwater

U T A H

to Salt Lake City and Oakland

N

Kms.   0   40

Miles   0   40

California Zephyr Route

Old Denver and Salt Lake Railroad (Moffat Road)

Royal Gorge Route of the Denver and Rio Grande Western

○ Station Stops

• Towns

◎ State Capital

mountain passes of southern Wyoming. In 1872, three years after the historic linkup of the westward-building Union Pacific and the eastbound Central Pacific at Promontory, Utah, the new Denver & Rio Grande Railroad drove south along the Front Range to Colorado Springs and Pueblo, aiming to follow the Rio Grande River to El Paso, Texas, then cross the stream and head for Mexico City. After skirmishing with the Santa Fe Railway over access to mountain passes near New Mexico, the Rio Grande gave up its lofty goal of spanning Texas and Mexico and instead pushed west through the spectacular Royal Gorge of the Arkansas River, finally reaching Utah in 1882.

The Rio Grande originally was a narrow-gauge line, its rails standing three feet apart instead of everybody else's four feet, eight and one-half inches. The only economical way to throw a railroad around the cliffs and over the chasms of the rugged Rockies to the precious metals within was to employ comparatively cheap narrow-gauge tracks under short cars and small locomotives that could handle tight curves and steep grades. A narrow-gauge railroad, the saying went, could "curve on the brim of a sombrero," and by the 1880s a large network of "baby railroad" crisscrossed the Colorado Rockies.

At the same time, however, the Rio Grande needed to carry the standard cars of other railroads, and began converting some of its through lines to dual-gauge track. By 1890 its main line from Denver through the Royal Gorge to Ogden, Utah, had been converted to standard gauge. When the precious-metal mines petered out, so did the "baby railroad" lines, rapidly abandoned after World War II. Surprisingly heavy traffic kept open the narrow-gauge branch between Durango and Silverton in the southwestern corner of the state until 1979, when the Rio Grande sold it to a private operator who still runs it as a tourist railroad.

The *California Zephyr* departs Denver not on the original Rio Grande tracks of the nineteenth century but those of an entirely different railroad, born in 1902 as the Denver, Northwestern & Pacific. It was the brainchild of a farsighted but underfunded Denver banker named David Moffat, who decided to build a railroad connecting Salt Lake City with the Burlington Route, which had merged its way into Denver by 1882. He aimed his line west from Denver through the forbidding Front Range of the Rockies, in 1905 surmounting 11,680-foot Rollins Pass hard by 13,260-foot James Peak. The line was so high and so rugged it was easily choked by snow, and during the bitter winter of 1904–5 it had to be shut down for several months when its new rotary plow became snowbound.

The next summer, Moffat ran out of money when his railroad reached Hot Sulphur Springs, and an infusion of new funds could take it only as far as Steamboat Springs in northwestern Colorado. In 1912 the "Moffat Road" was reorganized as the Denver & Salt Lake Railroad, which staggered only a few miles farther west, to Craig. It never reached Salt Lake City but struggled along through snowstorms, tunnel collapses, bankruptcy and strikes until 1922. That year the city of Denver and the state of Colorado at last recognized the importance of Moffat's railroad to the development of the northwestern part of the state, and passed a bill that funded the boring of a six-mile-long tunnel under Rollins Pass, ensuring the railroad's survival.

At the time it opened in 1928, the Moffat Tunnel was the longest railroad bore in North America; only the 7.2-mile Cascade and Flathead Tunnels on the Burlington Northern in Washington and Montana, and the 9.1-mile Mount Macdonald Tunnel on the Canadian Pacific in British Columbia, are longer. The circuitous twenty-three-mile-long journey over Rollins Pass had taken five hours; the tunnel, crossing the Continental Divide at more than nine thousand feet, cut the time to ten minutes. Not long after, the Rio Grande swallowed the Denver & Salt Lake.

Much later, in 1971, when Amtrak took over most of the nation's remaining long-distance passenger trains, the Rio Grande was one of the few holdouts. The maverick railroad's official reason was that it believed the grandeur of its Rockies scenery might attract enough passengers for it to turn a profit operating a daily train between Denver and Salt Lake City. The real reason was that management thought two Amtrak trains each day would interfere with the profitable running of freight trains on the single-track main-line. If the Rio Grande could keep its segment of the *Zephyr* operating between Denver and Salt Lake City, Amtrak would stay away. The Rio Grande believed, as did many observers at the time, that Amtrak had no future and the *Zephyr* could easily be dropped in a few years.

And so the Rio Grande renamed its share of the streamliner the *Rio Grande Zephyr*, and kept it going. Meanwhile, Amtrak rerouted what was left of the Burlington and Western Pacific train over the faster, less scenic, more northerly Overland Route—the Union Pacific Railroad main line north from Denver to Cheyenne, Wyoming, thence west to Ogden, Utah, bypassing Salt Lake City—and renamed it the *San Francisco Zephyr*. Amtrak's train also mounted the Sierra Nevada over the shorter and more direct Southern Pacific line rather than the slower and prettier Western Pacific route. The new route cut the total mileage of today's Amtrak *California Zephyr* run from 2,525 to 2,416.

By 1982—when Amtrak had demonstrated that it was here to stay—the *Rio Grande Zephyr* had become so popular, winning free and favorable publicity from Europe to Japan, that the Rio Grande faced a hard decision. Fine as the train was, the *Zephyr*'s cars were reaching the end of their serviceable life and needed to be replaced. The only way to avoid doing so was to reverse the decision of 1971, and Amtrak immediately rerouted its Superliner *Zephyr* across Colorado.

As Amtrak's *Zephyr* curved out of Denver Union Station toward the Moffat Tunnel fifty miles ahead, Burlington Northern territory lay to the right and Rio Grande yards to the left. I looked ahead. The three locomotives with which we had left Chicago were still at the head of the train. Even though the three cars of the *Pioneer* and one mail car had been dropped, three F40s still were needed to haul the remaining fourteen cars of the combined *Zephyr/Desert Wind* over the Rockies.

Barely two minutes after pulling out of the station, the train stopped . . . and then began backing. What? I thought irritatedly.

Don't tell me they've found another *Pioneer* orphan who should've had the sense to stay in his own part of the train! But then I noticed that the train was backing onto a different track, the second one away from the station.

"Your attention, please!" said the conductor. *"There will be just a short delay while we couple a private car on to the back of the train."*

Short delay? It was nearly 10:35 A.M. when the *Zephyr* stopped rocking forward and back, sulking a while like a colicky baby, then rocking forward and back again, and finally departed the Denver yards. I had no idea why it had taken so long to couple on that private car, but the reason, I thought, couldn't have been as absurd as the one that had caused a ninety-minute delay at Denver on a previous eastbound trip. The new engineer, we were told, didn't like a crack in the windshield of the leading F40 and demanded that the engines be turned so that one with a pristine windshield faced forward—although the crack didn't seem to have bothered the engineers who had brought the *Zephyr* from Oakland. This was inexcusable, especially with all those passengers with near-to-bursting bladders waiting for the train to leave so they could rush the restrooms.

Where, I thought, was Artemus Ward now that we needed his wit? During the Civil War, the humorist was riding in the last car of a particularly lackadaisical train when the conductor came by.

"Does this railroad allow passengers to give it advice," Ward asked the conductor, "if they do so in a respectful manner?"

"I guess it does," the conductor said.

"Well then, it occurred to me it would be well to detach the cowcatcher from the front of the engine, and hitch it to the rear of the train. For, you see, we are not liable to overtake a cow; but what's to prevent a cow from strolling into this car and biting a passenger?"

The assistant conductor apologetically interrupted my reverie as he came through the lounge car. "There were problems with the brake hose on the private car." Bending down to whisper, he added, "It happens, but Amtrak charges six thousand dollars to haul a private car from Denver to Oakland. Real moneymaker for us."

Nonetheless, the delay was irksome. Long dawdles in the Denver yards during the early spring mean that darkness may fall before the *Zephyr* passes through some of the best scenery in Colorado. I hoped we wouldn't drop further behind schedule.

Meanwhile, the train gathered speed through Arvada, a suburb whose trackside scenery is a mix of pretty houses and auto grave-yards. A few lonely horses grazed in scrubby backyards as Arvada thinned out, including a shapely Appaloosa that rose from the ground and shook itself gracefully as the train sped by at sixty miles per hour. Once past Arvada, the *Zephyr* stepped up onto the broad, bare, almost treeless front porch of the Rockies. The snowy roof of the Front Range loomed close over the train, but first we had to mount the foothills. Mule deer, startled from ditches and hedge-rows along the track, scattered like jackstraws.

Slowly the train swung north from its westerly course, then curved back west and south up a steepening grade, the locomotives slowing from the effort. The *Zephyr*'s headlight briefly pointed eastward as it climbed up and around the edge of a knob bulging from the foothills. The knob, called Rocky, is an enormous treeless Roman nose that juts from the brow of the Front Range. Clearly it gets its name from the moraine of boulders scattered like Brob-dingnagian marbles across its flat top.

The track curves in a giant loop south, then west and north again around the edge of the knob and across the foothills, gaining height all the way. On the inside of the curve—called the "Big Ten" by Rio Grande railroaders for the degree of its curvature—two dozen ancient hopper cars, laden with sand and gravel and sad brown bushes, squat rustily on detached rails, serving as a wind-break. Gusts up here can top one hundred miles per hour, periling the tall Superliners as well as excess-height freight cars. During a trip I'd taken three months earlier, the *Denver Post* reported that winds up to 117 miles per hour had blown out automobile windshields and toppled semitrailer trucks on the state highway nearby. The tempest, the paper said, was "typical January weather in Boulder County." It had been caused by the polar jet stream dipping southward as it flowed from Montana to Kansas, clipping northeastern Colorado.

The grade along the face of the foothills is a brisk 2 percent, meaning that the tracks gain two feet of altitude for every one hundred feet of rail. The locomotives leaned into their load like steel oxen, snorting plumes of exhaust skyward. They worked hard, their throaty revolutions rattling the rocks outside, but we could barely hear them inside the well-insulated lounge car, where latecomer standees groused loudly about "how some people hog seats and don't move all day so we can sit down too." Those who heard them adopted tough-cheese expressions and slid lower in their seats, driving home their claims.

"Look!" shouted a passenger. "Antelope!" They weren't; they were just one of the herds of mule deer ubiquitous to the Rockies. A few minutes past Rocky the train curtsied westward, then north again across Coal Creek Canyon and over a two-lane highway, a solitary coyote sitting sentinel on a low mound in a brown meadow, holding his lordly pose as the *Zephyr* rumbled by a hundred yards away. As the train wound around the canyon, the first of twenty-eight tunnels before the Continental Divide loomed ahead. There was just time to spot "TUNNEL NO. 1" emblazoned on its portal before the lounge car plunged into it. The *Zephyr* emerged a few seconds later onto Plainview, one of the great scenic stages of North America.

From Plainview the *Zephyr* is a rolling grandstand for gazing out upon the entire Denver metropolitan area, the high plains of eastern Colorado fading into infinity below. The view includes the Rocky Flats nuclear plant to the north, the nation's only processor of plutonium for atomic weapons, reputedly one of the most polluted in the nuclear industry. As the Cold War wound down in the early nineties, the federal government seemed certain to pull the plug on Rocky Flats. The hazy brown pall of air pollution that enshrouded the horizon from north to south seemed symbolic of the perilous cleanup task the nation faced.

Fortunate for the eastbound *Zephyr* riders, I thought, that they'd emerge from the mountains in the dark this evening to a world-class spectacle. Drifting down Plainview aboard the train at night is like a languorously extended landing approach to a big-city airport, the brilliant evening lights of the metropolitan area winking almost endlessly below.

For ten minutes the *Zephyr* traversed the beginning of the Rio Grande's "Tunnel District," one bore almost immediately followed by another. Massive broken anticlines testified to the enormous geological forces that thrust up the Rockies eons ago. Snow dusted crags, etching them in high relief like a tableau sprinkled with powdered sugar. The white background outlined deer and elk lurking in copses and brush below, and passengers hastened to unlimber their cameras. Some cursed quietly as they hurriedly focused, only to see their shots spoiled as the train plunged into tunnel after tunnel.

"Do not open the vestibule windows on the lower levels to take photographs!" the PA crackled. *"If you do, you will feel a wet breeze on your face. That's from the toilets in the car in front of yours!"*

In eleven minutes the *Zephyr* threaded seventeen tunnels. During this time, after it had slowed to twenty miles per hour on the constant tight curves, the *Zephyr* turned due west at Tunnel No. 8 and pierced the curtain of the Front Range. Scarcely fifty minutes had passed since the train departed Denver. At the one-hour mark, just before Tunnel No. 20, the crowd in the lounge car took a last glimpse through the mountains at the plains. Jaws dropped as gorge after breathtaking gorge passed below as the train twisted through South Boulder Canyon. A broadside of still and video cameras fired as a passenger pointed at the remnants of a wooden logging flume hugging the cliffside across the way. Suddenly a triangle of blue water peeked through the crags. It was Gross Reservoir, whose 340-foot-high concrete dam holds back billions of gallons from both eastern and western watersheds of the Rockies

for piping to the Denver area. (Water from the Pacific side of the
Continental Divide is sent under the mountains through a pipe
paralleling the Moffat Tunnel. At the eastern portal the water is
dumped into a creek to flow naturally down South Boulder Canyon
to Gross Reservoir.)

Between Tunnels No. 26 and 27 the train slowed to a funereal
ten miles per hour as it passed the site of a fatal wreck in September 1991. At four in the morning an eastbound freight train
rounded a curve and smashed into a truck-sized boulder that had
fallen onto the track from the canyon wall just a short time before.
The lead locomotive fell only partway down the embankment, but
the second engine toppled five hundred feet to the creek and was
struck by a tumbling freight car that killed a conductor and a
brakeman in the cab. With both his locomotive radios out of
action, the injured engineer staggered through 643-foot-long
Tunnel 27, pitch black and jammed tight with derailed cars, then
hiked three miles back to the village of Pinecliff and a wayside
phone to bring news of the calamity to his dispatcher, who had
been desperately calling the train crew on the radio.

It was a freakish accident; the rock had fallen in one of the few
spots where the Rio Grande does not maintain warning fences.
Rock that falls through such fences breaks wires and trips block
signals to red, halting trains until the source of the trouble is
discovered. Months after the wreck, deep gashes in the ground
remained unhealed and the remnants of a smashed freight car
peeked up from the bottom of the gorge. The scene was a sober
reminder that mountain railroading is still one of the most perilous industrial pursuits in America.

As the train slowly rolled by the small mountain town of Rollinsville
in the Roosevelt National Forest, Reggie's voice resounded over
the PA. *"We will be entering the Moffat Tunnel very shortly. While we
are in the tunnel please do not pass from car to car. Please stay in your
seat until we are out of the tunnel. We want to avoid getting fumes from
the locomotives in the cars."*

Minutes later the train plunged into darkness. Without the *Zephyr* to keep it in the public eye, the Moffat Tunnel, more than six miles from portal to portal, would be one of the great forgotten engineering marvels of the Western Hemisphere. Unfortunately, *Zephyr* riders have not been able to see more than a glimpse of the tunnel's majestic portals since 1983, when the Rio Grande finally threw in the towel on its money-losing remnant of the original *California Zephyr* and the last of the storied old glass-topped coaches gave way to Amtrak's Superliners, whose lounge cars don't afford much view of what's just ahead of and above the train.

As the *Zephyr* threaded the inky darkness of the Moffat Tunnel, I spotted down the lounge car the green-Mohawked youth I had seen the day before in Chicago Union Station. How I could have missed him since then, I don't know. He slept supine across a swiveling double seat turned partway into the aisle, the back of his head carefully propped on an armrest to protect his hairdo. Its long spikes protruded into the aisle. As I stepped carefully around the human hedgehog, I noticed a dark, swollen mouse under his left eye. Whether he had the shiner on departure, or perhaps had obtained it during a mild disagreement in the lounge car the night before, I couldn't say. Those deep scars on his cheek and chin, however, didn't look like cuts from shaving. He did not seem a person to awaken for casual conversation, and I let him be. But not until I had noticed, upside down, the legend in foot-high letters on his grimy white T-shirt: "тıнs." A high school athletic shirt? Nope. He was wearing it inside out.

Reggie stepped up from the lower level, and I pointed to the slumbering Mohawk. "Yeah, on departure yesterday I asked him to put on another shirt," the chief said, "but he doesn't have any other clothes. Turning it inside out was the best he could do." He chuckled. "Another guy got aboard yesterday wearing a T-shirt that said 'FUCK SADDAM.' He was sitting next to an old lady in the coach, and I called him into the vestibule and told him she might be offended. He shook his head and said, 'She's my ma.' "

Reggie shook his own head and continued. "He wasn't happy,

but he changed the shirt. Sometimes I've got to be a censor, trying to decide what isn't tasteful to wear in front of the other passengers. Being a censor isn't a lot of fun either."

Returning to the lower level, Reggie led a pack of a dozen or more ten- to twelve-year-olds behind his long, long legs like the Pied Piper. "Follow me! Follow me!" he said. What they were going to do I had no idea, but they all wore gaudy sweats, looking like an ambulatory explosion in a boutique. "GEOFFREY BEENE." "DIOR." "BEARS." "BULLS." "U2."

The American penchant for self-advertisement begins very young and grows with age, as I've seen more than once aboard the *Zephyr*. A sixteen-year-old had Marlboros for breakfast in the lower lounge while wearing a black T-shirt declaring, "D.A.R.E. TO TAKE KIDS OFF DRUGS." Another teenager wore "STOP THE BRUTAL GROOMING," whatever that meant. Still another dressed in a faded sweatshirt emblazoned "DIE YUPPIE SCUM!" A slatternly middle-aged woman favored a fire-engine-red T-shirt that proclaimed, "POLICE OFFICERS ARE ARRESTING PERSONALITIES." On a buxom bottled blonde of indeterminate age was a tight T-shirt marked, "IS THAT A PICKLE IN YOUR POCKET OR ARE YOU HAPPY TO SEE ME?" On her the line just didn't carry the ribald insouciance of Mae West, who said it first.

Once in a while there is some genuine wit, as with the young man whose T-shirt, advertising a Chicago bookstore on the back, opined on the front: "OUTSIDE OF A DOG A BOOK IS A MAN'S BEST FRIEND. INSIDE OF A DOG IT'S TOO DARK TO READ!—GROUCHO MARX." I remember fondly the shapely young women who wore "I PREFER IT ON TOP" and "WHEN I'M GOOD, I'M VERY, VERY GOOD. AND WHEN I'M BAD, I'M TERRIFIC!" One T-shirt that won my full admiration read, "THE LORD JESUS IS COMING. AND IS HE EVER PISSED." So did "ANKH IF YOU LOVE ISIS."

Why are Americans such walking billboards? Paul Fussell observed in his wickedly hilarious book *Class* that "by wearing a garment reading 'SPORTS ILLUSTRATED' or 'GATORADE' or 'LESTER LANIN,' [a person] associates himself with an enterprise the world judges successful, and thus, for the moment, he achieves some importance." Among the highbrow classes, he continued, "the T-shirts and carryalls stamped with the logo of the *New York Review of Books* . . . convey the point, 'I read hard books.' "

Remembering that, I looked down at my athletic-gray sweatshirt, emblazoned "KENYON" in large purple letters. Although I am not a graduate of that illustrious institution, I have earned by the sweat of my brow the right to wrap myself in that totem: sending my second son to Kenyon costs my exchequer $22,000 a year—at this writing. God knows what it'll be next year. On the other hand, highfalutin brand names like that can send mixed signals. In Denver Union Station the summer before, a sturdy salt-of-the-earth matron dashed up to me, tugged at the sleeve of the sweatshirt, and announced in a shower of dimples, "My husband's name is Kenyon, too!" Lord love those Real People.

My gaze alighted on a black mother who had spent hours at the far end of the lounge car combing out and knotting her twelve-year-old daughter's long, straightened hair into eight octopus braids, bedecking them gaily with small black, yellow and red pompons. Another African-American family, also dressed in bright colors, joined them. Immediately they exchanged wisdom on the relative efficiencies of various brands of curling irons, beginning a one-hundred-mile symposium, full of giggles and belly laughs, on the hairdressing arts. They were an oasis of sparkling good cheer in a sea of self-consciously reserved whites and Asians in the lounge car. When a dour white teenager with long, limp, straggly hair, clad all in punky black—tights, T-shirt, boots—passed by, the mothers and daughters gazed at her and shook their heads pityingly, in apparent amazement that one could *choose* to be so drab. Some people just don't know how to live.

Whoof! In a cloud of blowing snow, the *Zephyr* burst from the western portal of the Moffat Tunnel at forty miles per hour, the bright sun on the white ski slopes of Winter Park flooding the lounge car and blinding everyone's eyes. For the last three minutes ears had been popping as the train descended from the track's apex of 9,239 feet near the middle of the bore to 9,058 feet at the western portal. The odor of diesel fumes, which had grown stronger near the end of the tunnel despite the closed vestibule doors, began to dissipate. The train did not slow; the Winter Park ski area is not a *Zephyr* stop, though the timetable might lead one to think so. Only the *Rio Grande Ski Train* calls at the ski area. The *Zephyr* descends to the small town of Fraser, five miles farther west, to load and unload skiers.

Lunch turned out to be excellent. Bowls of a robust vegetable soup appeared on the table as soon as we were seated, and I chose the grilled chicken breast sandwich, new on the Amtrak menu that month. It was brought by Alfredo Gomez, who had served my table the previous night. The aisle was choked with a constant parade of passengers from the Los Angeles section to the lounge car. They jostled the waiters as they passed; patiently the waiters stopped to let them by, and their service was slowed a little—except for Alfredo's. He is a small man, an inch or two under my own diminutive height of five feet, six inches, but lean and wiry where I am chubby and heavy-muscled. Like a gymnast Alfredo expertly swiveled past the crowd, swinging to the side his plate-laden tray, spilling not a drop or a crumb.

"I'm an instructor as well as a service attendant—that's what Amtrak call waiters," he said. "We instruct our trainees that when someone is walking through the aisle, you have to swing to the side, move with your tray, and let the passenger come by. Or another waiter could be coming by. The waiter with the hot food has the right-of-way."

Does Alfredo's compactness make it easier to move around in the dining car, compared with a really big fellow? "Oh, most definitely. I used to like to work with big fellows so I could cut around them like Speedy Gonzales. They call me Go-Go Gomez." He laughed, his eyes crinkling behind his spectacles and mustache. "But no, it's easier when you're small. Big waiters do have trouble maneuvering, especially on a crowded train like the *Zephyr*. And I notice strain on some big people, especially when we're going through the higher altitudes in the mountains."

Alfredo was born in Elmhurst, a Chicago suburb, but speaks

with the slight drawl of south Texas, where he grew up in Brownsville. In 1979, when he was a music major at the University of Houston, he moved to Chicago to "cultivate a relationship" with his mother, whom he had not seen in twelve years. "It was a very difficult time," he said, "and I lost my musical goals." He decided to go into bartending instead of returning to school. A short time later "I saw an ad in the paper—'Wanted, Waiters and Bartenders'—and applied. That's what I want to do, I told myself. I went through a new thirteen-day training program Amtrak had just begun, and I fell in love with the railroad."

On the *Zephyr* there are three, sometimes four waiters, with the steward in charge. The division of labor seems simple but, like that in the galley, it's a little more intricate than a passenger would expect. "Every position has its description of side work," Alfredo said. "For example, the number-one service attendant—which I am in my crew—is responsible for the pantry, setting up supplies such as cups, water glasses, juice glasses, and maintaining the refrigerators, monitoring the expiration dates on certain items. We're like mini-chefs, in the sense that we work with packaged food items, like jellies and syrups. I get to work early the first day, at ten-thirty A.M., so I can help the steward and chef with the supplies and make sure everything's clean in the diner, to make sure the refrigeration and dumbwaiters are working properly. If the dumbwaiters jam, one of us has to be a human elevator up and down the stairs."

The number two and three attendants set up the tablecloths, salt and pepper shakers, sugar bowls, flower vase, and help roll silverware in napkins. "When I started in 1979, we were still using tablecloths and table felts underneath, and that was the number-three waiter's responsibility," Alfredo said. "We called him the linen person. We don't have the linens now, but they're coming back, I hope."

Some waiters from the extra board, I've been told, dread being called to work the *Zephyr*, because the six-day run, with its huge loads of passengers, is so long and exhausting. The "Train from Hell," they call the *Zephyr*. "If Five doesn't kill you, Six will."

Alfredo smiled at that. "It depends on the individual," he said.

"The *Zephyr* is one of the most popular runs with crews. I've worked all the trains that run out of Chicago, and each route has special qualities I enjoy immensely. But at the moment the *Zephyr* is my favorite. The tips are excellent, and the time off—seven days—is wonderful."

And what does Alfredo do during his seven days off? "I'm a musician, a trombonist, and last year I started playing several woodwinds, the clarinet, flute and oboe. I'm making my debut Sunday at church with a flute trio. I also collect cars from the fifties. I'm not a wild and crazy guy."

Tipping is a sore point with some Amtrak waiters. By law, Amtrak reports 8 percent of the total sales revenue to the Internal Revenue Service as tip income, dividing that sum among the waiters. Some of them contend that their actual tips don't add up to that 8 percent. Lela Janushkowsky thinks Amtrak ought to suggest on the meal checks, which don't mention gratuities at all, that tipping is at the diner's discretion.

"Yes, you have to report that eight percent even if you might not have received that much," Alfredo said. "A good example of that is with sleeping car passengers. The price of the meals is included in the ticket, but no gratuity. Sometimes sleeper passengers aren't aware of this. They figure that everything is included, and they'll have a meal and won't leave anything behind. It's not our place to solicit tips—it's against company policy. So you're left without a tip, yet Amtrak adds that eight percent to the check in its IRS reports."

Are the passengers on the *Zephyr* more generous than riders on other trains? Some sleeper attendants seem to think so. "No, everybody's pretty much the same on all trains. But I did encounter differences when I worked from New York to Albany. The people on that route are a little more assertive. I don't want to use the word 'demanding,' but they know what they want immediately. They're commuters. They come in the dining car and right off the bat they know absolutely what they want. On the long-haul trains, people are more relaxed, calmer, and take their time. Until dinner starts, anyway, and it's rush, rush, rush."

For the most part, Alfredo agrees, life on the train is good. Sending the chefs to the Culinary Institute has improved life immensely for the waiters as well as the passengers. "The chefs' attitudes are dramatically improved. Before, the food was such a simple generic thing, and now everyone is creative again. People weren't really complaining to me about the food, but they weren't saying it was great, either. Now they say, 'This is wonderful, this is fabulous!' And of course that helps my pocket."

Alfredo, however, feels that things are still too hectic in the *Zephyr* diners, thanks to the large passenger load. "We need another dining car," he said. "You're rushing everybody because they have to get a couple of eggs with bacon before they get off in Denver." The problem is just as acute for the eastbound *Zephyr*, which often must begin serving dinner at 4:30 P.M. the second day out of Oakland so that every passenger is fed before the train arrives in Denver at 7:45 P.M. "And I think everyone's attitude would improve dramatically if we had something nice to work with up here—real dishes, white linens, real flowers in the bud vases. We'd feel a sense of accomplishment. The personalities of some waiters would blossom if we had these things to enhance the appearance of the diner."

"If there is a doctor or nurse on board, please come to Car 512, the one just forward of the lounge car. This is not an emergency."

With a journalist's curiosity I excused myself and hurried from the dining car forward to Car 512, the second Oakland coach. There a nurse squatted before an elderly woman slumped in her seat, taking her pulse and chatting with her solicitously. The train chief hovered by. "She's okay," said the attendant calmly. "She has an altitude problem, and she had a breathing attack going through the tunnel. She's on medication for it. There's a paramedic at Fraser waiting to check her out. It happens all the time." A few more men and women from other cars arrived and offered their services. "Thank you," said the chief, "but everything's under control. We do not need any more doctors or nurses."

To flatlanders the symptoms of altitude sickness—more properly hypoxia, or decreased amounts of oxygen in the blood—come on quickly: headache and weakness, dehydration, mild nausea and loss of appetite. Most people don't experience symptoms until they reach an elevation of fourteen thousand feet, but many get the wobblies as low as eight thousand feet. The symptoms can be worse for those who suffer from respiratory difficulties, but rest and medication put them right. Some bring along their own oxygen tanks going through the mountains. On the *California Zephyr*, the problem seems to be greater for those going from west to east; paramedics meet the eastbound train in Denver more often than not. I had a bit of a headache myself, a slight throb behind the eyes, not helped by the coffee I'd had at lunch—caffeine dehydrates the body. Those who had had a nip or two of something stronger likely faced a daytime hangover, for a shot of alcohol has about twice the punch at higher elevations as it does at sea level.

Some passengers are so distressed by altitude sickness that they suffer strokes, even heart attacks. Crews are trained in cardiopulmonary resuscitation techniques, but there's only so much they can do, not being certified paramedics. From time to time a helicopter is flown into the mountains to pluck a severely ailing patient off the train. More often, however, the passenger manifest will show that there's a doctor or nurse on the train, and the chiefs will try to find out their specialties in case a child gets hurt, or a pregnant woman's time comes too soon.

If a medical crisis occurs near a town, the conductor can radio a dispatcher for an ambulance to meet the train. More than once aboard the *Zephyr*, I've watched as the engineer carefully stopped the train to put the vestibule door of a coach right in the middle of a grade crossing a few feet away from a waiting ambulance. Within five to ten minutes the paramedics gently removed their patients—usually heart-attack or stroke victims, and once a diabetic who had gone into insulin shock—from the train and placed them in ambulances.

Sometimes no medical professional is aboard and train chiefs and conductors must make decisions alone. "One time," a chief told me, "a guy had a stroke in the middle of Iowa, twenty minutes away from the next scheduled stop." That ordinarily would have been enough time for medical aid, "but he was in a bad way, and we decided to radio ahead for an ambulance to meet the train at the next highway crossing. Twenty minutes later and he might have died."

Another incident aboard a *Zephyr* demonstrated the quick thinking with which Amtrakers often must deal with medical crises. A sleeper passenger with two artificial hips suddenly dislocated both joints and fell across the aisle, his head and shoulders through one economy bedroom doorway and his hips and legs through the doorway opposite. The paramedics who met the *Zephyr* at Princeton, Illinois, were able to place their patient in a litter, but could not turn it in the aisle to carry him down the corridor and out the car. Nor could they tilt the litter up to clear the doorways, for fear of further damaging the patient's hips. The only way to get him out was through his sleeper compartment window. But that was two stories up.

Luckily a construction crew with a heavy bulldozer was working nearby. The train chief enlisted the 'dozer operator, who parked his machine parallel with the train and lifted his blade up to the window. Gingerly the paramedics opened the window and slid the litter onto the blade, to be lowered gently to the ground as cheering passengers with cameras captured the action.

Amtrak crews must be especially watchful over elderly passengers, because many suffer from Alzheimer's disease. A chief who came up through the ranks as a sleeper attendant recalled an occasion in which "this nice couple came aboard, put on by their son and daughter. 'I'll take care of them,' I told them. 'As if they were my own grandparents, I'll take care of them.' Well, the old guy was acting goofy, so I thought maybe he had Alzheimer's and was somebody I'd have to watch closely. I told his wife, 'I'll keep an eye on him.' And she said casually, 'Yeah, yeah, please do that.'

"The next morning I'm making coffee when the woman yells up the stairway at me, 'Are you coming down for breakfast?' I blinked. What did she mean by that? Then she shouted, 'You're going to be late for school.' Uh-oh, I thought. I went downstairs to put her back in her room, and I discovered that her husband had emptied a fifth of Jack Daniels overnight. He was an alcoholic, and she was the one with Alzheimer's."

High altitudes, the same chief added, often magnify the effects of Alzheimer's. As a sleeper attendant he hosted a group of women in their late sixties and early seventies who were traveling from New York City to Reno for the gambling. Not long after the train had descended from Soldier Summit, the *Zephyr*'s highest point in Utah, one of the women arose from bed and padded in her slippers to the back of the car, where the attendant lay drowsing in his compartment.

"She was peering one way and then the other. I said, 'Can I help you?' She said, 'No.' I waited a minute and said, 'Are you all right?' She said, 'Yes.' I said, 'What are you doing? It's two in the morning and everybody else is sleeping.' She said, 'I'm waiting for a bus.' I said, 'You're waiting for a *bus?*' She said, 'Yes, I have to catch the bus to go to La Guardia. My group is flying to Reno to go gambling.' Well, she did have part of the story right.

"I took the lady to her roommate, then woke up the tour leader and told him that the lady should be checked when she got to Reno. I also woke up a nurse and had her check the lady's pulse and look her over. We told her that she was on a train going to Reno, and that in about nine hours she would arrive with her group. She immediately came back to reality and realized she wasn't waiting for a bus. She was embarrassed, and I felt terribly sorry for her."

Sometimes such stories end tragically. Not long before our chat, the same chief had encountered still another passenger suffering from the dementia of advanced age. Almost as soon as she boarded the *Zephyr* at Sacramento, he said, she opened her bag, plucked her clothing out of it, and one by one threw each item over her shoulder into the aisle and the nearby seats.

" 'What are you doing?' I said. She said, 'Somebody stole my knives and forks.' I said, 'They stole your knives and forks?' She said, 'Yeah.' Maybe she had some silver, who knows? Then she went downstairs to the vestibule and tried to open the door, saying, 'I'm going out to my patio.'

"This is a very dangerous situation. People like that could walk off a train at seventy-nine miles per hour. I locked the door, but I don't like to do that unless I have to, and it's usually with Alzheimer's patients. Locked doors can be a safety problem in the event of a wreck. Finally I told the lady, 'Look, I packed your knives and forks. They're in your suitcase.' Then she settled down."

A week later, while the chief was off duty at home, the Indiana state police called him. They mentioned the woman's name, and asked about her behavior on the chief's train. She had been riding with her husband on the *Broadway Limited,* and after Fort Wayne, Indiana, he reported her missing. The conductor found the vestibule door open. At last she had succeeded in going out to her patio at seventy-nine miles an hour.

It was now 12:20 P.M., and the *Zephyr* glided past the frozen Fraser River into the Winter Park stop at Fraser, 1,100 miles from Chicago. We were now surrounded by the Arapaho National Forest, ski chalets and ranches, and it took a good ten minutes to unload the skiers from Galesburg and Denver. Their breaths hissed white into the noon air; I had no idea of the temperature, but it is often *cold* in Fraser, which once was a National Weather Service reporting station. The morning dailies used to report that the nation's low temperatures of the day before bottomed out at Fraser—minus 25 degrees, minus 35, once even minus 50. The Weather Service closed the station long ago, but the low temperatures remain. At 12:30 P.M., still fifty-five minutes late, we pulled out of Fraser. Half an hour later the train rolled into Granby at Mile 1,113.

Granby may be the gateway to the Rocky Mountain National Park as well as a host of summer resorts surrounding Lake Granby, but on this early-spring trip no one boarded or detrained the *Zephyr* at its tiny unmanned station. But we did pick up a spectacular watercourse and a bit of land that once fell through the cracks of nineteenth century diplomacy.

SEVEN

The sun hung high in the sky as the *California Zephyr* slipped through a piece of the nation, seventy miles long and thirty miles wide, that until well into this century was technically a no-man's-land. Middle Park, a high basin cradled between ranges of the Rockies, was overlooked by the United States, Spain and France in their slick nineteenth-century wheeling and dealing and did not officially become part of the United States until 1936.

The Louisiana Purchase of 1803 extended only to the eastern edge of the basin, while the territory ceded by Spain in the Adams-Onís Transcontinental Treaty of 1819 ranged just to the western edge. John Quincy Adams may have been the greatest American secretary of state (and the real author of the Monroe Doctrine), and though the treaty he negotiated with Spain gave the United States possession of all of Florida and for the first time fixed the southern boundary of the United States from sea to sea, he just missed Middle Park. John Fremont visited and named the region

173

in 1843, but only in a tract surrendered by Native Americans of the Ute tribe did the United States have formal possession.

By the time the legal anomaly was discovered, of course, the Americans had in practice established sovereignty, but the deal wasn't truly on the books until the governor of Colorado raised the American flag at Breckenridge on August 9, 1936, ceremoniously claiming Middle Park as part of the state.

Now the *Zephyr* sped west through Middle Park's long, rolling central alpine meadows, the crest of the high eastern Rockies fading astern as the Rio Grande tracks met the Colorado River at a point where the stream is almost narrow enough to leap with a running start. For the next 238 miles the *Zephyr* would hug its twisting, glistening, sometimes frozen path, descending all the way.

Once known as the Grand River, the stream tumbles 1,450 miles west and south through Colorado, Utah and Arizona to the Gulf of California and ultimately the Pacific, cutting the mighty continental gash called the Grand Canyon. A century and a half ago, trappers and mountain men used its upper reaches as a highway to the southwest, and a little later miners employed the waters of its tributary creeks for their sluices. (The railroad, however, is named not for the old Grand but the slow and muddy Rio Grande del Norte, the stream that rises in southern Colorado and marks the border between Texas and Mexico, its waters reaching the Gulf of Mexico and eventually the Atlantic.)

For all its strange provenance, Middle Park presents no breathtaking vistas for the *Zephyr* rider. The suddenly unspectacular scenery having emptied the lounge car, I decided to return to my compartment for a nap. Sliding open the door to Deluxe Room B, I sat down, sighed and started. Looming in the doorway was the attendant I had seen that morning in the vestibule as the train stopped in Denver.

"Good afternoon. Mr. Kisor, isn't it?" he said with a casual smile. "I'm Robert Heath." He entered the room, nearly filling it with his lanky six-foot-seven-inch frame. I proffered my hand and he grasped it firmly, my palm nearly disappearing into his enormous fist. "Do you know how the room works?" I did, but I never tire of hearing sleeper attendants explain their domains—*if* they do. (They're supposed to, but all too many don't.) The details are the same, but the spiels often are richly individual. "Tell me," I said.

"Those are the light switches," he said crisply, tapping each one with a long arm, like a mathematics professor at the blackboard, pausing expectantly after each sentence and glancing at me to see if the equation had sunk in. Many passengers don't listen to their attendants' instructions any more than they do announcements on the PA systems. Crews are forever complaining about having to repeat answers to questions they've just answered in detail. Either Bob thought he could save himself some breath if he got across to me the first time, or perhaps he simply was being extra solicitous of a deaf passenger. I noticed that he spoke slowly and carefully, making sure I could read his lips.

"You adjust the temperature with this here dial, and the sound systems with these dials. This is the call button. Pull it out and a bell will ring," he said, demonstrating, and a brief two-tone *ding-ping!* echoed from the corridor. "I'll be here in a second. This is your washbasin, and the towels and supplies are stored below." He opened a small cabinet below. "Here's the lever that allows your seat to recline. Okay?" I nodded. "Now, will you wish to sleep in the upper berth or the lower?"

The lower berth, I said, choosing its thin-mattressed three-quarters-of-a-double-bed over the thick, thirty-two-inch-wide up-per bunk. I like to sprawl, and a deluxe bedroom—for me a rare extravagance at as much as $280 a night on top of the regular fare—offers the long-distance traveler plenty of room. Floor space is triple that of the economy bedroom, with a soft armchair facing a long settee running the entire width of the compartment. Three adults can comfortably occupy the room, provided two of them don't mind snuggling all night in the lower berth. When split three ways, that $280 charge, which includes all meals, is not quite as painful as it might seem. Although many would-be passengers sometimes are stunned at the prices for the accommodations (an *economy* bedroom can cost as much as $180 over coach fare each night), Amtrak sleeping-car space still is booked up rapidly.

"Tomorrow morning at six-thirty I'll have coffee and juice at the station in the middle of the car. Do you want to be awakened at a certain hour?" I shook my head. "If you'd like ice or anything from the lounge car, or perhaps a meal in your room, I'll be happy to bring it. Just let me know. Oh, there's one more thing," he said, opening the narrow door to the tiny toilet-shower space. "This button flushes the toilet," he said, tapping the lower of two buttons set into the wall, one above the other just an inch higher. "*That* button turns on the shower." He looked at me with raised eyebrows.

"Aaaah," I said, displaying my understanding of the implications. Pressing the wrong button to flush the toilet in the middle of the night would be a soaking mistake.

"Yup," he said, his eyes widening with mine. "There's always one every trip." With a chuckle he took his leave.

Slowly Amtrak has been replacing those infamous shower buttons with a dial handle farther up on the wall. Other than that, the room looked good, its carpeting crisp, its corners only a little worn. I dropped to my hands and knees and peered under the seat. Weeks of dust-kitties blanketed the floor; the car cleaners in Chicago and Oakland hadn't been thorough. Moreover, a large chemical mousetrap squatted ominously in the corner. Ships host rats, trains entertain mice.

I decided not to stow my portable computer in the grime underneath the seat, but placed it on the armchair across from the bench seat and folded my down jacket over it. The computer, I thought, would be safe there. Unlike European trains, often plagued by thieves who steal suitcases en masse and even raid occupied second-class sleeper compartments at night, American long-distance trains see remarkably little theft. In my experience on the *Zephyr*, passengers risk little if they avoid leaving small objects such as purses and cameras out in the open, either locking them in the luggage or carrying them to lounge and diner. Yet I've seen Walkmans left untouched on coach seats all day while their owners rode elsewhere. It's probably not that there's anything particularly honest about American train riders; there simply are too many watchful eyes about, and if one is caught pilfering, there's nowhere to escape to.

Arranging the pillow against the window, I sank into the seat and closed my eyes. Thanks to the coffee in the lounge car, however, I was doomed to wakeful woolgathering, a state common among those who stare out train windows. The mood is far from mindless. Pleasant and almost hypnotic, the rocking of the train and the passing of the world without stirs the mind into a gumbo of loosely connected thoughts, recollections and glimmers of creativity. Sometimes entire strings of ideas emerge from the soup.

Slowly I became aware of the reflection in the window of the heavy steel latch on the sliding door, the latch that has given me so much concern as a deaf passenger, and my thoughts turned again to locked compartments. The progression continued: A locked room. The occupant doesn't respond to the attendant's knock. Does the attendant know the passenger is deaf? Deaf? He could be *dead.* Murdered? Murder and trains. *Murder on the Orient Express.* Agatha Christie. A modern locked-room murder mystery aboard an Amtrak train?

An idea began to take shape. Lela had said that because stewards carry a substantial amount of cash, they are assigned not a room in the dorm car with the rest of the crew but instead an economy bedroom on the lower level of the Oakland sleeper. Thanks to the presence of the passengers and the train chief, who also occupies a lower-level economy room, the security in the sleeper is better than that in the dorm car. Lela is responsible for as much as eight thousand dollars, and she must carry it on her person everywhere aboard the train—even to the bathroom in the middle of the night.

What if a beautiful blonde steward fails to appear at her post in the diner early one morning and does not answer the chief's irritated knock at the door of her compartment in the Oakland sleeper? Maybe the conductors could pry the door to her room off its sliding track, and there she lies strangled in glorious *déshabillé* among the bedclothes, her purse and its contents missing. But how could the killer lock that room behind him and make his escape? Not by slipping a slow-acting poison into the drink of the victim, who latches the door upon retiring—Christie already thought of that. Something more modern, even high-tech, is required to dispatch a victim in a rolling whodunit of the 1990s.

In an economy bedroom a few doors down sat Bob Locher, the Dorothy Sayers fan with whom I had chatted the previous afternoon. I found him there, again engrossed in the paperback. "A question," I ventured. "How could a locked-room mystery be set in one of these compartments?" He listened with bemused, but gathering, interest, idly fiddling with the lock on his door.

"Just about all the windows in this car are emergency exits, you know," I said, pointing to his. A large rubber grommet around the circumference of the plastic glass held it snugly in its frame. A red metal handle protruded from the lower inside surface of the grommet. When pried upward, the handle pulls out the grommet, freeing the window to swing out.

"Maybe the killer could arrange ahead of time for the train to derail, then in the confusion escape through the window," I said. "But then how could he shut it behind him and replace the grommet?"

"What's the premise?" asked Bob. "Who's the victim?"

"A beautiful blonde steward," I said. "Stewards always sleep in a downstairs economy bedroom in this car, and whenever they get up in the night for a pee they have to take their money with them, eight thousand bucks, because they have no safe place to leave it. I thought maybe the killer could meet the steward after dinner, keep topping up her soft drink so that she *has* to go to the bathroom, and lie in wait in another bathroom on the lower level of the car, and . . ."

"I like it," said Bob. "But how about a locked-room mystery that eventually turns out not to be a locked-room mystery at all? How did Sherlock Holmes put it? 'When you have eliminated the impos-

sible, whatever remains, however improbable, must be the truth.'
The Sign of Four."

He grinned at my expression of sudden respect. "I like the idea
of topping off her drink," he went on, "thereby allowing the killer
to enter her compartment and lie in wait to do her in. But that has
the disadvantage of not being terribly reliable so far as time is
concerned. Suppose the killer loads up her drink with a diuretic,
and also does something to cause her to hear the sound of running
water in her sleep? That's a powerful stimulus to go pee."

"This gets better and better," I said. "Needs a bit of refinement,
maybe. The stewards go to bed about ten-thirty or eleven on the
first night out of Chicago because they get up at five-thirty in the
morning to start serving breakfast at six. So we need to bump off
the steward at about two A.M., when everybody's asleep except the
conductors at a table in the dorm-coach.

"How finely can the killer time the diuretic?" I continued. "Say
a couple of milligrams of EZ-Pee per twenty-five pounds of body
weight, and our steward, a beautiful California blonde, weighs one
hundred twenty-five pounds. To give the rest of her dimensions
would be blatantly sexist and set off the Gender Police, wouldn't
you say? Anyway, perhaps the dose is on the conservative side so she
won't get up too early. And so the microcassette of Niagara Falls
comes into play to start the kidneys rolling."

I was on a roll. "Okay, we've got the killer inside her compartment now," I said. "What kind of weapon do we use to kill her? I
thought of strangling, but maybe it should be something not so
obvious. Maybe something that would come out only in an autopsy. But maybe an autopsy might be avoided if there's enough of
a derailment to kill a few passengers?"

Bob pursed his lips skeptically. I pressed on. "I guess a murder
mystery shouldn't have too many deaths. Should we stick to a single
victim?" Bob nodded. "Perhaps," I continued, "the killer breaks
her neck, then places her body in the bed so that her head is toward
the front of the train. So that in a derailment it looks as if her neck
was broken when her head struck the forward bulkhead of her

compartment. And perhaps her boyfriend, an amateur shamus, smells a rat when he hears that, because he knew she always slept feet forward because she was worried about just that—breaking her neck in a derailment. So with this clue he sets out to solve the case."

Bob ruminated for a moment. "I very much like that bit about sleeping feet forward," he said slowly. "And the microcassette. I have an idea about that—it would be one of those that has a clock radio so you can wake to music. The killer sets it to suit himself, and plants it in her compartment. The tape would be recorded to play very quietly with an increasing sound level, but still to a low maximum, and would quit in five minutes. Then it would start again in fifteen minutes in case she didn't wake the first time."

He rubbed his hands with relish. "And how about the killer planning to recover the tape player after he kills her, but she wakes up enough to find it, then hides it in her compartment before going to the john, thinking she knows who planted it? And maybe whispers a message, whispers so she won't wake the other passengers, into the recorder. Like, maybe, 'Thanks for that, Steve, you son of a bitch.' The killer can't find the recorder after he murders her, but the detective does, and is puzzled by the meaning of the tape. As for the actual means of death, I'd have the murderer knock her out with a pad of chloroform just as she returns to her compartment, just for quiet's sake, then break her neck while she's unconscious."

At that moment of unspeakable violence the *Zephyr* trundled past the picturesque mountain hamlet of Hot Sulphur Springs, known for its local geothermal pools as well as its history as the end of track for David Moffat's unlucky first railroad. A large green-rinded pool steamed so close to the tracks one could almost dive into it from the train. Almost immediately we plunged into Byers Canyon, whose striking red-and-gold sandstone spires and pagodas soar grandly up from the river bed like wind-carved sculptures. For ten minutes Bob and I fell silent, gazing out the compartment window as the train twisted through the canyon at thirty miles per hour. A few cars and trucks rolled past on the two narrow lanes of U.S. 40, blasted from the cliffs on the opposite side of the river.

By and by the train rolled out into treeless meadows dotted by weather-beaten shacks and scored by animal tracks, and feed-lots scratched muddy by still winter-shaggy herds of Herefords and Black Angus. These riverine lowlands, the train chief announced over the PA system, make up some of Colorado's best cattle country. Hunting country, too, it seems, for even at this time of year several shooters were squeezing off large-caliber rounds on half a dozen rifle ranges close to, but fortunately facing away from, the tracks. As the train picked up a bit of speed, Bob and I returned to bloodier matters.

"Now, for an overall motive," Bob said, "a few thousand dollars is really too picayune for this kind of murder. How about dope, instead? Could be a load of coke hidden in the ventilation ducts of the sleeping car, which are conveniently accessed in the steward's compartment. There's a gang of bad guys shipping the stuff, and a rival gang learns about it thanks to a turncoat, and plans to hijack the shipment. In the meantime, a snitch has told the Feds about the cocaine, and they're planning to meet the train in Oakland."

"Yes, you could smuggle the stuff onto the train easily in the Chicago coach yards before the crew gets aboard," I said. "I've been there, and believe me, the place looks *empty*. Early in the morning almost nobody's around, and whoever's there isn't going to question two guys in hard hats who look like they belong. But I don't think the ducts would work. They're not really big enough, and anyway it'd take too long to unscrew the grilles, hide the coke, and replace them. On the other hand, look at these headrests." I reached behind the large cushion against which Bob's head reclined and gave it a yank. With a screech of Velcro it came away easily. "You can replace the stuffing with bricks of coke in an instant."

Bob smiled and gazed up at the ceiling dreamily. "The gang shipping the stuff finds out its cover has been blown," he said. "They decide they need to get it off the train quickly, before the other gang or the Feds get to it, so they arrange the derailment to frustrate their rivals, figuring they can get the stuff off before anybody wises up. The other gang, the hijackers, murder the steward but the derailment comes almost immediately after, before the killer can grab the coke. He pops the safety window and is out before anybody sees him—leaving a victim apparently killed by the impact of the derailment. And her compartment window apparently popped open by the impact, too.

"Does any of this sound good? Ah. Here, how about this? A former steward who was fired is the guy who comes up with the idea for a train to carry the dope, because he knows where to hide the stuff as well as the routine for the steward and the other crew. And perhaps he once hit on the victim and she contemptuously spurned him—and so his humiliation has made him very willing to have her done in. And the former steward is a passenger. While he's not the big boss, he does mastermind the plan. And when he finds out that the hijackers are planning to snatch the coke, he flies out to Colorado to stage the derailment and save his dope."

I approved of the drug motive. It's not uncommon for drug runners to move loads by train. In recent years California has become a favorite point of entry for dope smugglers because of police heat on the Florida coast. Trains from the West Coast to Chicago are an attractive alternative for smugglers because of the direct route and because train stations, unlike airports, don't screen carry-on baggage for weapons and suspicious items.

Both Amtrak and the Drug Enforcement Agency are aware of all this. Often DEA agents with dope-sniffing dogs meet eastbound trains at Denver or Chicago, tipped off by ticket agents or train crews who spot passengers that conform to a profile: someone who asks for a one-way ticket shortly before departure, pays cash for it, carries just one bag and won't let the attendant stow it in the open luggage compartment below, never leaves his seat for meals, and seems excessively nervous. A passenger cannot be forced to consent to a search of his luggage, but the narcs can detain the bags to be sniffed by a dog. If the dog alerts, the narcs can obtain a search warrant to open the luggage. Frequently the smugglers try

Memorabilia of the *California Zephyr* of old: covers from a 1950 timetable *(left)* and a 1967 route guide. Today's *Zephyr* covers the distance from Chicago to California in almost the same time, though the Vista-Dome cars have been replaced by two-story Superliners. *(Courtesy of the Colorado Railroad Museum.)*

Reggie Howard, chief of on-board services for today's departing *California Zephyr*, on his way to work in Amtrak's 14th Street coach yards, with Chicago's Loop in the background.
(*Photo by the author.*)

Train chief Reggie Howard and a yard worker discuss a recurring problem with the power in the lounge car of Number 5.
(*Photo by the author.*)

Chef John Davis in his kitchen on the lower level of a *Zephyr* dining car. Food specialist Altagracia Romo is to his left, and at right is John's ubiquitous boom box. *(Photo by the author.)*

Lunchtime in Colorado: John Davis at the grill, fixing cheeseburgers Amtrak-style. *(Photo by the author.)*

Assistant conductor Mike Kemp collects the ticket of a passenger shortly after the *Zephyr*'s departure from Chicago Union Station. *(Photo by the author.)*

California Zephyr train manager Don Cushine, who rose through the ranks by doing nearly every job on or off the train, from laying track to cooking meals, from tickets to baggage. "I just love the *Zephyr*," he says. "It's my baby." *(Photo courtesy of Brian Kukla.)*

The *Chicago Daily News* heralds the terrible wreck of April 25, 1946, when a predecessor of the *Zephyr*, the *Exposition Flyer*, plowed at 80 miles per hour into the rear of its leading section, the *Advance Flyer*, at Naperville, Illinois. *(Reprinted with permission from the Chicago Sun-Times.)*

Wally Prince, an engineer who operates the *Zephyr* between Chicago and Galesburg, Illinois, with his train at Galesburg. *(New York Times Photo / Paul Meredith.)*

Luncheon

"As you travel over this bountiful land of ours, may you be ever reminded of the grace Almighty God has bestowed upon us. Let us acknowledge our debt to Him with prayers of thanksgiving."

To insure prompt service please write each item on meal check.
Waiters are not permitted to take oral orders.

"Table Flowers are Colorado Carnations"

Sandwich Plate — $2.35

Hot Corned Beef Sandwich
(Rye Bread, Own Gravy, Sweet Relish)
with
Whipped Potatoes
Choice of Dessert
Coffee   Tea   Milk

Combination Suggestions — $1.95

Includes:
Choice of Dessert and Beverage
Double-Deck Chicken Salad or Ham Sandwich with Julienne Potatoes and Pickle Garnish
Hamburger Sandwich on Toasted Bun with Grilled Onion Slice, Hashed Brown Potatoes and Sweet Pickles
Double-Deck Tunafish or Egg Salad Sandwich on Toast with Julienne Potatoes and Pickle Relish
Toasted Cheese and Bacon Sandwich with Potato Salad and Ripe Olives

À la Carte Selections

SOUP   Per Cup 40   Tureen 65   French Onion Soup, Parmesan   Hot or Jellied Consomme

ENTREES
Cooked to Order
Includes Beverage, Assorted Bread and Butter
Filet of Fresh Fish Saute, Tartar Sauce, 1.90
Cottage Fried Pork Chops, Hashed Brown Potatoes, 2.35
Sugar Cured Ham with Two Eggs, Hashed Brown Potatoes, 1.90
Broiled Double Rib Lamb Chop, Hashed Brown Potatoes, 2.10

Sandwiches   Chicken 1.35   Clubhouse 1.60   Lettuce, Bacon, Tomato 1.20
Double Deck   Ham 1.30   American Cream or Swiss Cheese 95
Single Deck   Peanut Butter and Jelly Sandwich 70   Imported Sardine Sandwich 1.30

SALADS
Chilled Fruit Salad Plate with Cottage Cheese 1.35
Avocado Stuffed with Crab Meat 1.55   Chicken Salad, Mayonnaise 1.45
California Zephyr Combination Salad 95   Iceberg Lettuce, 60   Crab Louis 1.85

DESSERTS
Ice Cream with Wafers 40   Bread & Butter Pudding, 40   Gingerbread Supreme 40
Peaches in Syrup 35   Chilled Grapefruit Maraschino 50

BEVERAGES
Pot Service for One—Coffee, Tea, Chocolate, Decaffeinated Coffee 35
Individual Bottle Milk or Buttermilk 20

Additional Charge will be made for Service Outside the Dining Car.

Steward in Charge of this Car is_____
Managers of Dining Car Service
2/62
No. 2-3
2-5   P. M. Scott, Burlington, Chicago • F. J. Corrigan, Rio Grande, Denver • H. G. Wyman, Western Pacific, Oakland

Aboard the Vista - Dome

California Zephyr

BURLINGTON • RIO GRANDE • WESTERN PACIFIC

Railroad cuisine à la *California Zephyr*, 1962, near the end of the storied era of epicurean dining-car fare. *(Courtesy of the Colorado Railroad Museum.)*

Steward Lela Janushkowsky charming her customers in the *Zephyr*'s dining car. *(Photo by the author.)*

No. 1 waiter Alfredo Gomez and a passenger consult over the dinner menu in the *Zephyr*'s diner. *(Photo by the author.)*

A steward's paperwork never ends: Lela Janushkowsky sorts meal checks after a sitting. *(Photo by the author.)*

Union Station, a well-kept classic American railroad depot, in the heart of Denver's recently gentrified downtown warehouse section.
(Photo by the author.)

On a crisp January day, the *California Zephyr* exits the west portal of the 6.2-mile Moffat Tunnel near the ski resort of Winter Park, Colorado.
(Photo courtesy of Steve Patterson.)

A mid-1960s photo of the *Zephyr* descending the western slope of the Colorado Rockies near Winter Park.
(Photo courtesy of the Colorado Railroad Museum.)

The *Zephyr* negotiates the confines of Little Gore Canyon near Radium, Colorado. Notice that two locomotives are needed to haul the train up the inclines in this section of its route.
(Photo courtesy of Steve Patterson.)

Classic and contemporary meetings: The eastbound and westbound *Zephyrs* passing in Glenwood Canyon during the 1950s *(left)* and near Dotsero during the 1990s *(inset)*. *(Left photo courtesy of the Colorado Railroad Museum; inset photo by the author.)*

The "monument to an idea" erected by the Denver & Rio Grande Western Railroad in Glenwood Canyon. The stainless steel replica of a Vista-Dome car marked the spot where Cyrus Osborn first envisioned a glass-domed cruise train through the Rockies. The monument has since been moved to the grounds of the Colorado Railroad Museum in Golden. *(Photo courtesy of the Colorado Railroad Museum.)*

Rafters in the Colorado River, a common sight from late spring to early fall. This staid group eschews the long tradition of "mooning" the passing *Zephyr*. *(Photo by the author.)*

Glenwood Springs as seen from the *Zephyr*, stopped at the depot across the Colorado River. At left, the old Hotel Colorado; behind the trees, the Hot Springs pool and hotel, and at right, the complex of old and new buildings serving the pool. *(Photo by the author.)*

"Don't go far, and be ready to get back aboard fast." Bob Heath, the *Zephyr*'s sleeper attendant, mother-henning the photographer.

(Photo by the author.)

Sandi Brown in the Glenwood Springs depot during a quiet moment between the arrivals of Number 5 and Number 6.

(Photo courtesy of Char Searl.)

Michael Parker at the wheel of the Cushman, hauling baggage to the Glenwood Springs depot as the westbound *Zephyr* accelerates away.

(Photo by the author.)

Engineer Ray Craig in Number 5's lead F40, the snowy forest of the Sierra Nevada's foothills visible through the windows. *(Photo by the author.)*

Ray at his "desk" in the F40. At upper left is the radiotelephone with which he communicates with the conductor and the dispatcher. Below it is the engine brake, and just to the right is the whistle lever. The white button below the whistle lever is the "Alertor" button the engineer must touch every half-minute or so, to show that he is awake and alert. Ray's left hand is on the engine throttle. At right is the speedometer, and the clipboard contains "track warrants" advising the crew of conditions on their route. *(Photo by the author.)*

Rogers E. M. Whitaker, the *New Yorker* editor who wrote about trains under the nom de plume E. M. Frimbo. *(Reprinted with permission from the Chicago Sun-Times.)*

Lucius Beebe *(standing)* and his sidekick, Charles Clegg, in the drawing room of their opulent private car, the *Virginia City*, in 1957. A copy of their newspaper, the *Territorial Enterprise*, is on the table at left. *(Photo courtesy of Maynard L. Parker Modern Photography, Los Angeles.)*

Bob Pimm, a tough, no-nonsense, by-the-book conductor who rules the *Zephyr* on its route over the Sierra Nevada, from Lovelock, Nevada, to Oakland. *(Photo by the author.)*

Bob Nicol, architect and railfan, at the drafting table in his Oakland office. *(Photo by the author.)*

Journey's end: The author climbs down from the *Zephyr*'s leading locomotive at the old Southern Pacific station in Oakland, California. *(Photo by Deborah Abbott Kisor.)*

to fool the sniffers by packing the dope with fish or perfume, but the dogs' noses are rarely deceived.

But why would anybody want to move coke westbound from Chicago to Oakland, instead of the other direction? Easy. A drug gang accustomed to importing its wares via ship at Oakland might be stymied on the docks by smart narcs. Logically, the gang could bring the dope in via the St. Lawrence Seaway and transship it to California by train. It'd be a roundabout way to ship narcotics to a seaport—so roundabout that the smugglers likely could get away with it for quite some time before the authorities cottoned to the plot.

But arranging that derailment bothered me, and I said so. "If this takes place in the Colorado Rockies it's not going to be easy. The Rio Grande is paranoid about its mountain track and often sends a trackman on a rail scooter ahead of trains to radio back track conditions. Also, the tracks are continuous welded rail, so the old trick of loosening the bolts on the rail joints won't work anymore. What's more, temperatures in the Rockies don't get very high, so 'sun kinks' in the rail—the usual cause of accidental derailments on the plains of North Dakota and Montana—won't work. How are we going to pull this off?"

Bob was unperturbed. "I don't see any problem," he said, "since the derailment will not be accidental, but rather very much the result of an intended criminal act. In reality it could still be difficult, but I think readers would accept that a band of felons intent on derailment could manage it. After all, a well-placed stick of dynamite is a persuasive argument."

He closed his eyes in thought. "Just how major a derailment do we want? A couple cars off the track but still sitting up, and only one injury—the dead steward? Or do you see a major mess, cars piled up on top of cars, with lots of injuries but miraculously only one fatality, the steward?"

I leaned back and replied, "I don't know, but it seems to me that *where* we stage this derailment is important. It's got to be in some place that's hard to get to, like a lonely canyon." I glanced out the window at the rolling meadows just as a block signal shack inscribed "TROUBLESOME" swept by six feet away. The train was rolling by a cattle hamlet called Kremmling, and just then the chief's voice crackled over the PA.

"We're entering the Gore Range. That's Mount Powell to the south. Thirteen thousand, five hundred thirty-four feet high."

Five minutes later we pierced the mouth of Gore Canyon. The narrow gorge is a jaw-dropping experience. More than any other sight on the journey, it demonstrates why, after the Rio Grande killed its remnant of the old *California Zephyr* in 1982, Amtrak chose to dispatch its Chicago–to–San Francisco train through rugged Colorado instead of over the lower, faster route through southern Wyoming. For seven minutes our train rolled slowly by—and through—beetling, bristling, jagged 1,500-foot cliffs looming so close that they seemed to threaten to collapse upon the track. Almost every hundred yards the train threaded short tunnels and cuts blasted from rock, the bubbling Colorado River corkscrewing and stairstepping in icy pirouettes from boulder to boulder a few feet below the train.

Here, I thought, is the perfect place to stage a railroad hijack. Gore Canyon is far too rugged for any sensible highway engineer to master; the nearest highway (actually a narrow country road) lies miles and mountains away. Rock slides near both ends of the canyon could stall the cavalry for a good long time, giving the crooks ample leisure to do their stuff. But how could the gang get there—and make its getaway? One or two might travel as passengers, but en masse they might be recognized, either by their rivals or the narcs.

"Helicopter," said Bob sagely, folding his hands over his belly. He is a private pilot, owner of a four-seater Cessna 172, and had noticed a wind sock high atop a cliff just east of Kremmling. Almost certainly the wind sock marked an airstrip where a chopper could alight and the dopers and the loot could be transferred to a twin-engine plane that would then flash low and fast over the mountains to Mexico and safety.

Immediately I saw the possibilities. Wind roaring through the canyon likely would prevent the latter-day James Gang from dropping on ropes from the helicopter. They could, however, land on the summit of the cliffs, then rappel down not only to track level but also to a couple of spots high up. There they could set off charges small enough not to be heard far away, but large enough to bracket the *Zephyr* fore and aft with a few thousand tons of rock.

The rocks would break through the multistranded slide warning fence that parallels the roadbed between the tracks and the cliffs, tripping block signals to red, forcing the engineer to stop his train immediately. Timed right, the explosion would cause the *Zephyr* to halt safely just short of the slide. A slight miscalculation by the crooks, and the train might strike the rocks and derail, but at a speed slow enough to avoid a major disaster, in which the smugglers aboard could themselves be injured or even killed.

Having fallen upon the train and removed the cocaine from the headrests in the derailed sleeper, the gang could then be winched back up the cliffs by confederates above, board the chopper and escape.

One thing bothered me. "What about radio communications?" I asked. "Couldn't the engineer get through to the dispatcher in Denver or to neighboring train crews to report the hijack and call for immediate help?"

"The gang could knock out the repeaters," Bob said.

"Repeaters?"

"From time to time along the way," he replied, "you must have noticed those white saucer dishes on top of high points." I had; they are affixed to squat towers that also bore several antennas, just barely visible. Next to the assemblies sit tiny white shacks. "They repeat, or relay, radio calls that otherwise couldn't get out of the canyon or around mountains," he said. "There are a bunch of them around, all in line of sight with each other. The dish antenna sends the signals to the next station, and the smaller antennas pick up the signals from the train for relay. Coaxial cables run from the antennas to the shack, which contains the radio equipment."

Immediately I had visions of a well-placed grenade, or perhaps a bazooka rocket, or maybe a sharpshooter with a heavy rifle and eight-power scope clipping the wire with a bullet.

"Not necessarily," said Bob. "All you need is to get a hijacker up there a few hours before—if a human being built the repeater, anybody can climb up to it—with a tiny pin. All you have to do is push the pin into the cable that leads from the antenna. That shorts it out. The sabotage is almost invisible up close and certainly so from the air. Or for that matter you could simply cut the cables."

It had been building up for a while, and now a nagging thought intruded into my eager complicity. "Wait a minute," I said. "There are a couple of flaws in this plot. For one thing, the steward's supposed to get up at five A.M., and at that hour the *Zephyr* is still in Nebraska. We don't get to Gore Canyon till about one-thirty in the afternoon. We can't kill the steward before breakfast in this place. And are we sure there are any radio repeaters in Gore Canyon? Verisimilitude, you know, is important to both mystery readers and railroad buffs.

"Besides, what's the motive for killing the steward if drugs, not a few thousand bucks, are going to be the loot? And we've gone from an apparent locked-room mystery to a Rambo-style drug thriller. This isn't Agatha Christie, for God's sake, it's Sly Stallone!"

"Think about the movie rights," replied Bob. "That's where the real money is."

He had a point. With Hollywood as our grail, I mused aloud, we could solve those problems easily. Instead of a diuretic, the killer could slip a nauseous drug into the steward's morning coffee, sending her ill to her compartment before lunch. And while everybody on the lower level of the Oakland sleeper had gone either to the diner or lounge car at the noon hour, the murder could be accomplished in privacy. Furthermore, the motive for the killing could be simple: Perhaps our beautiful blonde steward, instead of being an innocent tragic heroine, could be up to her soon-to-be-broken neck in the smuggling plot. She could be the on-board escort for the drugs, maybe even the snitch who tipped the Feds. Perhaps she had recognized one of the hijackers and simply had to be eliminated at the moment of the hijack.

"There are, however, a good many flies in this ointment," Bob said. "We are still hung with the cause of the derailment being somehow secret. We are talking about sabotaging the repeaters in such a way that nobody will later notice the real cause of the failure, and that everything will seem a series of unfortunate accidents leading to the derailment. On the other hand, we are talking about a gang making an escape with the coke. I see no problem with simply having a gang member go cut the coaxial cables of the repeater just before the heist. By the time anybody goes to check out those cables, the whole world will know that a crime has taken place." (So taken was I with the idea of sabotaging the relay stations, I was disappointed to learn later that although the Rio Grande maintains plenty of repeaters along the route of the Zephyr, none lie in the vicinity of Gore Canyon.)

As the *Zephyr* approached the western end of the canyon, a rough footpath appeared through the patchy snow on the opposite slope. During the summer, fishing enthusiasts hike in a mile or so from a rocky meadow just west of the canyon where they park their four-wheelers and trailers by a dirt road. The field lies cheek by jowl with a rustic parking lot at the edge of the river, a station for river-rafting and kayaking parties.

Bob pointed up the trail. "The hijackers could send up the swag to the chopper, and to save time escape on that footpath to the field—and a couple of waiting Blazers."

"The river's pretty rough there," I said. "How're they going to get across? How about kayaks? They could be checked to, say, Glenwood Springs in the baggage car at Chicago. After the job's done, the half-dozen or so hijackers could retrieve the kayaks and be off. Round the bend they go, and when they arrive at the meadow they look like ordinary river rats and nobody pays attention. As in the Chicago coach yards, they look as if they belong."

"We may be seriously overdoing things," said Bob, rubbing his jaw. "There are too many irreconcilable elements in this plot. Let's go back to the notion of a conventional mystery. Suppose we forget the idea of derailing the train. The original murder as we had set it up is pulled off, but the murderer pulls out the emergency window at some point where he knows the train will slow on a curve, and dumps all the coke out the window for recovery by his confederates. Then he quickly returns to his compartment and feigns innocence when the conductor rushes in to see where the wind noise is coming from, and discovers the body of the steward."

Could our hero perhaps be riding in the private car on the rear of the *Zephyr*? I asked. Perhaps a guest in that party is a visiting chief superintendent from Scotland Yard, the sleuth who eventually cracks the case?

"Nooo," said Bob, shaking his head in distaste. "That's *reaching*. Let's go back to the steward's boyfriend. That would mix in well with romance on the rails, though we end the romance almost before we begin."

"What about making the boyfriend the train chief?" I suggested.

"Sounds fine to me. We could develop a durable hero here. Dick Francis has a good thing going with horses. Tony Hillerman, too, with Indian cops. How about an on-board chief that's an amateur sleuth who solves a series of mysteries set on trains?"

Before I could tell Bob I liked that idea very much, a woman swept past the compartment door, smiling at us as she went by. She was the elegant Québecoise with the disabled husband I had met on departure, and Bob had had dinner at her table the night before.

As she disappeared down the corridor Bob said, "Maybe her husband's a fake, disguised as a cripple. How about making him the brains behind the heist? We could have him actually doing the murder, then throwing a dummy load out the window and hiding the real coke in the handicapped compartment. Being an apparent stroke victim could be a real good disguise. But the case could be broken open when the train chief suddenly recalls that at one time he noticed that the stroke victim's *right* side was paralyzed—the wrong side.

"Meanwhile, the train chief has to deal with the police, keep the train running, grieve for his dead love and all the while work desperately to solve the crime—which he might perhaps not manage even at the end of the trip. Perhaps he has to take a vacation, and, riding the train back and forth, work out what happened and finger the villains.

"Look, we could take either approach—a dirty little murder with at first no apparent motive, with all the important characters remaining on the train, with the mystery solved either on the train or afterward. Or we can go the Railbo approach, with a derailment and a gang of merciless druggies dropping from the sky. But I don't think we can take a middle ground. I could, however, happily proceed with either approach."

At that moment I recalled an article I had read not long before about a new satellite communications system being tested on the *Empire Builder*. A self-contained, computerized keyboard allows train chiefs to call ahead for medical assistance, kitchen and bar supplies, and to report no-shows so that unoccupied seats and compartments can be resold down the line. The signals from an antenna mounted on the crew dorm bounce off a satellite hanging above North America, eliminating the need for line-of-sight radio repeaters.

What's more, the system also reports the train's exact location. Many trucking companies use this idea. Visible just behind the wind deflectors on top of a tractor roof lies a small microwave dish, pointing straight up. Every few minutes it transmits the truck's location to the home office via satellites. Several stolen trucks have been recovered quickly, thanks to that equipment.

"Would this pose a problem for our plot if Amtrak adopted this system for all its trains?" I asked. "If the authorities knew that the train had been stopped, wouldn't they be concerned? What if the crooks had a second transmitter, its antenna mounted on the top of one of those little 'track speeders' track workers ride to the job site? Perhaps a hijacker playing the role of a train chief could ride aboard a speeder up the tracks at normal train speed, regularly transmitting its location and making the dispatchers think all is well while the hijackers loot the *Zephyr* stopped miles behind in Gore Canyon?"

Bob's brow furrowed and he sat back in his seat. "I would be a little concerned about sending a phony second transmitter ahead of the train," he said. "There are several reasons. One is that getting hold of a second transceiver would be difficult; that is not exactly the stuff one could pick up at any Radio Shack. For another, I suspect that Amtrak has some rather fancy coding impressed on the signal that would be extremely difficult to replicate. Satellite stuff often does; the codes are used to carry instructions to the relay satellite and that sort of thing."

Bob, however, did not see the new technology as an impediment to our story. "Our plan, you know, is to arrange the heist at a spot where there is no quick way for the authorities to get to the train. Indeed, we've just discussed the thieves recognizing the technology they are up against and making allowances. I surely see no problem with the felons sabotaging the train's satellite system—or trying to and not getting it done."

Ideas beget ideas, goes the old saw, and Bob proved it once again. After all, he added, we are considering that a disgruntled former Amtrak employee is involved. "Of course, we could play with the idea that the ex-employee did not tell the felons everything, figuring that perhaps they would get caught and he would have a chance to get away with his own loot, his own loot being perhaps the valuables he steals from train passengers while the gang is getting the drugs out of the compartment, and maybe that is the deal the gang cuts with him—he can rob the passengers while they rob the drugs.

"But then maybe they shoot him at the end of the robbery so that he can't turn against them if he gets caught. That ploy has another value to the gang—the passengers would be much more likely to remember the robber who took their belongings than they would the rest of the gang who they don't have any real contact with.

"Then, when the ex-employee gets bumped off, that becomes irrelevant. Also, the ex-employee would be the one who robs the steward, since he knows her routine, and the possibilities of the money she is responsible for. Then he gets plugged, leaving more of a mystery. Whatcha think?"

"Not bad, not bad," I replied admiringly.

We fell silent for a few minutes. "What about a title?" I asked.

"*Rocky Mountain High?*"

I blinked. A penchant for puns as well as a mind for crime! This notion had real possibilities, and this was a fellow worth cultivating. "Perhaps," I suggested, "at some future time we could collaborate on the writing?"

"I thought you'd never ask!" Bob said.

Half an hour before, the *Zephyr* had left behind Gore and Little Gore Canyons and now approached a hamlet called Bond, so shabby and weather-beaten that a casual passerby never would imagine its historic importance in mountain railroading. It's the eastern terminus of a thirty-eight-mile stretch of track known to railroaders and railfans the world over as the "Dotsero Cutoff."

All that's visible from the train is a branch line climbing into the mountains, heading 103 miles northwest to Oak Creek, Steamboat Springs and Craig. This was David Moffat's old Denver & Salt Lake Railroad, over whose original route the *Zephyr* had been running ever since it departed Denver.

Before the 1930s the Rio Grande's old main line to Salt Lake City, the circuitous "Royal Gorge" route, had curved south along the Front Range 117 miles from Denver through Colorado Springs to Pueblo before turning west to Utah. Not until a "cutoff" track could be built along the Colorado River through the mountains to link the southerly Rio Grande main with the northerly Denver & Salt Lake could the Denver & Rio Grande Western truly compete for transcontinental traffic with its rivals, the Union Pacific to the north and the Santa Fe to the south. The dream was born before the turn of the century, but thanks to the railroad wars endemic to the West, it was not until 1934 that the cutoff was finally built. It shortened the route from Denver to Salt Lake City by 176 miles. The Rio Grande leased it until 1947, when it finally swallowed the Moffat Road.

The western end of the cutoff is at Dotsero, the junction of the Colorado and Eagle rivers, marked as ".0" (dot zero) on the maps of a surveying team that charted the Colorado River in 1885. The other end is just east of Bond, at the point (called "Orestod"—Dotsero backward) where today's branch to Steamboat Springs curves away from the main line. Following the Colorado River at its calmest, the cutoff takes an hour for the *Zephyr* to traverse, and it affords spectacular sights of wildlife, especially in winter and early spring, when birds and animals can be seen without green cover to block the view from the train.

The lounge car had filled up again during the runs through the canyons, but I found an empty seat next to a veteran *Zephyr* rider who luckily had both sharp eyes and binoculars. A few minutes outside Bond the train passed what appeared to be a tumbledown Ferris wheel by the river. "It's an old irrigation wheel," said the white-haired conductor, standing in the center of the car and serving as an impromptu tour guide. "It used to scoop up water and empty it into a ditch there."

A minute later the train threaded the ruddy rock pagodas of Red Canyon (one of the reasons the Spanish named the country and its river "Colorado"), then emerged onto a low plateau full of small ranches. The name of one such struggling spread, emblazoned on its barn, was "Rancho Starvo."

"Look!" said the conductor. "Bald eagles!" A majestic black-and-white bird soared on six-foot wings a few feet above the water, swooped up and settled into its eyrie in a sixty-foot snag high above the river. Everyone in the car searched for its mate, finding it gliding low above the water a hundred yards downstream. Here the river dipped above and below its icy cover, thousands of animal tracks crisscrossing the snow to open patches of water. Every mile or so the fellow with the binoculars pointed out a beaver dam, its builders slapping the water with their tails as the *Zephyr* roared by.

Everyone in the car stood to peer ahead at the locomotives, curving in a tight arc toward the river. A dozen mule deer had bolted in panic from below the train, racing the locomotives to the high ground on the other side of the track. Before our horrified eyes, as the engineer frantically leaned on his horn to warn them off, three of the deer leaped across the track and up the embank-

ment a hoof-width ahead of the onrushing locomotives, the others
veering away to the low ground. We let out a collective sigh. Deer
are as mindless as teenagers racing a train to a grade crossing.
During a population explosion of the species in the 1930s, so
many deer died in collisions with Rio Grande locomotives that the
railroad was reduced to sending track speeders ahead of all its
trains, the men aboard waving their arms, firing pistols and shouting to scare the deer away from the line.

It was nearing four o'clock, and the afternoon shadows began to
lengthen as the *Zephyr* reached Dotsero. Briefly the train waited in
a siding to let its eastbound mate go by. As it was a pretty spot by
the Colorado River, I decided to go down to the vestibule and open
a window while the train was stopped so that I could poke my
camera out and get a couple of shots unfettered by streaked compartment windows. Yes, the act was irregular—if the attendant or
a conductor had come by, he'd have slammed the window and
chewed me out—but photojournalists, I reasoned, never allow a
few rules to keep them from getting a good picture. The chances
were good that I could get away with it. And, although I kept
glancing behind me nervously, expecting the wrath of officialdom,
I did. My luck had held.

What's more, John Davis leaned from the tiny window of his
galley door, deep in conversation with a young fisherman standing
by the tracks. He was carrying a stringer of perhaps a dozen dripping fish a good fourteen or sixteen inches long. Suddenly John
dipped into his pocket and handed the young man a fistful of cash,
and the young man passed up the stringer in return. It was an act
with a history almost as distinguished as that of the dining car;
railroad chefs long have kept a weather eye out for likely spots
along their routes where they can restock their larders with the
freshest possible fish.

Later that afternoon I asked John about it. "Yep," he said.
"Bought a dozen fresh rainbow trout off the guy. I'll broil 'em with
a little lemon for the crew tonight."

"Lucky bastards," I said, wishing mightily that I could invoke journalist's privilege. Really, shouldn't I live the crew's experience as closely as possible, eating the same food they do, even the special treats? I didn't have the gall to suggest so. And John did not offer.

"What *really* makes me feel good," he said, "is when a train attendant or waiter says, 'Well, now we can *eat* this trip. We got a decent chef downstairs.' "

To make sure I got the point, John told me about a dinner Amtrak gave for its employees at the end of a safety campaign. "They put up notices about who the chef of the day was going to be, and the guys came in and looked to see who it was. We got some good cooks out there. I'm not knocking them, you know? But when everybody found out who the chef was, they came. I used seven cases of chicken, twenty-four chickens in the case, plus spaghetti with meat sauce. All Amtrak issue. I made everything from scratch. I made three pans of banana pudding, I made fudge brownies, rice pilaf, baked chicken and dressing. *Everybody* came."

"Lord, it tires me out to listen to you," I said, shaking my head.

"They enjoy my cooking," John said, tapping my chest with a finger, "because I put pride in my work all my life."

In a moment the eastbound *Zephyr* rolled by. It had left Salt Lake City at dawn and also was running late. Moving again, our westbound train rolled under Interstate 70 and met the highway again at the eastern mouth of Glenwood Canyon. Beginning at this point is a man-made structure that drives Earth Firsters into a frenzy, but has led many thoughtful conservationists to admit that human engineering does not always destroy the environment, and indeed in important ways can enhance it.

Interstate 70 was the last link of the national superhighway system to be constructed, and probably its most controversial. Environmentalists exploded in the late seventies when plans were announced to drive the four-lane road through the 12½-mile-long Glenwood Canyon. The quiet grandeur of the great gorge would be destroyed, they said, by the clamor of truck and automobile traffic, and the limestone, granite and red sandstone cliffs would forever be scarred by the concrete snake slashed into their sides. In a celebrated riverside press conference in the early eighties, pop singer John Denver loftily informed reporters that the proposed highway would all but fill up the narrow canyon, "just a stone's throw between walls." To illustrate his point, he picked up a stone and threw. Into the river it splashed. His second rock went no farther. Nor did the third. "Phooey," he said, and stalked home to glittering Aspen.

As the *Zephyr* coursed through the soaring, gold-tinged gray cliffs of the canyon, however, I thought that if a superhighway had to be built here, this was the way to do it. The highway, which has cost $40 million per mile to build, is not merely utilitarian steel and concrete, but an exercise in roadbuilding as a visual art. In places the highway soars grandly on viaducts designed to preserve trees and vegetation below. The viaducts, tapered to make them look less massive, are borne on slim columns, not heavy spraddle-legged bridge supports. Bridge railings are rusting into a natural-looking brown. Concrete retaining walls, underpinnings and rock cuts have been textured and stained to blend with the surrounding cliffs, and the builders are even healing damage done half a century ago when the old two-lane U.S. 6 was driven through the canyon.

A paved bicycle path has been built along the river's edge, and near the western end of the canyon lie several small parking lots and concrete ramps leading to the river for rafters and kayakers. (During the summer, rafters on the Colorado consider mooning the passing *Zephyr* great sport. The more exhibitionistic of both sexes strip to full frontal glory and stand line abreast, hands on hips, grinning broadly as the train grinds by.)

The road, sailing over the river here and hugging the cliffs there, tunneling in two spots through whole mountains, is a magnificent engineering marvel. Withal, I thought, here is an effective compromise of commercial and conservationist interests as well as an architectural structure to be admired for its own sake. Perhaps in time the highway will come to be thought one of the canyon's beauties, as the Golden Gate Bridge—which would have been reviled if it were being built today—is considered a glory of San Francisco Bay.

The only truly ugly structure in the canyon is the old dam of the Shoshone hydroelectric plant of the Public Service Company of Colorado between the cliffs in the shadow of Interstate 70, and it long antedates the highway. Two large underground penstocks carry water from the dam farther downstream to the power plant, the Colorado River thinning to a trickle between the two installations. Below the plant the river surges again into wild rapids that are among the favorite haunts of central Colorado rafters.

Near this spot in 1950, across the river from the main line at Grizzly Siding, where the eastbound and westbound *Zephyrs* were scheduled to meet daily from 1949 until 1970, the Rio Grande erected "a monument to an idea." It was a nine-foot-long, five-hundred-pound stainless steel replica Vista-Dome car, welded to two steel rails mounted on a twelve-foot arch of native stone. For a quarter of a century the twenty-nine-ton monument stood spraddle-legged by the highway, honoring Cyrus Osborn's 1944 vision of a glass-domed cruise train in Glenwood Canyon.

As the years passed, the decline of American passenger trains encouraged vandals, who shot the windows out of the monument, one flattening the dome with a bat. In the mid-1970s the Rio Grande rescued the car, storing it for a while and donating it to the Colorado Railroad Museum in Golden. When, in 1985, the construction of Interstate 70 reached the site, the Colorado Highway Department gave the stone arch to the museum, uniting the two artifacts. On its grounds today the monument shines still, restored to its stainless-steel splendor.

Five miles past the original site of the monument the *California Zephyr*, wending the twisting, turning tracks at about twenty miles per hour and spooking colonies of white-throated swifts and tiny mouse-colored canyon wrens, rounded a bend in the river across from a small settlement called "No Name." It then entered a tunnel and emerged from the canyon into Glenwood Springs at Mile 1,222, almost exactly halfway between Chicago and Oakland. At 4:07 P.M. the *Zephyr* still was running fifty-five minutes late.

EIGHT

As the *California Zephyr* slid to a stop by the picturesque old Rio Grande station in Glenwood Springs, I recalled a memorable visit a few months earlier—one that had begun in, of all places, O'Hare Airport, in a United Airlines passenger lounge.

"*Glenwood Springs?* Ugh! You don't want to go *there!*" Ray, a boyhood friend, had said with a discernible sneer. We had encountered each other for the first time in two decades at O'Hare, where we and our spouses were waiting for a late-afternoon flight to Denver. I and mine were going on to Glenwood Springs by *Zephyr* the next morning (our long weekend schedule didn't offer enough time to travel all the way from Chicago by train); he and his were picking up a rented car for the drive to Vail, where they owned a cottage.

"Glenwood Springs is so . . . ah . . . *middle-class*," Ray added, vainly searching his mind for a suitably colorful pejorative. "In Vail and Aspen you'll find far more . . . *interesting* people." He sniffed in distaste, and I sighed inwardly. Though we had grown up in the same dead-center-middle-class Eisenhower-era cloth-coat-Republican milieu in Evanston, Illinois, we'd taken different roads. I still lived in Evanston, but Ray, a bright and ambitious fellow who had risen high in a large Chicago corporation, had left behind his roots to move north to superexclusive Kenilworth, the nation's wealthiest suburb. It's amusing and a little sad, I thought, how so many people's social cocoons retain the same constricted dimensions instead of enlarging with every rung they climb on the status ladder. It occurs to very few of them that keeping one foot solidly planted in their origins can confer generous benefits of membership in multiple strata of human society. In their world it's always Us versus Them, even when they used to be Them. The class system, America's dirty little secret, is one constant the frontier never changed. Pity.

That evening we said our restrained good-byes to Ray and his wife at Stapleton Airport, and by the next afternoon he had faded from my mind when I turned to Debby in our Glenwood Springs hotel room and asked, in an ersatz *Mitteleuropa* accent, "Vell, shall ve take der vaters?"

"Ach, ja," replied *meine Frau,* slipping into her swimsuit as well as into my jocular mood. "Off ve go."

And off we went next door to one of the great attractions of *déclassé* Glenwood Springs: the huge Yampa Hot Springs thermal pools, where every accent known to the world is heard amid the rising steam. Evenings in the pools are a symphony of languages as well as unselfconscious bodies of all ages and shapes. Many of them belong to budget-conscious Americans, including academics and journalists—and vacationing Europeans.

Why take the waters? On the most superficial level, because they're there. The "World's Largest Outdoor Mineral Hot-Springs Pool" is actually two adjoining tanks arranged in an enormous coffin shape next to a three-story red-brick Victorian structure that used to be the Hot Springs Hotel. The bigger pool is longer than a football field and contains more than a million gallons of water. Its temperature hovers at 86 to 89 degrees in the summer, 90 degrees in the winter. The smaller tank, called the "therapy pool," is kept at 102 to 104 degrees. The idea is to parboil yourself up to the neck for about ten minutes, then hop into the big pool for a short cool-off before returning to the steaming stuff.

Except for its odd shape, the larger tank looks like a super-Olympic-sized swimming pool, with diving boards at the deep end and half a dozen lap-swimming lanes adjacent. Every time I've been there, a dozen serious distance swimmers have been at work, although I wonder about the effect of high water temperatures on a body already overheated by exercise. In any event, the only concession to touristiness seems to be a huge, twisting water slide near the diving boards, with its own tiny pool at the business end. I guess it helps keep youngsters out of the hair of adults determined to "take the waters."

And what's so special about the waters? According to the spa's literature, Yampa Hot Springs and the adjacent vapor caves are awash in industrial-strength quantities of sodium, magnesium, potassium, lime and sulphur dissolved in various chlorides, bromides, iodides and fluorides as well as bicarbonates, phosphates and biborates. Any soup that tastes that bad must be good for you, eh? (I caught an accidental mouthful when I collided with another lap swimmer.) I don't know; I'm not one who believes in healing powers of mineral waters. But a good soak does have beneficial effects. An hour or so in the pools each evening so utterly relaxed our sore and weary hikers' muscles that Debby and I slept deeply the night through.

Much of the attraction of thermal pools lies in simply letting one's imagination float upon the passing scene. Sitting on a ledge in the shallows of the larger tank during our visit was a quartet of stout matrons in their seventies, chattering animatedly in age-old fashion. Throughout history women have gathered to exchange gossip at watering places, and these ladies, despite their floppy straw hats and voluminous skirted bathing costumes—"swimsuits" is inadequate—wouldn't have looked out of place in linen robes, with amphorae on their shoulders.

Next to them four men of similar vintage—their husbands?—sat in silent line abreast like basilisks brooding on a cornice. Four leathery bald heads remained rigid as four pairs of reptilian eyes slowly trailed into the pool a thong-clad beauty who brought to life Raymond Chandler's line about "a blonde to make a bishop kick a hole in a stained-glass window."

Behind them in the therapy pool a middle-aged man, his eyes heavy with tragedy, cradled an unmoving teenage boy. The youth's painfully thin limbs drifted in rubbery paralysis amid the ripples, his eyes staring fixedly at the sky. The father, if he was that—and he must have been—arose from the water and bore his limp burden to the next pool, slowly immersing the boy with gentleness and great love. Were they hoping for a cure, or just an easing of their pain? The scene was almost too much to bear, and I looked away.

On thermal springs bobs a good deal of historical flotsam. Since antiquity water has been celebrated as a source of energy, both physical and metaphysical, even to being sanctified as the source of life. For millennia sacred springs have been places of pilgrimage for healing, both physical and spiritual. The medical establishment may scoff, but it's the competition.

Healing waters may be pagan indulgences, but they're also scenes of solace and society. In Rome, *thermae* were a public pleasure, the focus of communal life, a place of relaxation, gathering and worship. *"Sanitas per aquas"* (health through water), Nero was supposed to have declared upon seeing the magnificent fountains of Rome. The word "spa," some think, is an acronym for this phrase. Bathing, however, tends to spark the libido, and the Romans ruined it for everybody by welcoming prostitutes to the pools. Soon bathhouses became synonymous with brothels, and by A.D. 527 Justinian, the officially stiff-necked (though privately licentious) Christian emperor of Byzantium, forbade mixed bathing, except for married couples. Bluenoses from the beginning, Christians made bodily dirt a badge of holiness. Soon everybody stank, which famously gave rise to the perfume industry. In the fifteenth century Isabella of Castile took noisome pride in taking only two baths during her life, first at birth and then before her wedding.

(In Europe only Jews, whose religious obligations required them to do so, bathed regularly.)

Christendom took on a better odor when John Wesley, founder of Methodism, began to preach in the 1730s that cleanliness was next to godliness. Of course there were holdouts; Napoleon, for instance, sent messages to Josephine ordering her not to bathe for several days before his return from a campaign. Her rankness turned him on. But the idea of bathing had breached the dam and spread like floodwaters. Shortly after World War I, Aurora, Illinois—birthplace of the Burlington Northern—decreed that every citizen must bathe at least once a week or go to jail. (Sooner or later everything is connected to the railroad.)

The world's great spa communities—Evian-les-Bains, Baden-Baden, Marienbad, Salsomaggiore, Saratoga Springs among them—prospered when railroads enabled the wealthy and famous to travel at will to their favorite thermal baths. Grand hotels, casinos and theaters followed. Compared with such places, Glenwood Springs is decidedly minor-league, without a luxury hotel or four-star restaurant to its name. It is not a glittering mecca of pampering for wealthy matrons hiding out after a tummy tuck or jowl hoist. It is not even a backwoods version of social-climbing Vail or moneyed Aspen. Its very unpretentiousness is a good part of its charm, and I fell in love with the place the first time I stepped off the *California Zephyr* there. I suspect even my friend Ray would enjoy it despite his striving self.

Like so many towns in the Rocky Mountains, Glenwood Springs (population 3,500) is a touristy village ("Last Resting Place of Doc Holliday, Famous Gunslinger"), but its touristiness is low-key and unselfconscious, shunning both sleaze and ostentation. Like so many other Rocky Mountain towns, it seems to have escaped the decline so sadly visible everywhere on the Great Plains during the last decade of the century. That shouldn't be surprising. The economy of the Rockies always has been based in great part on tourism, which did not dip as drastically as other industries during the recession of the early nineties.

At first glance Glenwood Springs is not the usual pretty mountain town. A triple barrier—the Rio Grande tracks, the Colorado River and Interstate 70—bisects the northern and southern portions of the community. On the north lies the Hot Springs Pool, its sprawling new hotel and, next door, the Hotel Colorado, a turn-of-the century brick pile so picturesquely Old Western that through its doors one half expects Teddy Roosevelt to charge in, all teeth and mustache, aboard a bronc.

In their turn-of-the-century brick buildings the downtown curio shops push the wares of local artisans—leather crafts, wood carvings, Indian jewelry and pottery, much of which is surprisingly artful. True, the shops also sell mountain kitsch made in Hong Kong as well as "Glenwood Springs" and "Rocky Mountains" sweatshirts, but nowhere did I spot the pornographic postcards and witless T-shirts that mar so many American resort villages.

Praise be to God, Glenwood Springs shelters no New Testament Wax Museums so characteristic of redneck vacation spots, like the Wisconsin Dells and the Black Hills. There isn't a Jellystone Park Campground within miles. The town does, however, host many small shoestring husband-and-wife businesses too poor to afford a storefront. One private residence on the main street is a combination women's dress shop and ranch plumber's establishment. "TINA'S BOUTIQUE," says the top line of the sign out front. Right underneath is printed "HIGHLANDER IRRIGATION."

Many of the people who live in Glenwood Springs seem to come there from somewhere else. The dark-haired pixie who brought my breakfast at the Daily Bread Bakery, a Main Street storefront establishment, confided that she was from Cleveland and had graduated from Kent State the previous June. Unable to land a decent job at home, she had spent the winter ski-bumming at Aspen and supporting herself baking and waiting on tables in Glenwood Springs, where she shared a tiny apartment with two other young women.

"When times get better I'll go to grad school," she said. "There are lots of us in the same boat here. One of my roommates has a master's, and another used to be a kindergarten teacher in Boston.

But this isn't a bad place to be, though it can be a little expensive, being a resort town and all."

Clearly this young woman was an urban sophisticate, and that should have prepared me for the surprising greeting I had later the same day at Florindo's, a restaurant in the next block that serves excellent everyday Italian cuisine. The hostess, upon seating me and Debby, inquired solicitously if I'd like more light at my table, even though I hadn't asked. She had recognized my deafness as soon as I'd asked for a table for two; my "deaf speech" is a dead giveaway to those knowledgeable about hearing impairment. Restaurant hostesses who understand lip-readers' need for a well-lighted table are rare in any cosmopolitan city and almost unheard of in a small town. I was therefore not surprised to learn that in the elections of 1992, the citizens of Glenwood Springs bucked a state-wide trend and voted against a constitutional amendment whose effect would be to limit the rights of gays and lesbians.

If I needed more evidence that Glenwood Springs is warm and caring, comfortable and unpretentious—well, at least compared to New York City or Paris—I found it in the two women who run Glenwood Springs's Amtrak depot, a picturesque stone-and-brick pile recently spiffed up to attract the summer resort crowd as well as skiers in the winter. Most days, *Zephyr* passengers can spot agents Michael Parker and Sandi Brown trundling a baggage cart loaded with skis, suitcases and trunks to the station behind their little tractor.

They seemed taken aback by my interest when I introduced myself in the station. "Nothing goes on here, really," they said in genuine puzzlement. "We sell tickets. We take care of the baggage. We shovel snow. We do the janitorial work. If there's any mechanical work we can accomplish, we do that, too." Michael is homey, merry-eyed and in her fifties. As agent in charge, she wore a smart blue uniform vest and slacks. Sandi, smiling, honey-blonde and in her early thirties, had just returned from maternity leave. As number two, she is the baggage person and wore blue coveralls. However, there seems to be no pecking order between the pair. They do all the jobs together and help each other where they can; while Sandi goes over the station with a dry mop, Michael polishes the brass railings on the stairway.

Born and reared in the Tacoma-Seattle area ("It's a plain background—my dad was a dentist, my mother a housewife"), Michael came to Amtrak from the travel industry. She worked for a Denver tour operator that sold Amtrak tickets, and when it went out of business in 1984, she won a job on Amtrak's extra board in Denver selling tickets and humping baggage. The following year she was transferred to Glenwood Springs, and has been chief agent there since 1989.

Sandi, a native Coloradan, has the Rio Grande in her blood; her stepfather, grandfather, an uncle and countless cousins all worked for the railroad. She began her career as a brakeman in 1978, teaming with another female brakie—the only other one on the Rio Grande—in what used to be a hairy-chested man's world, and she met immediate resentment. When a fellow crewman made a clumsy pass at her in a caboose, she brushed him off. "After that, male crew members were quick to criticize me and reported my mistakes to management all the time. I was being punished for not responding to the guy the way he wanted. I had no witnesses and no proof. The guys were real hard on you. They didn't want women taking a man's job."

After six months on the road, Sandi switched to a clerk's job, holding it until a layoff in the summer of 1987. In 1988 she joined Amtrak, first at the Grand Junction station, then moved to Glenwood Springs to be closer to her husband, who works in Aspen as a telephone repairman.

Twenty-five years ago, women labored as clerks and maybe dispatchers, but with the odd exception (such as the old Zephyrette) never on the trains and rarely as agents. Now they're everywhere in Amtrak—in service crews, on operating crews, behind desks. Women have been in charge of districts that embrace several states.

Not all agree, however, that Amtrak has elevated women far enough. Mimi Earley, Mike and Sandi's boss in Denver, who was acting district chief when I met her on one *Zephyr* layover, thinks women's advancement in Amtrak is "a touchy question. They don't do poorly. That's about all I can say." When I pressed, she said, "Amtrak does have quite a few women in management positions, but they're not high up. All the vice presidents and assistant vice presidents and directors are male. It looks nice on paper when Amtrak says, 'We have this many women management employees,' but in reality all the higher jobs are still dominated by men."

A quick look later at Amtrak's 1992 annual report corroborated Mimi's contention. All nine members of the board of directors were white males. All fifteen members of the executive staff were male. Just one woman was a corporate officer—Jane E. Bass, assistant corporate secretary. The lone black was William S. Norman, the executive vice president and number two in Amtrak's hierarchy.

All the same, though Mike and Sandi are quick to say that they experienced gender discrimination early in their careers, they see little or none today—a sentiment I've heard echoed many times among on-board crew members.

"I feel there's a respect now, a mutual respect," Sandi said forthrightly.

"In Denver when I first started there might have been some sexism," Mike added. "Not a whole lot. It was just a feeling you got. Now the older men, the ones that have been there the longest time, are getting used to it. They're realizing that women can handle a job most of the time—that just like in anything else, there are some *men* that can and some that can't."

In practical terms the biggest problem Mike and Sandi face is the obvious one of upper body strength and oversized luggage. The Amtrak weight limit is seventy-five pounds, and Mike and Sandi each can handle that easily enough. If a duffle bag or steamer trunk in the baggage car goes over the limit, however, "we have to figure out other ways of getting it where it needs to go," Mike said. Some chivalrous passengers offer to help, "and if it gets too rough we might say yes, but the conductors are helping us out now."

These women may be liberated, but they are not unfeminine. To get what they want, they said with sly smiles, they unholster a bag of chocolate chip cookies, whose contents are spread where they will do the most good.

They also decorate their station during the holidays. Few male agents do that, partly because it's just not something guys do, and partly because Amtrak doesn't provide funds. The two women supply their own decorations, two trees and all the trimmings. To pay for other comforts, Mike and Sandi recycle cans from the pop machine. So far they have bought a refrigerator and coffee percolator for their station office.

Except for the reservations computer, radio, modern telephones and yellow Amtrak hard hats, the station looks as it must have a century ago. The oaken wainscoting and curved arches in the waiting room were recently refinished, and the carved oaken benches are in good shape. In an office corner lies an enormous steel strongbox on wheels—the kind Butch Cassidy once dynamited—and on an old oaken desk is an ancient Remington upright typewriter. Sometimes dispatchers call in orders, and Sandi and Mike type them out to hand to engineers and conductors on train arrival. An old-fashioned long-handled order hoop leans against the station wall, but the women no longer use it—*Zephyr* stops at Glenwood Springs are always leisurely enough for the crews to climb down to pick up their orders.

Occasionally a train chief will radio ahead, asking the agents to go out for a few cases of beer, soda pop, or kitchen essentials to replenish shortages. "Trouble is they never tell us what size they want, assuming we'll know," Mike said. "Once a chief called ahead and requested four cans of gravy. I went out and got four eight-ounce cans—but he meant *gallon* cans."

One of the agents in Grand Junction, the next stop eighty miles west, sometimes gets in a jam when working alone, Mike said. "He rides a motorcycle to work, and occasionally a chief will radio ahead for a few cases of beer—and it's not easy to get eight cases of Bud on the back of a motorcycle!"

Passengers sometimes rub Mike and Sandi the wrong way, especially, said Mike, "when they get grouchy, when they get nasty, when they try to take advantage of our good natures and pass bad checks."

"Most of the time they're okay," Sandi said, "but sometimes no matter what you do you can't make 'em happy. The other day I had both trains coming in at almost the same time, and I needed all the boarding passengers' baggage to be in thirty minutes before the trains came in. This passenger didn't show up till just as the train was due in, and I couldn't check his bags through and he got very irate with me."

Sometimes the point of contention is over a local resident's inability to get a ticket on the train. Like the airlines, Amtrak sets aside large blocks of seats to be used only by tour operators or long-distance riders, say from Chicago to Glenwood Springs. Low-cost excursion fares may be available only between certain stations. Hence, residents of Glenwood Springs who want to go to Denver, 185 miles away, may be told even six months in advance that no seats are available. "You can get tickets from here to Fort Morgan," Mike said, "but you can't get tickets from here to Denver. People get angry."

How do Mike and Sandi handle these would-be passengers? "Mostly all we can tell them is that we don't have the space right now, and to try again later," Mike said. "Sometimes space will open up later on, close to the time they want to go. There's too many people that aren't spontaneous, though. They have to make their plans far ahead."

"When the seats open up twenty-four to forty-eight hours ahead of time, when a travel agency turns back the unsold seats, we can sell them," Sandi added. "But by that time it's often too late."

"There are days where we can't get excursion seats say, from here to Sacramento for the whole month of August," Mike said. "People are looking for the lower excursion fares, like all of us, and they don't want to pay the regular coach fares. They end up having to pay the most expensive fares. If it's about the same as an airline ticket, they're going to take the plane."

The system of computerized "yield management" is one borrowing from the airlines that I hope Amtrak will turn away from soon, as it did airline-style meals. (Airline-style videos, I am afraid, are in the lounge cars to stay.) While Amtrak management must try every means to maximize income, something remains outrageously unfair about a small-town taxpayer being unable to book seats or cheap fares on a federally subsidized transportation system because those seats and fares are reserved for travelers from big cities and profit-making tour operators. And that transportation system may be the only public conveyance out of town. Besides, fat lot of good yield management has done the airlines, sinking ever deeper into clouds of red ink.

All the same, Mike and Sandi can and do go out of their way for their customers. "Sometimes we'll ask, 'What date do you want to go?' 'What date do you want to return?' " Sandi said. "And we'll keep checking, and if space opens up we'll book the ticket and then call them. Other times we'll just give them the '800' national reservations number and tell them to keep checking periodically. Sometimes we'll send them to the travel agency—but if we do that, it cuts into our ticket sales, and if they're down, it's good-bye job."

While most of their morning is low-key—an occasional call from a passenger, an occasional drop-in to pick up a ticket—things start moving just before 1:00 P.M., when eastbound passengers arrive half an hour before train time. There are pockets of excitement. It can get hairy in midafternoon if the eastbound *Zephyr* (due out at 1:25 P.M.) is running late and arrives at the same time as the westbound (due out at 3:20 P.M.). There is only one platform, and when one train arrives, the other must wait on a siding just out of sight. "Lots of times," Sandi said, "we announce both trains at the same time, and it makes it real interesting if we've got sixty or seventy bags coming off the first train and we've got only five minutes between trains. It happened just last Sunday."

Occasionally at these hectic times passengers with no sense of direction will try to board the wrong train. Normally the conductors check the tickets in time, but more than once the *Zephyr* has had to stop after starting up to let off a wayward rider. "Sometimes," Sandi said, "we say, 'If you're going to Denver, the engine's going that way. If you're going to California, the engine's going *that* way."

The biggest excitement Mike can remember was the derailment of the westbound *Zephyr* ten miles up Glenwood Canyon on Christmas night, 1988, with 294 passengers aboard. Somehow the rails spread, and the slow-moving train gently slid off the tracks. "Nobody was hurt," Mike said, "but it took a while to bring all the passengers down here to the station." The Rio Grande brought them back, caroling all the way, aboard seven cabooses in two trips, and wresting the train back on the track took work crews two days. "We had to keep the station open and answer the phones, and keep clearing the snow off the platform—it was cold and snowing a lot—and help get the passengers out of here by bus to Denver and Salt Lake City airports."

As one might expect, the town of Glenwood Springs came to the rescue, too. "Everybody provided coffee, and that night one of the stores opened up real early so we could go and raid 'em of all their doughnuts and stuff. The police department, the state patrol and the sheriff helped, and on the whole everything was well taken care of. That was the biggest excitement we had. I don't want to have that one again."

Then there was the time Hollywood came to Glenwood Springs to use the picturesque station as a set for *Flashback,* the 1990 film with Dennis Hopper as an unrepentant hippie and Kiefer Sutherland as the straight-arrow FBI agent bringing him to justice. "I stayed in the station all night for three days to keep an eye on things," Michael said. "The producers replaced everything as it was—almost. They didn't quite secure the big Amtrak sign out in front of the station the way it should have been, and it blew down in a windstorm. They broke the fluorescent lights above the dispatcher's desk, but fixed them. And they did leave a hundred-dollar ladder here, so we came out ahead."

When a train comes in, either Sandi or Mike takes the Cushman tractor and baggage wagon to a point about two hundred yards up the track. The other remains in the station to watch for the train coming around a distant curve and announce its arrival.

"May I have your attention, please? Amtrak Number Five westbound now arriving," Sandi said on the PA. *"Please stay behind the yellow line until the train is stopped. Thank you. The* California Zephyr, *for Grand Junction, Provo, Salt Lake City, Winnemucca, Reno, Sacramento, Oakland and intermediate points. All tickets will be pulled from passengers by the conductors and by the station. Aaaaaall aboard!"*

And out she rolled from the station on a dead run, ponytail flying, on a two-hundred-yard dash for the spot far up the platform where Michael waited with the baggage wagon. Just ahead of the decelerating locomotives Sandi arrived, breathless but ready.

Michael and Sandi work together only three days of the week, on Fridays, Saturdays and Sundays, the heaviest days. One of them is always off on the other four days. But they look out for each other nevertheless. "If there's a lot of snow," Michael said, "the one whose day off it is will come down to the station and help shovel."

Sandi lives west of the station, Michael east. On their days off the one at home often will call the other at the station when she sees the train coming, to let the other know so that she can get out the train announcement in timely fashion and sprint to the baggage wagon spotted on the platform a few minutes earlier. These two Amtrakers take care of each other.

Pleasant memories of that summer visit to Glenwood Springs percolated in my mind as Bob Heath pulled shut the sleeper's vestibule door and yanked open the window so that I could get a glimpse of the agents before the *Zephyr* pulled out. Sure enough, here came the Cushman tractor trundling the baggage wagon, Mike at the wheel, Sandi beside her. "Mike! Sandi!" I shouted as the train began to roll. "Remember me?"

"H-e-e-enry!" they called back, smiling and waving broadly, as Superliner and Cushman passed close aboard like ships in a narrow channel. As the women disappeared around the curve I shut the window and dogged it with a smile as wide as Mike's and Sandi's. Of all American rites, this is one of the most charming: People wave at trains, and people on trains wave back. Why? Maybe

it's just a habit of long-forgotten origins, but when I'm in a generous mood I like to think those who wave at and from trains are simply acknowledging the special place railroads occupy in American hearts, that it is a grand and mutual gesture of recognition. And when you know the people at whom you're waving, there's an added joy in the fleeting acknowledgment of friendship, of lasting connections.

It was just after 4:15 P.M. when the *Zephyr* cleared the outskirts of Glenwood Springs, having detrained forty-five passengers, mostly skiers, and picked up a dozen. The serpentine mountain canyons of the central Rockies now were gone, the scenery changing to that of a broad river valley. Here the Colorado River is no longer a frothy, narrow mountain torrent but a wide, ambling stream. The open spaces allow straight track and sweeping curves, and the *Zephyr* picked up speed.

A few minutes later the train flashed past New Castle, site of the infamous Vulcan coal mine, whose black slash is still visible on a nearby mountainside. There, in 1896, an explosion set off by careless blasting tore through the shaft, killed fifty-four miners and shot timbers four hundred feet from the mine adit into the river. A blast in 1931 killed all thirty-seven people in and around the mine. Far below the surface of the earth, the mine is still burning, smoldering veins of coal yielding enough heat to melt snow on the ground hundreds of feet above. This part of Colorado is full of old mines whose fires have never been put out, and which may burn quietly, barely noticed, for a century to come.

Dusk was beginning to fall when the *Zephyr* left behind the hamlet of Silt and the evocatively named ranching and shale-oil towns of Rifle and Parachute near the Parachute Mountains, so named for their billowing shapes. Soon the train roared through DeBeque Canyon and into the wide Grand Valley, the center of western Colorado's fruit-orchard region. During summer daylight passengers can view rank upon rank of fruit trees—peach, pear, apricot, apple, cherry—marching away from the tracks, as well as look back toward the east and behold the ten-thousand-foot Grand

Mesa, the world's largest flat-topped mountain and the beginning of the Book Cliffs, enormous palisaded rocks that disappear far into the north.

Here, also, is the beginning of the high intermountain desert between the Rockies and the California Sierra, eight hundred miles away. The aspens and grasses of the eastern mountains had vanished; now, away from the riverine lowlands, only rocks, sand, sagebrush and low, scrubby pines are visible.

As I sat down to dinner, the *Zephyr* glided into Grand Junction (Mile 1,312), named for the confluence of the Grand—that is, the Colorado—and the Gunnison Rivers. Tacked to the shabby yellow Rio Grande station, built in 1905, is a faded sign that records the elevation at 4,578 feet and the population at seemingly a permanent 28,000. Grand Junction, the largest settlement in western Colorado, used to be a railroad town, but now it's a center for fruit shipping as well as coal, oil shale and uranium mining—and retirement. The average age of the thirty or so detraining passengers must, I thought, be about seventy.

I made a mental note to get off the train here someday and explore the tall monoliths and red cliffs at the nearby Colorado National Monument as well as the Grand Mesa National Forest and visit a couple of dinosaur digs nearby. And, I mused, I'd like to talk with the sturdy woman in her forties, clad in snug denim overalls, who had dismounted from the locomotive, walked back to the station and given the stationmaster an enormous smiling embrace. She was, I later would learn, an assistant engineer.

At 6:15 P.M., the very moment when John Davis's baked chicken (not too dry, either) arrived on the table, the *Zephyr* departed Grand Junction, still nearly an hour late.

This time the seating was serendipitous. As if to make up for the morning's disaster with the rat-faced man, Lela carefully placed me across the table from a courtly, white-haired man with a ruddy Irish face. Reaching across the table to shake my hand gravely, he identified himself as Byron Broderick, and said he had just retired from teaching in a Harlem public school and was headed to California on vacation. Next to me was a diminutive Chicagoan in her forties, Lynn Scherer, a public school librarian. The fourth in our party, a blonde woman also in her forties, introduced herself as Jackie Park, a public school principal from Connecticut who also taught as an adjunct professor at Western Connecticut State in Danbury.

The conversation was thoughtful, touching on such issues as political correctness ("it's an exaggerated issue," Byron said, speaking with the quiet authority of long experience) and philosophies of teaching. "I'm liberal on social issues," said Jackie, "but I'm very conservative in the classroom, and I just *wearied* of open walls in education. I believe in structure." Before I could feel odd man out as a journalist trapped in heavy shop talk among teachers, Lynn asked solicitously, "What do you do?"

"I'm a newspaper book-review editor," I began, immediately precipitating a small explosion from Jackie. "You're a book editor? I'm an author!" she exclaimed. "I'm on a tour promoting a novel!" Naturally newspaper book editors, as well as TV talk shows, are primary targets of such publicity tours, and we marveled for a few moments over the odds against such specialized subjects and objects meeting at dinner on a train in the lonely Western desert.

The title of her novel, Jackie said, was *A Stone Gone Mad*, published under her full name, Jacquelyn Holt Park. She does not fly, so her publisher, Random House, allowed her to travel by train. She was headed to San Francisco on the first leg of the publicity tour.

The jacket of her novel bore a generous blurb from William Styron, a novelist not given to indiscriminate praise. I asked her how she scored that coup.

"It was 1983 and I was living in a literary colony near Los Angeles, writing the book," Jackie replied. "Styron was slated to keynote a literary convention in L.A. I wrote a letter to Styron asking him to be my guest at dinner, and sent it to him through a friend's aunt who had typed the manuscript of Styron's novel *Lie Down in Darkness*.

"Styron accepted, and I spent the evening with him and his

daughter, who was filming a documentary on Eudora Welty. We had sushi, and I hated it, but I was so in awe of him I ate it anyway. I paid for the dinner on my American Express card. He said, 'I *never* do this,' but I insisted. And he said, 'I owe you.'

That gave Jackie her opening, and she asked if Styron would read her manuscript. Oh no, he said, throwing up his hands. Every week he's buried in manuscripts from hopeful first novelists. Jackie persisted, later calling him at his home in Connecticut. Finally Styron gave in.

The fantasy of every budding writer is for a distinguished novelist to be so stunned by a proffered manuscript that he sends it to his own publisher. That's exactly what happened. "He liked it, and he sent it to Robert Loomis, a top editor at Random House. And Random loved it—the first forty-four pages, though they felt the rest didn't work. They put me under contract for fifteen thousand dollars on the basis of the first pages."

For the next six years she rewrote the novel, reducing it from eight hundred pages to three hundred. "And so Mr. Styron endorsed it on the jacket, and I'm on a tour, and that's how I met you!"

A Stone Gone Mad is a very good novel of a woman's coming to grips with her homosexuality in the late 1940s through the 1970s. She is not "gay," but in the cruel terms of her era, a "lesbo," a "queer," a "homo" ostracized by family and friends. For thirty years she lives a double life, denying the core of her being, until she can emerge in wholeness. Owing to my deafness, I felt a strong kinship with the character, because she vividly reflected the fears and feelings of human beings isolated from their neighbors because of differences over which they have no control.

As dessert was served (apple pie à la mode, Amtrak style, is a deplorable weakness of mine) I reflected on another book that deals with gayness—and railroading as well. *Boomer: Railroad Memories* is the autobiographical story of Linda Niemann, one of the first women to go to work for a Western railroad as a "boomer," or itinerant brakeman, the quintessential trade of American railroading. (Not brakewoman or brakeperson, please; in that tough and muscular profession, "brakeman" is genderless.)

Boomer is about railroading the way *Moby-Dick* is about whaling. Locomotives and boxcars and marshaling yards and ribbons of high iron are just the graveled roadbed under a grander adventure—the oldest one in literature: the spiritual journey, an exorcising of personal devils and the discovery of self. When Linda Niemann went to work for the Southern Pacific in 1979, her life was in a shambles. Holding a Ph.D. in English from Berkeley, she was an "intellectual who looked like an all-American bimbo." Divorced and unemployed, a bisexual with a collapsing lesbian relationship, she was increasingly plagued by her mother's battle with mental illness. She was also a heavy drug user and well started down the long slide into alcoholism.

Why did a person so thoroughly screwed up choose to become a brakeman, one of the world's dirtiest, most difficult and dangerous jobs? "The railroad transformed the metaphor of my life," she wrote. "Nine thousand tons moving at sixty miles an hour into the fearful night. I now would ride that image, trying to stay alive within it. I know that later when I sat behind the moving train in the darkness of the caboose, window open and the unknown fragrances of the land filling the space, the blackness of the night was my friend. It felt good to be powerless and carried along by the destiny of that motion. I felt happy and at peace. I was where I belonged."

Brakemen, it seems, often are social misfits of one kind or another. Perhaps only such erratics can stand the life. Even today the rough-and-tumble work is extremely dangerous. At all hours in all kinds of weather, brakemen must hang with one hand on side ladders of free-rolling cars, lanterns in the other hand. Frequently they must dart along moving cars to pull uncoupling pins, all the while keeping an eye out for perils on the adjoining track.

Then there is the "brakeman's reward." The job puts the boomer way out on the line in the desert at those magic times of morning when you can "smell the dew on everything before true colors can exist—the red spectrum just waking up." As trains meet there is rhythm and peace on the land. Eventually Niemann struggled out of her self-inflicted hell of drugs, booze and stormy love affairs into a semblance of stability, and emerges from her book as a thoroughly likable and intelligent human being.

In person she doesn't look the least bit like a callused, hard-nosed brakie. When I met her in San Francisco after a *Zephyr* run, I was surprised that she was not husky and rugged but small and attractively weather-beaten, with a sea of freckles, sun-crinkled eyes, a throaty chuckle and a brilliant smile. During the time she wrote *Boomer*, she was an Amtrak assistant conductor for three years on the *Zephyr* and the *Coast Starlight*. She didn't have a steady job, but worked the extra board, which meant that she was on call all hours of the night and day.

When she joined during the summer of 1987, she said, "Amtrak was chronically shorthanded, and the extra board turned over real fast. I worked all the time. I lived in Santa Cruz and I started my day in Oakland. Often I would sleep overnight with my beeper in my truck in the parking lot. Some of the crews lived way down the valley in Fresno and others lived far up the coast. They'd be sleeping in the yards, in empty coaches, trucks, campers. We turned into zombies, but it still beat working freight."

I asked Linda whether she thought that Amtrak might be a step or two ahead of the rest of society so far as homophobia is concerned. Her response was sad confirmation that although many straight Americans are intelligent and aware enough to accept homosexuality as a natural phenomenon, they are still uneasy in its presence. She started off with the good points, characterizing Amtrak as a well-integrated organization especially in its hiring. "A lot of the on-board crew are gay," she said, because "service is something that gay people are good at. We're more sensitive, so we're in caring industries—nursing, teaching, service."

Other Amtrakers concur, at least about the numbers of gays in the organization. Reggie Howard says one of his concerns before a *Zephyr* trip starts is to make sure that the crew members he assigns to double rooms in the dormitory car will be comfortable with one another, because some straights can't handle the idea of rooming with a gay person.

The majority of Amtrak crew members are straight, and most are quick to profess tolerance toward gays, indeed showing them an everyday civility. Nonetheless, a latent homophobia sometimes surfaces, especially late in the evening in the dining car after hours. There "the discourse is controlled by the straight crews," Linda said. "You have to listen to a lot of gay-bashing. Straights are being forced to deal with the fact that a lot of gays work for Amtrak, and their first response is defensive. Some of the straight on-board chiefs go out of their way to let everybody know they aren't queer. You have to listen in detail to their sex stories. They say to themselves, We're going to stake out our territory, and this is going to be a straight table, and we're going to talk about being in the war and sleeping with prostitutes." Linda chuckled. "For hours they'll talk about that. So many of their sex stories go back to Vietnam I felt like I was in Nam myself."

In an atmosphere like this, Linda continued, gay crew members cannot talk about their personal lives, but must keep quiet. The atmosphere becomes oppressive, poisoning the camaraderie of the railroad.

But that wasn't what caused Linda to return to the Southern Pacific after three years on Amtrak. Rather, she said, she felt "claustrophobic" dealing with passengers. She's naturally shy, and "the worst thing for me is not being able to have my own personal emotions when I'm working with the public, and when you work all the time and suffer from lack of sleep, it's very hard to be a public person and suppress your feelings."

Still, she does get more respect from her fellow workers for having written a book. "It's been hard for me on the railroad because I've been shy about revealing who I am to the people I work with because of being a lesbian. Now I think it's better. Even though people don't like certain things about me, at least they know me now. The whole thing feels better. There are a few people I work with that don't talk to me, but those guys are assholes, and who wants to talk to them anyway?" She laughs.

Linda has a particular crotchet about Amtrak: the corporate term "assistant conductor." Applied to female crew members, the term, she says, "makes passengers think they are basically stewardesses, mere ticket-takers. In fact, the train crew is responsible for the safety of the train, and it's too bad the public doesn't understand the complexity of the job. Too often it has no idea that the train is anything more than a rolling restaurant."

When Linda joined Amtrak in 1987, it was hiring its engineers and conductors from the freight roads. "Amtrak is very lucky to have us with all this freight experience. Some of us have thirty years on the railroad. Amtrak was a haven for old heads, people who had retired or were about to retire. They already knew everything about the railroad. They were the safest people for passengers to be with."

Now, she said, Amtrak hires new operating crews who have never worked on the railroad. "Somebody who just comes off the street is going to be dealing with tickets, passenger problems, stuff like that. They won't get the benefit of training in freight railroading, where they can see what's happening. I think Amtrak could do more railroad training of engineers, conductors, assistant conductors. That's hard to do when people don't get freight experience. To me that's the biggest problem Amtrak has, next to the equipment—the cars. We can't get them serviced. We can't get replacements or parts. It's a miracle we're rolling along. There's one car whose rear door I used to have to close with a broomstick this way," she said, demonstrating with an imaginary lever on a recalcitrant door. "We never could get it fixed. You have to become an expert in the quirks of each car, because you're stuck with them."

During the half hour after the *California Zephyr* left Grand Junction, it had passed the hamlet of Fruita, famous for dinosaur fossils, and the town of Mack, known to rail buffs as the home of the old narrow-gauge Uintah Railway, and entered the spectacular—at least in summer daylight—Ruby Canyon, eastern gateway to the deserts of Utah. The Colorado River carved the mesmerizingly shaped red cliffs out of a high plateau called Uncompahgre.

No roads cut through the chasm, which looks very much like a minor-league Grand Canyon.

"We're crossing over the Colorado-Utah state line now," said the chief on the PA. We were still in Ruby Canyon, and in summer twilight westbound *Zephyr* passengers can see high on a cliffside the dividing line painted by Rio Grande track workers long ago. The place, aptly, is called Utaline.

Just two miles later, at Westwater, the Colorado River parts company with the Rio Grande main line, heading south through Westwater Canyon, a rafter's paradise, to Arizona, Glen Canyon and Lake Powell. Night had fallen, and against the dark sky the light of the full moon etched the Book Cliffs, and high beyond them, the mesa tops of the lonely Roan Cliffs. And then the *California Zephyr* plunged out into the enormous forlorn expanse of the Utah desert.

NINE

On the way through the last Oak-
land coach toward my sleeper, I glanced down at two teenaged girls
sitting together. A heavy woolen blanket lay mussed in the lap of
the one sitting next to the aisle. The car wasn't particularly cool—
in fact, the temperature actually was a bit warmer than normal. But
before my mind could form the question, I saw the little brown tail
wiggling from under the blanket. Parking myself in the seat across
from the girls, I smiled and whispered, "How'd you get him past
the conductors?"

"It's a *she*," said the girl, "and the conductors *know*. Shhh."
Surreptitiously she peered back toward the lounge car. "But the
chief doesn't." She smiled and pulled back a fold of the blanket.
What appeared to be a cross between a Shih Tzu and a toy wire-
haired terrier eyed me expectantly, its stubby tail windmilling. The
little dog, however, lay quietly, as if it thought the slightest miscon-
duct would result in banishment to the wilderness.

"She *is* well-behaved," I said. "Are you going far?"

"No," said the girl, adding that she and her friend had boarded at Grand Junction and were getting off at Helper, three hours away in the Wasatch Range. She'd done it before, she said, adding that the trip was short, "and nobody's going to put us off the train in the desert just because of her."

I took another look at the girl, a petite green-eyed, freckle-nosed redhead with a snub nose, and understood. Nobody could refuse such adorable brazenness. A little later, when I encountered the conductor in the lounge car, I inclined my head toward the coach and said with a wink, "Woof woof." He shook his head slowly and theatrically, stared me in the eye and said lugubriously, "What dog? No animals on *my* train. They wouldn't *dare*."

Maybe the girls were just lucky. Except for guide dogs for the blind and signal dogs for the deaf, animals are expressly forbidden on Amtrak. Not in sleeper compartments, nor in pet carriers, nor even in cages in the baggage car. When I later asked a spokeswoman about the policy, suggesting that maybe a few genial conductors winked at the occasional well-behaved pup, the response was far from kindly. "What you apparently witnessed on the *California Zephyr* was an infraction of Amtrak's pet policy," she said with corporate iciness. "This is not a practice that Amtrak would like to continue." And she asked me to rat on the culprits, to tell her where I'd "apparently witnessed" the incident, as if she couldn't quite believe I had.

"While we understand the desire to take pets on board a train," she added somewhat less glacially, "we do not presently possess the ability to comfortably accommodate their travel at this time." In these litigious times, I suspect, it is simply prudent to ban four-legged beasties from the rails. Just one snap from a cranky Peke might attract hordes of personal-injury lawyers charging Amtrak with negligence in following strict federal rules regarding the transport of pets on common carriers.

On the other hand, the spokeswoman said, Amtrak was considering a change of heart—for one train, the *Auto-Train* between Lorton, Virginia, and Sanford, Florida. Most passengers on that train are headed for Florida for a two- to three-month stay with their automobiles, and there are no intermediate stops. That makes feasible a special area, perhaps part of a baggage car, for handling caged animals. When the *Auto-Train* is re-equipped with Superliners, Amtrak may once again allow pets on that train.

Meantime, train crews don't complain about the stiff regulations, even though pet-loving Americans and Europeans, accustomed to taking their animals on trains with them, might demur. Animals can be extraordinary headaches. Not only dogs and cats but rats and ferrets have gotten loose in coaches and stirred pandemonium. So have more exotic animals. Kurt Olsson, a veteran *Zephyr* chief, tells a vivid tale about one.

"One night the conductors asked me to work the door of one of the Los Angeles coaches coming into Denver eastbound," he said. "I was down in the vestibule as the train backed into the station when an attendant yelled over the PA, *'Immediate assistance to the 12 car!'* I ran down through three cars to the second Oakland coach, and the attendant was standing by a seat with a woman and a man. The attendant was unhappy, the woman angry and the man sheepish.

"The attendant said, 'The lady says this man has been kicking under her seat from behind for hours. She finally got so upset she needed something done.' I turned to the man, who had boarded four hours before. He said, 'I wasn't doin' nothin', but I know what the problem is.'

"I said, 'And what is that?'

"He said, 'I brought a pet on board. It kind of got loose. It's under the seat.'

"I said, 'What kind of pet?'

"He said, 'A boa constrictor.' "

Kurt clapped his forehead. "*A boa constrictor!* There's a kind of rubber trampoline in the seat just under the upholstery, and the snake had got in under it and wrapped himself around and around in there and had been thumping around for four hours trying to get himself comfortable.

"We're backing into Denver, and everybody is draped over the seat trying to get the rubber up and the snake out. Sure enough, he's that thick"—Kurt cupped his palms around an imaginary pipe six inches in diameter—"nine feet long, forty-five pounds. Everybody's ready to grab. Then the lights went out. I yelled, 'Don't move, everybody!' We got flashlights and started working again. That snake was *hard* to move.

"Then somebody came along with a flash camera and fired a good one. The snake shot straight up into the air and we all fell upon him. We're wrestling all over the place with this thing, and the guy is yelling, 'Don't hurt him, don't hurt him! He's a *good* snake!'

"For me no snake is a good snake," Kurt said with a sigh. Then he smiled wryly. "We have a mechanical map in the car—"

The Map 21-A? I asked. The sheet on which car defects are reported?

"Yeah. And I wrote on it, 'This car has *no mice.*' "

Meantime, plenty of riders less appealing than winsome teenage girls try to con the crews—and fail. The usual hustle is to claim that an unlikely beast is a seeing-eye dog. One elderly woman tried to board with a perfumed pink standard poodle that had just been to the hairdresser, claiming it was a guide dog she was transporting to a blind friend in another city. Instead of a working collar and leash, it sported a red silken ribbon around its neck.

Another rider, a man, tried the same scam with his huge tricolor collie. This example, however, had the breed's deplorable habit of greeting people by enthusiastically jamming its long, lever-like muzzle into their crotches. When the conductor finally returned to earth after the collie's big hello, he banished dog and owner from the platform under a hail of fulmination.

Another of Kurt Olsson's animal tales helps explain Amtrak's stern policy. Once he was helping board a party of seven Soviet citizens, and spotted a small dog hiding inside the greatcoat of a young Russian woman, the last to arrive. *Nyet,* Kurt said. No dogs. *No dogs.* Period.

What could she do? the young woman wailed. She could, Kurt replied, ship the dog by plane to her destination, and take the next day's train. No, she replied, bursting into tears. The dog was thirteen years old and couldn't possibly survive the trip.

By this time the other Russians had returned to the platform. One leaned toward the conductor, who by the time had joined the milling group, and proffered a large bill. Though the conductor seemed receptive, Kurt held up his hand and shook his head. Passengers may be adamant, but train chiefs are adamanter. Now all the Russians burst into tears.

A woman passenger who had witnessed the scene spoke up. Her son-in-law, she volunteered, had seen her to the train and would be happy to make sure the dog was safely shipped by air to its destination. The son-in-law nodded. He liked dogs and the animal would be in good hands.

The Russians dried their tears, and the girl took out of her greatcoat the little dog and placed it on the ground. "Come!" said the son-in-law, clapping his hands. The dog charged and sank its teeth into the son-in-law's ankle.

Kurt swept the Russians back aboard his train. "Good luck!" he said to the son-in-law, hopping on one foot, clutching his bleeding ankle and cursing, partly in pain and partly at the prospect of waiting out the rabies quarantine. "Now you've got the dog for thirty days!"

Bob Heath, my Oakland sleeper attendant, told a story that illustrates more than any other I've heard why Amtrak in the late seventies decided to forbid pets after the Feds posted their regulations: They are simply too much of a nuisance. In addition, the tale provides a powerful echo of the often vexatious experience of the old-time Pullman porter.

Bob was working the old *Inter-American*, predecessor of the *Texas Eagle*, at a time Amtrak still allowed dogs to accompany passengers in the sleepers. "I had a lady get on the train at St. Louis going to San Antonio," he said. "She had a big German shepherd in her roomette. I'm not keen on dogs at all. I dislike dogs. Maybe it's because when I was growing up in the Chicago ghetto, I'd walk through the neighborhood past a gang of kids with a dog, and they would all sic the dog on me and it'd chase me for miles.

"As it was my job, I had to accept the presence of this dog. He was well mannered, but those roomettes in the old sleepers from the fifties were small ones, and the dog would lie out in the middle of the aisle. Every five minutes I would have to go ask the lady to put her dog back in her room."

The woman was a tippler, and drink turned her both immodest and imperious. "Every time she rang the bell for me, I would go to her room and there she would be half dressed. I would say, 'Excuse me, ma'am. Would you kindly put some clothes on before I come here to answer this bell?' She's sitting there in her panties and a bra.

"She said to me like I was a servant, 'I want you to give me enough time to get ready when we come to a station where I can walk my dog.' She gave me a seven-dollar tip. When the time came, I went to her roomette and knocked on her door and said, 'Ma'am, in a few minutes we're going to arrive at a stop where you can walk your dog for ten minutes or so.'

"But she was full of alcohol, and she just wouldn't wake up. After we passed the stop, she came to and yelled at me, 'I *told* you to wake me up to walk my dog!' I said, 'Ma'am, I came and knocked on your door and gave you plenty of enough time!'

"She said, 'Well, I want you to walk my dog for me.' I said, 'My, that ain't my job to be walking a dog. I don't even like dogs.' She got very, very loud and started cursing at me. Then she shouted, 'I want to see a conductor!' So I went and got him. She started cussing *him* out, and the conductor says, 'Wait just a minute, ma'am. I don't have to take this from you. If you don't slow your voice down and you remark one more vulgar word to me, I'm going to put you off this train.'

"She said, 'Well, I gave this attendant seven dollars to wake me up, and he didn't.' I had already explained to the conductor that I had gone to her room to wake her up, and furthermore I did not ask for the seven dollars she gave me. So I gave it back, and she calmed down. I told her that at our next stop we'd be there for about fifteen minutes, so she could get off and walk her dog. So we came to the stop, and she got out and walked the dog without its leash.

"Soon it's time to get back on the train. I'm standing right there at the vestibule by the door with my step box. The conductor yells, 'All aboard.' She gets on. Now the dog decides *he* doesn't want to get on. The train's getting ready to move, the conductor's looking down the platform at us yelling 'All aboard, all aboard!' and she's standing there yelling, 'My dog, my dog, my dog!' And the dog ain't paying attention to her at all, just sniffing the weeds across the platform. I said, 'Well, if the dog doesn't want to get onto this train, *I* am not going to be left behind.' And I swing the step box aboard. At the very last minute the dog decides to get on the train, and we're moving before I get the door shut.

"When we got to San Antonio and she got off I all but fell on my knees and said, 'God, thank you.' "

A fortnight later, on Bob's next trip, "Guess who I ran into on the way back to Chicago? Yes, indeed. Her and this dog. But this time before she got on the train, I said, 'Now look. We had problems two weeks ago, and I ain't going to go through this same thing on the way back home. Please, if you got any problems now before you get on this train, let's stop it right here and you can catch another train, and we'll both be happy.' "

And once the conductor, tipped off by Bob, "told her if she said one nasty word he was going to put her off the train, she stayed calm. She had a regular bedroom with plenty of room for the dog, and she laid off the booze. Going home everything went okay."

Before A. Philip Randolph and the Brotherhood of Sleeping Car Porters came along just before World War II, the Pullman porters of old frequently had to endure supercilious behavior such as that woman displayed. To many if not most white patrons of the first half of the century, black porters—who were universally, if impersonally, called "George"—merely were part of the furniture with which their namesake George M. Pullman kitted out his sleeping cars. Passengers knew they'd never encounter away from the train the men who served them aboard it and therefore felt comfortable in their indiscretions.

That built-in social distance was one reason Pullman hired only blacks—many of them former slaves—as attendants. Furthermore, Pullman knew that to many whites, having a black servant was an elegant way to travel. With a straight face he said he was doing black men a favor by giving them jobs, but he paid them cheaply for their labor, for he knew that nobody else would employ them except as menials.

The Pullman car conductor always was a white man; the company explicitly excluded blacks from holding the title, although they often "ran in charge," or collected tickets when conductors were in short supply. Pullman conductors had no special skills the porters lacked, and they worried that the black men might take over their jobs. To the conductor, a black man running in charge had risen above his subordinate status; he had become "uppity." Friction between porters and conductors therefore always was high. Not so ironically, the Pullman Company often encouraged blacks running in charge, because it saved money; porters were paid half the conductors' wages. To survive, they relied on tips.

Out of their pittance, porters had to pay for their own uniforms, their food, even their shoe polish and rags. If they wanted to keep their jobs, they had to "double out" willingly—being sent on another run without rest immediately after completing a trip. Porters who worked the extra board had to put up with "P.M. time." If a run left at midnight, the extra-board porters' time began at 12:01 A.M., even if they had worked two hours, from 10:00 P.M. to midnight, preparing for the run. They were denied those two hours of pay.

If that were not demeaning enough, it was unthinkable that a white person should sleep under a blanket a black man had used. Hence Pullman passenger blankets were brown, but blankets issued to porters were always blue, and God help them if they got caught sleeping under a brown one.

Pullman's dining car waiters fared no better. Many railroads specified that the black men employed in their dining cars "must be of the same shade of color, and as near the same size as possible, in every car." And they received no respect from restaurant waiters, even black ones, for dining-car waiters performed more than one task. As well as serving food, they were also busboys, pantry cleanup men and silver polishers, all unskilled chores. The same thing occurred in the galleys, where fry cooks might also be dishwashers.

Despite these humiliations, porters and waiters took great pride in their work, knowing they did a good job in the worst possible circumstances. They recognized their chief adversaries as their employers, not their passengers. The old-timers among the porters often say they got along well with the majority of their patrons, for sleeping-car passengers tended not to be rude and boorish, but refined and mannered—especially if they came from aristocratic families. "Old money asks, new money demands," porters often said.

They also had status within the black community. They traveled all over the United States and brought back fascinating stories of strange and wonderful things—as well as hilarious tales about wayward passengers. In fact, storytelling was one of the mechanisms the porters employed to cope with the humiliations they suffered at the hands of the high and mighty.

The Duke of Windsor, one of modern history's sorriest characters, is the centerpiece of a tale passed along by Jack Santino in his absorbing book of Pullman porters' stories, *Miles of Smiles, Years of Struggle*. Far from being regal and benevolent, the duke was every bit as cruel and arrogant as the traveling salesmen in cheap suits who liked to tear five-dollar bills in half, present a porter with one of the halves and promise him the second at the end of the trip if he jumped to his work.

Every time a veteran porter named Ernest Ford Jr. rendered a service, the duke gave him a dime. "By the end of the trip, Mr. Ford had been given eight dimes, but had spent three of them. As he looked at the coins, he thought, Is this my tip? Five dimes? Then the Duke of Windsor approached him and asked for the dimes back. Mr. Ford gladly returned the five coins. The Duke took the coins and handed porter Ford five new ten-dollar bills. . . . Mr. Ford was finally given a good tip, but he was put through psychological torture to get it. He was demeaned, humiliated, and reminded of his lowly status."

Despite all these indignities, many of the old porters never lost their humanity; they *cared* about their passengers. Santino tells how one Chicago-based porter dealt with a wayward mother of two children. After putting her youngsters to bed in their berths, the mother shacked up in a neighboring drawing room with a male passenger she had met on the train. Early the next morning the porter noticed that she hadn't slept in her berth the night before— just as the woman's husband, intending to surprise her, boarded the train to make the rest of the journey with his family. The swift-thinking porter parked the husband in the smoking room, dashed into the drawing room and got the wife out of there and into her own berth before her husband could suspect a thing. "I saved that family," the porter declared.

One of the lasting historical icons of the long-suffering old-time porter is the memory of passengers stowing shoes at bedtime in a little locker in the compartment bulkhead, then opening the locker the next morning to find the shoes freshly shined. It was a service for which a tip was expected, to help porters augment their meager salaries. Oddly enough, the Pullman Company did not require the porters to shine shoes, although it assumed they would, just for the tips. The old porters, Santino writes, didn't consider shining shoes an act of Uncle Tomming. They believed that providing a service to a fellow human being did not necessarily lack in dignity. It was the scraping and bowing and the constant "yessir" and "nosir" that stuck in their craws.

In these more righteous times, ironically, Amtrak requires shoe shining of its attendants. "Shoe-shines are an advertised part of First Class service," the on-board services employee's manual says, instructing attendants to explain to each sleeper passenger how the shoe locker works. In my experience as a passenger, the white attendants follow through, and sometimes—but not often—so do the black ones. The historical image of the "shine boy" is not one most will accept anymore, and they remain at loggerheads with Amtrak management over the issue.

. . .

As for racism aboard the train today, in all my trips on the *Zephyr* I heard different answers from different crew members; the acuteness of the problem is at least partly a matter of individual perception. Perhaps because blacks are still in the majority among on-board service crews, they by and large did not seem to consider racism an everyday issue. Only one of a dozen I spoke with said he considered it a problem, and his complaint involved a long-running dispute with a particular white superior. Most everybody offered a variation on "Hey, it's there sometimes, but you can't let it bother you."

In most situations, sheer force of personality may be all that's needed to keep racism at bay. Sam Jenkins, a sleeper attendant and the president of the Chicago local of the Amtrak Service Workers Union, said he has never heard a racial slur from a passenger, though he has had to cope with his share of drunks and lunatics. There is an air of friendly authority about Sam, an erect and handsome man who says he has little trouble with passengers "because I establish control of the car from the beginning."

To maintain his authority, he said, he refuses to react to derogatory statements. "You can't take control if you lose control over yourself," he says. "If I keep my cool, all the other passengers will support me. The old-timers in the Brotherhood taught me that, and they went through a lot more than we do today."

Sam's colleague Bob Heath concurs. So far as blatantly racist passengers are concerned, Bob said, he may have encountered "one or two in the whole eighteen years" he has been working for Amtrak. "But when it happens I don't let it faze me, because this is my livelihood. I'm not going to let you take away my livelihood just because you're being stupid."

Bob said he draws strength from the collegiality of his crewmates of all races. "Pretty much we are a family," he declared. I blinked in mild astonishment—one does not often encounter such statements in American society—but he nodded insistently. "You'd be surprised at the unity we have. Look, we're in close quarters traveling together for ninety hours straight. We rely on one another.

Suppose one of us gets sick on the train in the middle of nowhere? You don't want to get off the train and go to some clinic in some little hick town. You want to wait till you get to Oakland and get to a decent hospital. One of your coworkers—black or white—will cover for you. We're close-knit."

Many of today's conductors, unlike those of old, support the service crews, Bob added. They won't tolerate displays of racism; they'll stop the train and put off passengers who use racial epithets, and in some cases will call the police to drive home the lesson.

"A couple years ago, on Number Five, I saw a case like that," Bob said. "A guy in my sleeper was making racial remarks to the waiters in the dining car. He never once said anything like that to me in the sleeper, but one of the waiters just had enough, and he came back to my car and got me and we went and talked to our conductor, Art Gilmore, a white man who works out of Denver. Conductor Gilmore is the Marshal Dillon of Amtrak. He does not take any mess.

"He said, 'Well, Bob, if he was up here in the dining car making racial slurs, and if it's not directed at you, what do you think we should do about it?'

"I said, 'Mr. Gilmore, if he's up in the diner making racial remarks at my coworkers, and I'm the same color they are, he may not be making them to me, but he might be feeling it. He may not have been vocal with me, but if he's thinking it, he's just as guilty. If he's in there saying that to them, it's just a matter of time before he says it to me. I think we should get him off the train.'

"Mr. Gilmore said, 'That's all I wanted to hear.' And when we got to Winter Park, the police was waiting. He said to the guy, 'We are not going to tolerate your kind on the train. These men work over twenty hours a day. They're trying to provide the best service they can to anyone, and they don't need this from you. You take your attitude somewhere else.' And he put him off the train.

"See, we *are* a family."

Families, however, can bicker. Sometimes, Lela Janushkowsky said, she can be the only white person on the crew. "Maybe when you're part of the majority you don't see racism, but if you're in the minority you sometimes see it." For example, she said, some black crew members may automatically support a wayward colleague against a white supervisor simply for reasons of shared race, no matter the culpability of their crewmate.

"But I don't think it's unbearable," Lela said. "I just think it's there, and every time I see it I point it out. I say, 'Do you see what you're doing?' I let them look from another view. It happens both ways, even today, just like in society. It's still here, but it's getting better."

Reggie Howard sees racism, but of an inverse kind. "I may encounter a racial remark by one of my subordinates," he said, "but I've noticed that as a black supervisor, I get more respect—I would say eighty percent more respect—from a white employee than I do from a black one. And I have talked with some white chiefs who will say the opposite, that they get more respect from a black employee than they do from whites.

"I don't know why a white supervisor would get more respect from blacks—I don't know if the blacks feel intimidated or not. I know as a black supervisor that the whites don't feel intimidated by me, but it just seems like the blacks think I'm on a pedestal and looking down on them. Some people can't take constructive criticism.

"I don't know if blacks are jealous or what, but when I first started as a chief three years ago, I really found out who my true friends were. The people I thought were my friends when I was in rank and file would call me names behind my back, or say, 'He ain't this, he ain't that, he think he's Mr. Good Stuff.' It kind of hurt me at first. I said, 'Well, when I was in the rank and file with you, everything was okay, but now I'm trying to mature as a person and move up in the company, and if you want to try to keep me down, you want me to just stay where you're at.' It used to hurt, but now I don't look at it like that. People are going to say what they want to say. So I just take it with a grain of salt, let it go in one ear and out the other. I don't have a problem with racism."

Sexual harassment may be more common than racism. Sam Jenkins's wife, Linda—who happens to be Reggie Howard's sister—is
a coach attendant. Sam never works the same train with her because, he says, "I don't like to see male passengers hit on her. I
don't know if I wouldn't lose it if I saw a man grasp my wife by the
haunch. It happens all the time, and my union complains to Amtrak, which does nothing. The women can handle it, though, and
the conductors can and do put repeated offenders off the train."

Displays of sexism can be far subtler than sexual advances. When
his wife was a sleeper attendant, Reggie said, her tips were less than
the male attendants. "I know she did a good job. However, sleeping car passengers are geared to seeing men back there, and they
will give a man more of a gratuity than they will give a woman. In
the coaches and the dining car there's not that much discrimination between male and female in tips."

Some of the discrimination, Reggie thinks, may be laid at the
door of physical strength. "If females cannot lift a certain heavy
bag, they'll ask a male counterpart or a conductor or myself to give
them a hand. Which I do. But if I want to play devil's advocate or
male chauvinist, well, these women are getting paid the same salary
as the male attendants. I know it's teamwork, that we're all a team,
but for the same salary you should be able to lift this bag, one
hundred pounds, something reasonable. That sometimes gets to
me. There should be a line drawn somewhere."

Occasionally, Reggie said, there can be an incident of sexual
harassment between employees, usually off the job during layovers,
but Amtrak is as quick to deal with them as any other enlightened
corporation. It discourages "fraternization" on the job between
employees, Reggie said, and layovers during runs are considered
being on the job.

Whenever I asked a female crew member if sexual harassment
was bothersome, she almost invariably shrugged in dismissal, reinforcing my growing impression that "hitting on" women is more
of a problem for their male colleagues who witness it than it is to
the women. Aboard the train, female attendants seem to share that

same feeling of security with female passengers seeking romance: There's nowhere for an offender to escape to, and in any case help is just a shout away.

Perhaps the social milieu that produces most female Amtrak crew members enables them to deal effortlessly with clumsy sexual approaches. The maverick feminist critic Camille Paglia believes that black and working-class white ethnic women, in whose cultures men are expected to be horny and unmannered, cope with sexual harassment far more readily than naïve and inexperienced white upper-middle-class women who make up the majority of feminists. Whatever the truth of that contention, the women who work on the trains are good at putting the jerks in their place.

I watched Lela do that once. In the dining car one evening after dinner while she worked on her accounts and I tapped away on my laptop as several crewmen on an evening break sat drinking coffee behind her, a well-dressed, distinguished-looking middle-aged man stopped at our table. "Ma'am," he said in the tones of one used to being obeyed, "I have a bottle of very fine wine in my bedroom. Would you like to come back later and share it with me?"

My jaw dropped at the blatantly public nature of the pass. Without looking up Lela said, not a trace of bite in her voice, "Sorry, sir. I've got plans."

The man slunk away.

In my snug sleeper compartment I stretched languorously. Outside, night had long fallen when the *Zephyr* glided at 7:30 P.M. through a tightly curving cut into tiny Thompson, Utah (Mile 1,390), the only flag stop on the route. Yes, Amtrak still services flag stops, tiny towns that produce too few passengers to rate the honor of a scheduled stop.

While the engineer will halt his train at the sight of an unexpected passenger who signals with an arm-wave on the platform, most often a boarding passenger will have telephoned Amtrak to make a reservation. The agent in turn will enter into the reservations computer a note that a passenger will be waiting at the flag stop. When the conductors print out their manifest from the computer, they will spot the note and radio the engineer to halt at the stop—in fact, they often specify which car they want spotted at the platform. Today nobody was in sight, and the train immediately accelerated away.

During the summers the *Zephyr* more often than not calls at this lonely little desert community of forty people, the only Amtrak stop in a desolate region known far and wide as "the nation's atomic warehouse" for its rich uranium deposits. But it's not radio-activity that attracts riders. Thompson is also the gateway to the southeastern Utah attractions of the Canyonlands and the Arches National Parks, Monument Valley and Dead Horse Point, all favorite stomping grounds of backpackers.

Past Thompson, the Rio Grande main line curves to the north-west and hugs the eroding mesas of the Roan Cliffs for several miles as it enters the broad basin between the cliffs and the mighty Wasatch Range to the west. Not half an hour out of Thompson, the *Zephyr* crossed the Green River and rolled through the town that is its namesake. By day the riverside is a pretty green oasis that snakes through the desert, nourishing the watermelons and cantaloupes that have made the town of Green River famous throughout the West.

Ever since the *Zephyr* had left the Moffat Tunnel in the early afternoon, it had been steadily losing altitude, coasting much of the way, and at Green River it bottomed out at 4,066 feet, the lowest point of the day's run. Now the train began a steady climb up a one percent grade all the way to Helper, seventy-one miles distant. The throaty roar of the engines deepened subtly as their prime movers increased revolutions for the ascent. I got to my feet and headed for the lounge car.

As I traversed the train it suddenly braked briskly to a stop. I squinted into the blackness—the moon had disappeared behind a cloud—but could see nothing. We seemed to be "in the hole," sitting on a siding waiting for an eastbound freight to approach and pass on the main line. For five minutes we parked in the darkness, with no sign of a freight.

In the lounge car I took a seat next to a young black woman in a red-and-orange catsuit apparently painted on her sleek body. Gazelle-like and extraordinarily fashionable, with close-cropped hair and large golden loop earrings, she looked like a younger version of Iman, the high-fashion model who brought long-necked African grace to the pages of *Vogue*. Ah, was the young woman herself a model? No, she was an Air Force noncom going home to San Francisco after a month's furlough. Two days hence she'd be on a C-141 heading for Turkey, her destination the U.S. Air Force base at Incirlik. I just couldn't picture this lissome vision on a scaffold in greasy coveralls, messing around the innards of jet engines. How times have changed! I felt superannuated and out of touch.

A woman in her late thirties, small, skinny and with a prognathous overbite, who had been watching me scribble in my notebook, introduced herself as a minor Amtrak personnel official traveling incognito between Denver and Salt Lake City, "partly to write a report on the crew and partly for vacation." Ah, a company snitch! I asked about her background, and she replied that she had worked for Trans World Airlines before joining Amtrak five years before. She hoped to be a train chief someday, she said, adding that she had recently applied for the job as agent of the new Amtrak station at Laramie in Wyoming on the *Pioneer* route. (She looked neither assertive enough for the former nor big enough to hump seventy-five-pound luggage, a requirement for the latter.)

I had been thinking about the on-board collegiality Bob Heath had mentioned, and asked if she had observed a "family atmosphere" within Amtrak. Mistake. She snickered into her handkerchief, her frail frame quaking. "Oh? Is there great friction between management and employees?" I pressed. She did not answer, dutiful corporate soldier that she was. But when I asked why Amtrak recently had broken up its train crews—sleeper, diner, lounge and coach attendants now all work varying schedules with different days off, losing what some see as a delicate trust and rapport that often is built up among crewmates—she forthrightly replied, "It's the recession. We're trying to make them go further, to get by with fewer employees and less overtime."

Even during the recession of the early 1990s, Amtrak had been rolling toward a bright future in the estimation of both the traveling public and the politicians responsible for the purse strings of subsidies. Amtrak's crusty old president, Graham Claytor, was even suggesting that the railroad could reach the break-even point by the year 2000.

An eighty-year-old former destroyer escort skipper, onetime Secretary of the Navy and longtime chief of the Southern Railway, Claytor had expertly massaged the politicians on Capitol Hill into benevolence toward Amtrak, partly by trimming the number of employees to the bone to show that the railroad was, in corporate parlance, "lean and mean." Aboard the *California Zephyr*, the most visible result was fewer coach attendants. Instead of overseeing one coach, each attendant was responsible for two. Although he'd said he'd rather have kept the previous level of service, Don Cushine, the *Zephyr* train manager, had said he believed the added work had not been onerous. At some station stops in the beginning, there weren't enough attendants to open all the doors, place step boxes on the platform, and help passengers detrain. One attendant had to sprint down the platform to open the next car's door before an impatient passenger did the job himself and perhaps tumbled out onto his head. Now, however, the train chief, the conductor and assistant conductors were plugging the holes. So far it had worked out, Don said, but he hoped further cutbacks wouldn't be necessary. (As it turned out, he was too optimistic. During the ensuing months, winter and summer storms, wrecks, and the continuing depredations of the long recession stretched Amtrak's limited resources to the utmost.)

As I made departing pleasantries to the Amtrak personnel official, a heavy hand descended upon my shoulder. It belonged to Matt Skonieczny, the tall, sleepy-eyed train-hater, Las Vegas-bound friend of the gas-station incidentals salesman I had encountered the previous afternoon. "It gets *worse*," he said with a growl. "No, it gets better," said Tom Hankins behind him, laughing.

Matt's eyes, I noticed, looked sleepier and red-rimmed. "Last night I got up at three in the morning to pee, and hit the shower button instead of the flush button," he said. "I was just *soaked*! And all night I had to sleep in hell. There's not enough room even in those expensive deluxe bedrooms. And above my head is this cold air vent that just blew in my face. So I got up and remade my bed so that my head was on the other side—and there's a cold air vent *there*, too." (There isn't; I suspect Matt, perhaps fuddled by sleepiness, might just have remade his bed as it originally was.)

Tom chuckled and chuckled as his friend related his tale of woe. If he had been wearing a tie, he'd have wiggled it just like Oliver Hardy, to whom he bore more than a passing resemblance.

"My friends who left home this morning are already in Vegas at the gambling tables and winning money," Matt continued, "and I'm not going to get there till nine o'clock tomorrow morning!" Then he choked out a final confession. That five hundred dollars Tom had paid Matt's wife to let him go on the trip hadn't come out of the goodness of Tom's heart. Tom had agreed to it only after his friend promised to repay him fifty dollars out of every paycheck.

Just then the train began moving . . . *backward*. Everyone in the lounge car peered around in confusion, but the only Amtrak employee there was the lead service attendant downstairs, and he didn't have a clue. For perhaps five minutes the *Zephyr* backed up, then stopped. Suddenly the lights went out for thirty seconds, then flashed back on. The train moved forward for a couple of minutes, then stopped again—and backed up once more. What the Sam Hill? As the train backed up, a dark shadow passed us on the right. Two red lights marked its end. The train stopped once more, for about five minutes, then resumed its progress, this time forward. Again the cat-eyed red lamps approached, and this time I saw through the gloom the outlines of an old-fashioned, open-platform observation car. Was it the private car we had picked up at Denver?

It was, said the conductor a few minutes later when he arrived in the lounge car, and its problem was one of the oldest in railroading: It had a hotbox. Although Amtrak requires the wheels of all private cars it hauls to be equipped with slippery modern roller bearings instead of old-fashioned friction bearings, hotboxes do occur, although less frequently. If the oil in the bearings should run dry, the lack of lubrication will cause axle and bearings to overheat. Sometimes they can turn cherry red and even burst into flames before the heat fractures the axle, causing the wheel to shear off and dumping the car on the ground. Fortunately a trackside hotbox detector had sensed the elevated temperature in the private car's wheel as the *Zephyr* rolled by and warned the engineers of the problem before it could grow worse.

The *Zephyr* had stopped on the main line, then backed onto a parallel siding where it uncoupled and left behind the private car. The *Zephyr* then returned to the main line and backed down it until the train's coach-dorm car lay across from the private car on the siding. There the private car's dozen passengers and their attendants boarded the coach-dorm. That explained all the to-ing and fro-ing we had done.

What's more, the conductor said, shaking his head, back in Denver it had taken the crew three tries before the private car's brakes could be set open, and that was what had caused the long delay in departure. "These cars are a nightmare," he said. The car would be left behind on the lonely siding until a switch engine could come down from a yard, fix the bearing and hook the car to a freight for the trip back to Denver. Amtrak was responsible for the car, and the conductor hoped it wouldn't be vandalized over the several days it'd have to sit unattended.

Not long after that, a man in civilian attire sat down and introduced himself. He was Gregg Konstanzer, trainmaster of Amtrak's Rocky Mountain division. At first he looked far too young for his responsibilities, bossing eighty-five conductors and engineers from Salt Lake City to Grand Junction in the east and Sparks, Nevada, in the west. Close up, however, I could see deep crow's-feet at his eyes and the beginning of salt-and-pepper gray in his hair.

After we chatted a bit about the engineer's job, I asked Konstanzer his opinion of private cars. "They bring in a lot of money for Amtrak, and I'm going to leave it at that," he said with a tight smile.

A few minutes later, after he had left, the conductor, who had overheard our conversation, volunteered what Konstanzer presumably wouldn't, or couldn't, say. Passenger cars owned by private citizens, said the conductor, give fits to Amtrak operating personnel. They are antiquated and hard to keep in shape. Although their running gear and electric power have been upgraded to Amtrak standards and are inspected every year, Amtrak doesn't do the maintenance, so cannot be certain that the cars are indeed well maintained. Still, he said, they represent considerable extra revenue for Amtrak, and in any case the owners of the cars—tour operators and wealthy private citizens—are often well connected politically. Amtrak, ever dependent on Congress for its subsidies, must cultivate these influential men.

Couldn't he give his bosses a piece of his mind about this particular private car, perhaps in a stiff letter? "No way," he said. "Amtrak makes a lot of money off these cars, and if I came down too hard on them I'd end up in hot water because their congressmen would get on Amtrak's case, and it'd all come down on my head."

Meantime, that private car had put him fifteen minutes further behind schedule and handed him some additional passengers to nursemaid. They were irked because they'd expected to be treated like royalty all the way to Salt Lake City, and now there were no sleeper compartments for them. Instead, they had to sit up till well past midnight in the tatty old coach-dorm, and they took out their frustrations on the conductor.

Private cars are relics of the gilded age of privilege, in which every American millionaire owned a "business car" of unimaginable splendor, coupled on the rear of whatever fast passenger train was convenient. Besides the usual open observation platforms and carved mahogany fretwork, some cars featured marble bathtubs, Venetian glass and gold dinner services. So plush were they that the wife of one American plutocrat boasted that the only economical feature of her husband's private car was the gold water taps. "It saves polishing, you know," she said.

The rolling temples of luxury that belonged to railroad presidents were symbols of power as well as wealth. The cutthroat financier and railroader Jay Gould traveled in a private *train* of four cars, which included such amenities as a personal physician, a personal chef and a personal cow for the freshest possible milk. Such cars announced that the men who occupied them were part of the American aristocracy, many levels above the blue-collar employees who sometimes resentfully watched them roll by. In this more egalitarian age owner's cars still can spark resentment. In 1992 Graham Claytor's Amtrak business car was stoned in Boston by maintenance workers angered by its luxury while they suffered layoffs and tough labor negotiations.

To be fair to Amtrak and to the parties who own private cars, not all operating crews dislike them. Some engineers, especially on the East Coast, have told me they've never had a problem with a private car on the rear of their trains. Moreover, an owner of a West Coast fleet of private cars leased to tourist groups contended that many of the delays are Amtrak's own fault: "Most typically, Amtrak or the terminal company doing the switching fails to provide the required switcher or crew in a timely manner." It may simply have been that with private cars tonight's *Zephyr* crew had had a long run of bad luck, like Joe Btfsplk, the "Li'l Abner" comic-strip character constantly trailed by a rain cloud of misfortune.

As the *Zephyr* gathered speed again, lounge-car riders returned to their seats and rooms to prepare for the night. I followed and, in my sleeper room, picked up the Rumpole novel unread since the previous night. Fitfully I dipped into it, every few minutes switching off the light and peering out into the darkness, trying to identify the rocky shapes appearing and disappearing in the fading moonlight. It's a pity for winter and early-spring passengers that the westbound *Zephyr* travels the 174 miles from Thompson to Provo in darkness, for the route offers some of the most spectacular sights to be found in mountain railroading. The Rio Grande main line cuts northward across a broad plateau that grows narrower and narrower until the train reaches the beginning of a box canyon separating the Wasatch Range from the Book Cliffs at Helper (Mile 1,489) and nearby Price.

Helper sits atop coal reserves so rich they could supply the

United States for three hundred years, but its major claim to railroad fame is in its steam-era namesake as a site for "helper" locomotives that shoved long westbound freights over the Wasatch Range. The commercial area, much of it boarded up, looks the picture of an old Western town, and early-morning risers in the eastbound *Zephyr*'s lounge car often unlimber their cameras to capture a weather-beaten hand-painted Coca-Cola sign on the north side of an apartment building.

Helper lies at 5,830 feet at the beginning of a strenuous 2.4 percent uphill grade. Just outside town the *Zephyr* passed a curious sight on a ridge high above the tracks on the east side: two enormous rocks shaped like children's building blocks, one seemingly teetering atop the other in the breeze. A bare flagpole juts up from the topmost block. The wind at Balanced Rock is so intense, legend has it, that three attempts to plant the American flag there failed miserably, including a thick steel imitation banner that snapped off its standard after two days.

Five minutes later the train threaded the shadowy battlements of Castle Gate, so named for the castellated rock formations guarding the entrance to Price River Canyon. A huge iron portcullis from the land of the giants wouldn't look out of place above the tracks. The little settlement here used to be one of Utah's largest coal mining camps, and it was the site of one of the Old West's notable robberies.

Butch Cassidy (born George LeRoy Parker of Mormon parents) was not as stupid and thuggish as most badmen of the West. He had certain smarts. He knew that a gang couldn't just ride into a town and knock off the bank. It had to scout the place, determining the strength of the sheriff's force or local vigilantes, and find out how much money was to be had.

When Cassidy arrived at Castle Gate with two of his Hole-in-the-Wall Gang confrères one day in April 1897, he already knew the town, having worked as a miner there. Dressed as an itinerant cowpuncher, he spent several days hanging around the railroad station, apparently getting his horse used to the roar of the locomotives, and applying to local ranchers for a job to camouflage his intentions.

On April 21, just as the Rio Grande train from Salt Lake City pulled in, Cassidy and a sidekick rode in, dismounted, left their horses with reins dangling, and walked to a mining-company office near the depot, standing casually by the stairs. After the mail and express were offloaded and rolled into the baggage room, a mining paymaster and two aides emerged with more than $8,000 ($136,000 in today's dollars) in gold and silver.

As they brushed past the two loafers below the office, Cassidy and his confederate suddenly pulled six-shooters and relieved them of the payroll. The other robber cut the telegraph wire so that word of the robbery could not immediately be flashed to neighboring lawmen, and in a instant the trio was back aboard its horses, leaving town in a cloud of dust.

Posses eventually were called out, but the gang had made good its escape into the inhospitable country. Instead of spending the loot conspicuously, Cassidy and one of his henchmen rode south to Lay, New Mexico. There they took jobs as cowboys and blended into the countryside while the posses rode madly in all directions searching for high-living outlaws. Once again Butch had outsmarted the law.

For ten circuitous miles past Castle Gate the *Zephyr* clawed its way upward through the narrow canyon, its exhaust booming off the rock walls. Soon the train emerged onto a long plateau that sloped gently upward, the grade relaxing to an easy one percent for twenty miles until the track reached 7,440-foot-high Soldier Summit.

The pass is named, the Amtrak route guide says, for the "Union soldiers in Johnson's [sic] Army buried there in 1860." How could they be Yankees if the first shot in the Civil War wasn't fired at Fort Sumter until 1861?

Actually, Utah saw no Civil War clashes between rebels and bluecoats; the Union Army there fought only the Indians. Before 1860 U.S. soldiers in the region were led by Colonel Albert Sidney Johnston, later to win immortality as a Confederate general. In

1858 "Johnston's Army," sent by President Buchanan to put down a Mormon rebellion, arrived in Utah spoiling for a fight. Cooler heads prevailed, a truce was struck and the soldiers settled at Camp Floyd south of Salt Lake City in an impromptu occupation.

Although historians don't know for sure, their best guess is that the summit is named for members of a detachment from Camp Floyd who died there, either from illness or perhaps in a blizzard, in 1860 or 1861.

Soon my ears began to pop. The *Zephyr* had crested Soldier Summit and had plunged into a long, winding coast down a negative 2 percent grade. Far ahead, the engineers cut in their locomotives' dynamic brakes to keep the train from running away down the three tight horseshoe curves just below the summit. In dynamic braking, the engineer reverses the electric current to the traction motors on the locomotive's axles, turning them into drag brakes. Just think of putting your car in second gear to slow it as you drive down a steep hill, and you'll get the idea.

The forward motion downslope causes the locomotives' traction motors to become dynamos, generating electricity that in turn is conducted to steel grids on the roofs of the locomotives to be dissipated as heat. Running downhill, in effect, converts the locomotives into gigantic space heaters. If you stand at the bottom of a long hill and watch a train whining downhill under dynamic brakes, you can spot above the engines tall columns of air shimmying violently from the radiated heat.

At what used to be called Thistle, the train threaded a three-thousand-foot tunnel, built after an enormous mud slide in April, 1983, swept the entire town into Spanish Fork Canyon and blocked the Rio Grande main line for three months until a six-mile-long bypass, including the tunnel, could be built. By day the wreckage of roofs and houses is still visible in the dried mud near the tracks.

The *Zephyr* picked up speed, streaking north across the Salt Lake Valley at sixty miles per hour until, at 11:40 P.M., it rolled into Provo (Mile 1,564), three-fifths of a mile in altitude below Soldier Summit. Tonight only about a dozen passengers detrained at the station, normally a busy one at vacation time, thanks to students at

Brigham Young University. Quickly we were away, skirting the freshwater Utah Lake, almost invisible in the darkness, and breezing close by the tailings of the Kennecott Copper open-pit mine a few miles away. Soon the train passed through the brightly lighted industrial outskirts of Salt Lake City, and at 12:30 A.M. the *Zephyr* pulled up at the Rio Grande depot (Mile 1,609). It was just twenty-nine minutes behind time, thanks to the generous forty-one-minute slop built into the schedule between Provo and Salt Lake City.

The servicing stop took half an hour while locomotives and cars gulped deep drafts of fuel and water. (In the summers, they also hold their cheeks up to be scrubbed by a mobile window washer.) As I left my sleeper and wandered toward the station, a sudden thunder of diesel horns a few steps away nearly launched me into orbit. A locomotive, coach-dorm and diner on the track between the *Zephyr* and the station began backing down to couple on to the three Los Angeles cars, unhooked from our train by a switch engine. Though I couldn't hear the horns, their powerful vibrations had startled me nearly out of my skin.

I once spent a Sunday in Salt Lake City, to break a westward *Zephyr* trip, and I have to say that it is not my kind of town—no offense meant to Utahns. My beef is not with Mormons, whom I have always found memorably polite and pleasant even though a couple of brightly scrubbed young missionaries to the deaf—themselves deaf—turned up uninvited on my doorstep one day not very long ago. They ignored the "NO SOLICITING" sign on my front door, rang the doorbell and greeted me with an incomprehensible hail of sign language.

Now I do not mind being disturbed by Girl Scouts bearing cookies and other small children who thankfully don't know what "soliciting" is, but my home is also my workplace, and uninvited adult callers who disturb my concentration make me testy. I'm afraid I was unnecessarily rude to the two well-meaning young Mormons, who at the very worst were guilty only of naïveté about urban privacy. "Can't you read?" I demanded. "If the Jehovah's Witnesses respect that sign, why can't the Latter-day Saints? I am *not* interested!"

I doubt that they could read my lips, but they got the message when I slammed the door. They left, visibly crestfallen, and I quailed in shame at my irascibility. I could have invited them in for lemonade and cookies, gently deflected their pitch and sent them away smiling. After all, they were deaf, too, and for a few gentle moments with pencil and paper we could have shared our humanity. I felt so guilty that it was hours before I could concentrate again on my work.

During my brief Salt Lake City visit, however, I behaved much more amiably with the young missionary-guide who welcomed me at the entry to the grounds of the Mormon Temple. "Just having a quick look," I said, "but thanks." She smiled winningly, asked where I was from, said, "Have a good time," and moved on to the next potential convert. So charmed was I that I didn't mind not being able to see the interior of the Salt Lake Temple; visitors must be Latter-day Saints with "recommends" from their bishops. Instead, a vicarious tour is provided for gentiles in two large visitor centers. The enormous scenes from the Book of Mormon painted on their walls didn't strike me as being theologically absurd; they seemed no more preposterous than the doctrines of any other religion founded on divine revelation.

Two things discombobulated me about Salt Lake City. The first is its streets. The heavily trafficked boulevards are so wide that I worried about getting to the other side before nightfall, let alone before the Walk signs changed. In the middle of the broad avenues I felt like a deer jacklighted in a football stadium full of fans with rifles. I much prefer the narrow canyons of Chicago, where a nimble pedestrian has a fighting chance against traffic.

Then there are the weird Utah liquor laws. In the bar of the Holiday Inn, I was told that before I could be served a Heineken on a Sunday, I would have to join their private club, and dues were a dollar. I looked around. Not a single black, Hispanic or Asian face was visible in the busy lounge. I drew the wrong conclusion. "Thanks but no thanks," I snarled, and stalked off to the restaurant for supper.

"Can you bring me a beer?" I growled. The waitress nodded. "Doesn't it cost a dollar to join, like that 'private club' over there?" I asked. She shook her head and smiled. Ten times an evening she explains the facts of Utah liquor life to ignorant outlanders. Alcohol by the drink cannot be sold to the public on the sabbath except in "private clubs," unless it is served with food in restaurants. A "private club," however, is easy for anybody to join. This is how the Mormons accommodate both their abstemious God and thirsty tourists, not to mention gentile Utahns. Piety often goes hand in hand with good business hypocrisy, but I prefer the latter well camouflaged, not right out in the open like that.

Upon leaving I spotted a sign by the cash register. It warned that "alcohol purchased on these premises" might cause disease and endanger pregnant women. "What's so particular about the booze for sale here?" I asked the cashier, pointing to the sign.

"You have to understand," he said. "This is *Utah.*"

Of course there was not an alcoholic drink of any sort to be had out in the station parking lot, where Reggie (Danish roll and newly updated passenger manifest in hand), Lela and other crew clustered for a midnight snack around a catering truck they fondly call the "Roach Coach." The chocolate chip cookies, however, looked good, so I bought two.

Back aboard the *Zephyr* I turned into my compartment, undressed and fell into bed, so tired I skipped the mints Bob Heath had arranged on my pillow earlier in the evening. It had been a long day, and I didn't stir when, shortly after 1:00 A.M., the *Zephyr*—minus the *Desert Wind,* which would leave for Las Vegas and Los Angeles a few minutes later—slowly rolled out of Salt Lake City just thirty minutes late.

TEN

To lie awake in a darkened sleeper berth, window shades open as the train races across the Utah desert under a full moon, is an experience in eerie beauty. Not that most people aboard the *California Zephyr* would notice, except for insomniacs. The train crosses the godforsaken wastes of Utah in the small hours when just about everyone is asleep. So far as the Amtrak route guide is concerned, the barren gray salt desert is not worth acknowledging, except to mention in passing that the train follows the southern shore of the Great Salt Lake for fifteen miles and later traverses the Bonneville Salt Flats, where the world's automobile speed records are set. Yet the passing land is fascinating for both its geology and its history.

Just west of Salt Lake City the train plunged into the Great Basin, a large misshapen bowl full of valleys and ridges that spreads over Utah and Nevada. The water in the Basin finds no escape to the sea, because rainfall is too sparse to fill it to overflowing. It was not always thus. For a 250,000-year span that ended only about ten thousand years ago, much of the Great Basin was covered by Lake

Bonneville, a freshwater sea 145 miles wide by 346 miles long, and more than 1,000 feet deep. The Great Salt Lake is one of the remnants of this ancient sea.

Sleeping fitfully, I awakened frequently to slip on my glasses for a glimpse at the passing basin-and-range country of the Great Basin, where parade grounds of flat alkali sands—the basins—play host to silvery regiments of mountains—the ranges. Where early adventurers dared death from thirst and sunstroke, I'm snug in a climate-controlled compartment. By day, mirages that once tortured thirst-crazed minds are now no more than interesting optical illusions: small mountains that look like floating islands in broad seas.

Fifty miles west of Salt Lake City the train flashed through desolate Skull Valley. Trucks on neighboring Interstate 80 kicked up dust devils, dim in the moonlight. Were they ghosts belonging to the Indian skeletons the pioneers found here a century and a half ago? This is extraordinarily arid country, the sparse rain evaporating almost immediately upon touching the low mountains. So parched is the country, it is hard to believe anyone ever lived here, but as late as 1843 travelers found small bands of Gosiute Indians scratching a crabbed existence out of the rocks and sand. "They wear no clothing of any description," wrote Thomas J. Farnham, an early settler. They "build no shelter. They eat roots, lizards, and snails. . . . And when the lizards and snails and wild roots are buried in the snows in winter, they . . . dig holes and sleep and fast till the weather permits them to go abroad again for food. . . . These poor creatures are hunted in the spring of the year, when weak and helpless . . . and when taken, are fattened, carried to Santa Fe and sold as slaves."

A little more than thirty miles farther west, the *Zephyr* shimmered past a memorial to a group whose fate was even sorrier than that of the Gosiutes. The Donner-Reed Trail Monument commemorates the crossing of a wealthy party of California-bound emigrants for whom the frontier dream turned into a nightmare. Led by George and Tamsen Donner, they set off for their grail from Springfield, Illinois, in April 1846, with James Frazier Reed and his clan, picking up several other families on the way. Altogether the party numbered eighty-seven souls.

During the summer they lost valuable days breaking a trail across the Wasatch Mountains. Their guide, a reckless adventurer named Lansford W. Hastings, had never been across the Great Salt Lake Desert, and the route he thought he had found was twice as long as the known way. The desert "is the most desolate country on the whole globe, there being not one spear of vegetation, and of course no kind of animal can subsist," wrote James Clyman, trapper and guide, that same year of 1846. Added Horace Greeley thirteen years later: "If Uncle Sam should ever sell that tract for one cent per acre, he will swindle the purchaser outrageously."

The Donner Party's desert crossing took five waterless days and nights, during which they lost many of their wagons and cattle. (Their tracks are still visible in the salt crust from the air.) The unexpected delays caused the now impoverished party to reach the Sierra Nevada too late to cross before winter. There they were trapped by early snows. To survive, they ate their remaining cattle, then their dogs, and finally each other. Only forty-six of the original eighty-seven still lived in the spring of 1847.

Though the *Zephyr* had been running over Union Pacific tracks ever since it left Salt Lake City, this is not the route of the first transcontinental railroad. That one ran much farther north. The UP had constructed its 1,085.5-mile line from Omaha westward to Ogden, thirty-nine miles north of Salt Lake City, thence northward around the Great Salt Lake, meeting the 690-mile-long Central Pacific at Promontory on May 10, 1869, ending one of the most colorful, well-documented and expensive chapters of American history—the railroad cost $165 million to build, the equivalent of $1.5 *billion* today.

The route over which the *Zephyr* skirts the southern end of the Great Salt Lake and traverses Utah and Nevada to California is more direct, and it follows the old Western Pacific Railway line, built eastward in 1907 (and swallowed up by the Union Pacific in 1982), to Winnemucca in Nevada. At Winnemucca the train crosses over to the historic old Central Pacific line from Sacramento—which long ago became the modern Southern Pacific.

At Salt Lake City I had set my watch back an hour before turning in and fell asleep well before the Utah-Nevada state line at Wendover, where Mountain Time becomes Pacific Time. I did not stir as the train clattered over the siding turnouts at Elko (Mile 1,871) at 3:45 A.M., and slept deeply until first light peeked over the eastern horizon. Yes, of course, it was 5:00 A.M.

I sat up in my bunk, peering out the window, chin on forearm. Dawn in the Nevada desert is so heartbreakingly lonely that even an auto graveyard is a welcome sight in the vastness. From time to time an occasional settlement of mobile homes and tar-paper shacks clustered around a gas station, the whole hardly worth a name. No animals, not even a scrawny cow, were to be seen. In the distance snow dusted high mountain ranges. I felt small, insignificant and far from God.

The *Zephyr* tootled along at a sedate sixty miles per hour on straight track that apparently had not been designed for higher passenger-train speeds. A few lonely cars and trucks swept by on neighboring Interstate 80. For about twenty miles an eighteen-wheeler paced us, as if glad for a companion across the empty desert. By and by the truck pulled ahead, apparently bored with escort duty.

During the night, just west of Elko, we had picked up the eccentric Humboldt River, Nevada's largest stream, a waterway without a truly discernible beginning and end. From rivulets in the mountains of Elko County it flows westward for three hundred miles, then, trapped by the Great Basin, simply disappears into the wide and shallow Humboldt Sink. During summer water evaporates from the sink, leaving salty mud flats and dry lakes.

Suddenly we plunged into a low-lying bank of fog—so thick I could barely make out the trackside signal boxes twenty-five feet away—and in another instant we were out of it. For mile upon mile we threaded patch after patch of fog, like an airplane stolidly flying through clouds, deviating not an inch from its course, as if it were on—rails. I sighed, then smiled. This was a special day, I remembered, not one for dour early-morning woolgathering. As the *Zephyr* slowed for its scheduled 5:45 A.M. call at Winnemucca (Mile 2,005), I arose in an expectant mood, and not because Butch Cassidy knocked off the local First National Bank here in 1900, nor because the town is named for the last great Paiute chief, nor because we were now running just fifteen minutes behind schedule. Because—well, to say why would be to get ahead of the story.

Entering the lounge car, lively even at this early hour before the diner opened for breakfast, I looked around to see what the night's passenger rollover at Salt Lake City had brought. Many of the new faces belonged to rural white Westerners in scruffy boots and stained jeans. Among them a surprisingly large number of mothers, some still in their teens, towed ill-behaved toddlers. Almost as soon as I sat down there came a loud wail, followed by a sharp thwack and, quite out of sequence, "I'm fixin' to spank your butt!"

"Can't you control your child, please?" growled a tall, tanned young man trying to read a paperback at the next table. Multiple earrings framed his dark ponytail, hanging low over a pink "QUEER NATION" T-shirt.

"Ain't no way to control a baby!" shouted the young mother.

"*You* are louder than the kid!" he replied. "Perhaps you could control *yourself!*" He stood up and stalked back to his coach.

Under his mother's glare the offending toddler snuffled and fell silent. Nearby another young mother sat quietly, nursing her baby so discreetly behind a voluminous blouse that only a few passersby noticed, and those who did softened visibly. A few minutes passed before the quiet was broken by a yuppie couple in brand-new L.L. Bean togs, ascending noisily from the lower level with a double handful of Bloody Marys.

Across the aisle they sat, boasting to a trapped middle-aged pair in high, brittle voices about how they had partied their way across Europe the previous summer. At first bright and harmless, they grew increasingly repellent as alcohol fueled their self-regard. Like so many young Americans to whom drinking is a participatory sport, they considered their inane conversation witty, their habits worth emulating.

"We're not going to breakfast," announced the young woman grandly. "We bring our own *healthy* food." Out of her Lands' End carryall she pulled a large plastic bag of hiker's "gorp"—mixed nuts, raisins, dried apricots, grain and M&Ms. Alcohol, I thought, also must be one of their major food groups.

Close by, a young man, left arm in a cast, was telling his three companions—another young man and two young women—that upon graduation from Macalester College the summer before, his parents had given him a choice between a year's medical insurance and a long vacation before graduate school. He'd promptly racked himself up in a motorcycle accident, had to have a couple of rounds of surgery and had rolled up thousands of dollars in medical bills. "I don't know how I'm going to pay them," he said, "but I'm not giving up my vacation."

Macalester, he added in a bored voice, was "more fun when they had drugs," but was "not much fun now that they've cracked down."

Moments later one of the young women in the group—whose members apparently had just met on the train—identified herself. She was, she said, an Israeli soldier recently graduated from secondary school and vacationing after basic training. I was surprised. She was no robust, tanned sabra of *National Geographic* color spreads, but red-haired and wan, like an undernourished waif from Belfast. Her voice, however, carried a quiet steeliness that hushed her acquaintances.

In Chicago the previous week, she said, she'd encountered a street demonstration in front of the Israeli consulate exhorting her countrymen to give up the West Bank. "I was resentful because they didn't know zip about the situation," she said of the demonstrators. She spoke calmly, in excellent American idiom, with only a trace of the Middle East in her accent. "They had no inkling of the whole history of the West Bank."

There was a brief hush, then the injured young man said as if chastened by the Israeli's solemnity, "Well, there wasn't much diversity at Macalester—it's just white middle class. *That* was really why I didn't like it very much."

Without acknowledging the non sequitur the Israeli continued quietly, launching into a long, detailed and engrossingly lucid outline of life for both Arabs and Jews in the occupied territories. Perhaps a Palestinian might have debated her partisan point of view, but she summarized it expertly. Between the Israeli and the now respectful Americans clustered about her, the emotional and intellectual chasm seemed deep and wide. In the Middle East, young people grow up early. In America, some never do.

Just as Reggie began rolling a Disney video movie at one end of the car to occupy the rumbustious youngsters, Lela sang, "First call for breakfast!"—cheery as always. It was 6:30 A.M., and only a few scattered patrons responded. I followed them into the dining car. Through the rear window door—the diner was now the last car in the train—the low red sun flooded the tables with warm light. My awakening expectancy had taken on a tinge of mellowness, even though I immediately noticed that instead of stainless steel flatware, "four-in-ones"—plastic knife, fork, spoon and napkin wrapped in cellophane—sat on the tables.

Lela followed my disapproving glance. "There's no water in the diner," she said. "We can't wash the silverware. Back in Salt Lake, somebody forgot to close a valve after filling the water tanks, and all the water was dumped overnight. See why I always backorder four-in-ones?"

She pointed at a waiter shouldering his way into the diner from the lounge car with large plastic containers of water, a one-man bucket brigade. "We've been using four-in-ones a lot lately, anyway," she added. For the last few weeks the third cook had not worked the Salt Lake City–to–Oakland leg aboard the *Zephyr*, but had been getting off at Provo during the night and swinging back on the eastbound train the next morning. With only half the passenger load leaving Chicago, the second cook assumes the third cook's dishwashing responsibilities. It's one of myriad little ways Amtrak has saved money during the recession.

"That's just a temporary measure, though," Lela said. "When we finally get real china on the *Zephyr*, we'll need that third cook all the way to wash all those dishes."

My table companions at this breakfast were unmemorable, primarily because none of them said much beyond "good morning." We were all too fascinated with the conversation from a singular fellow at the table across the aisle, who seemed to be a convict just sprung from prison. He was a thirtyish Hispanic in bib overalls and a sleeveless undershirt, his bare shoulders and upper arms covered with crude jailhouse tattoos.

"José! My man!" A young black man sat down across from José, exchanging an elaborate soul handshake that ended with a snap and flourish. "Partner!" José replied. He reached into his bib pocket and peeled off a fifty-dollar bill, slipping it to Partner. Then José tucked into his breakfast prison fashion, grasping the back of his plate with his left hand as he shoveled in bacon and eggs like a rottweiler wolfing Ken-L Ration. With a manic cast in his eye he glanced around repeatedly, as if checking for guards.

It seemed a reasonable surmise. A number of state prisons lie near the route of the *Zephyr*, and from time to time a felon who has completed his sentence arrives at a station in a prison bus and boards the train under the watchful gaze of guards making sure the new ex-con gets out of town.

Partner began telling José about his experiences with the law. "The po-leece hassle me just 'cause I'm black," he began. He, however, couldn't go on, because José cut in immediately with the story of *his* life. Seemingly every other word out of José's mouth was "shit" or a variation thereof. He used "shit" as an all-purpose noun, verb, adverb, participle and exclamation. Here is a lightly bowdlerized version of his conversation:

"Shit, my dad left my mom when I was two and all that shit. My brothers were in the Navy, so, shit, I lived in a house with all women—my mother and sister. Ma used to knock the shit out of me for no reason. My brothers came back from the Navy and set up an import business in the front of the house but sold other shit in the back. I had been doing shit on the streets but soon I was helping my homeboys. I was smoking shit and drinking all sorts of shit and got sent up at fifteen for armed robbery and did two years. Shit, if I'd been older I'd still be in the shit up there."

I was wondering what sort of shit had most recently landed José in prison when he said, "Shit, people are happier to see ya when you go back up than when you come out. I still like to shoot things . . . but, shit, not *people*." He offered that last in what apparently was meant to be a reassuring tone.

A conductor who had been listening to the conversation got up from the crew table, walked over to José, leaned close to his ear and said quietly, "There's a good movie in the lounge car. Want to eat up and go there?"

"Shit, no," said José.

At this point a young black female attendant stepped over and said quietly but firmly, "I been telling you to watch your mouth. If you don't stop I'll tape it shut."

Without missing a beat José said in a placating tone, "One of my teachers in school said 'shit' must be my middle name, 'cause I say it so much. Hey, I won't eat in the dining car for lunch."

"Oh, it's all right," the attendant said, softening slightly. "We'll just put you in a special place."

A tall coach attendant ambled by, and José said, "You look like Tommy 'The Hitman' Hearns!"

"Tommy 'The Hitman' Hearns?" replied the attendant without surprise. "Yeah, sure."

For the rest of breakfast the crew kept a weather eye on José, treating him gingerly, but not as if he were an unfamiliar sort. What "special place" the waiter had in mind for José I never discovered, because it was nearly 7:00 A.M., and I had to get back to my compartment to pack before the appointment with destiny I had eagerly anticipated since awakening. I was almost hyperventilating.

You would be, too, if for the last 340 miles of the trip to Oakland—over the Sierra, yet!—you were going to achieve a boyhood dream and *ride up front in the cab of the locomotive*. No shit, José!

No platform greeted me at Lovelock (Mile 2,078) at the foot of the Humboldt Range, the last crew change point before Oakland. As I swung carefully down to the roadbed, one hand gripping the slippery grab iron and the other my two bags, I saw a familiar face up by the lead locomotive.

The evening before, engineer Ray Craig had brought Number 6, the eastbound *Zephyr*, up from Oakland, overnighting with his crewmates at Sturgeon's Motel a few hundred yards down the dusty street. On an earlier trip a few months before, my wife, Debby, and I had spoken with Ray in the dining room of Sturgeon's, a gaudy, low-roofed forty-dollars-a-night restaurant-motel-casino complex. Outside, a staggering stench rose from a huge feedlot next door. Inside, bracketing keno and faro tables, lay rows and rows of one-armed bandits, a few of them swallowing nickels, most quarters, and some silver dollars. The patrons were ranchers and interstate truckers, seemingly all men; as we walked in, a hundred pairs of male eyes hungrily fastened on Debby, an attractive woman but one close to age fifty. This is Marlboro country, where men are men and women are scarce.

By way of beginning our conversation I asked if Amtrak picks up the crew's meals on an overnight layover. Well, said Ray with a sigh, Amtrak pays $4.15 per diem for meals if the layover is less than twelve hours, as his is; if it's more than twelve hours, it will pay $8.30. Four dollars and fifteen cents is barely enough for a ham sandwich and a cup of coffee, and after a shift that long—ten and a half hours, sometimes eleven, sitting four feet in front of a bellowing 3,000-horsepower diesel prime mover—both Ray and Chris Younger, his assistant engineer, ordered steaks the size of hubcaps. Each cost only twelve dollars, half the price it would bring in a Chicago cholesterol emporium. "Railroaders," Chris offered, "always know the best places to eat for the least money in any town."

Chris, in his early thirties, is a large and hearty fellow with a belly to match. Ray is a slim six-footer in his mid-fifties, with thick salt-and-pepper hair and a warm, easy smile that brings back memories of Gary Cooper. (Debby later opined, "He's s-o-o-o hand-some!") As I spoke, Ray strained toward me, and often asked Debby to repeat what I had said. He suffers from the old railroad engineer's malaise, diminished hearing.

"It's been a gradual loss over the last thirty years," he said. "It's caused by blowing the whistle and going through tunnels and stepping back into the engine room, and every once in a while a warning torpedo will explode under the wheels. And we've got a radio right next to our head, blasting in our ears constantly."

As the locomotives go through rebuilding, Amtrak adds a sec-ond, outside door to the engine compartment, like a storm door on a house. That helps insulate the cab from the yowling prime mover, but, Ray says, most of the engines are not air-conditioned; in the desert heat "you have the window open, so the whistle still gets ya." Amtrak also provides ear protection, thick foam plugs, but with them Ray can't hear either his fireman or the radio.

His hearing loss sometimes frustrates Ray. "I can't hear birds and I can't hear crickets and I can't hear cats meowing. Any high-frequency sound I can't hear at all. Some of these watches," he said, tapping his own, "have alarms, and I can't hear them. Or the newer alarm clocks that have little beeps. You do learn to live with it."

I nodded in agreement. You do. You have to.

Ray began his railroad career with the Southern Pacific in 1959. His father was a Southern Pacific fireman, "a real meticulous kind of guy. He had the reputation of being one of the very best steam engine firemen on the railroad. Everybody liked him. When I first went to work for SP, his experience and reputation helped lay a little groundwork for me. Until everybody gets to know you, the old engineers are hesitant about letting a young guy run the engine, but because of my dad they let me do it sooner than normal. He died in 1963, the day John Kennedy was buried."

A year later Ray lost his job in a move to eliminate firemen from diesel engines. In 1965 he opened a Shell service station in San Luis Obispo, "on the day my second daughter was born." (His two daughters are now grown, and he has a three-year-old granddaughter.) Many railroaders used his service station, and one day in 1967 a road foreman of engines "come in the station and says, 'Raymond, you want to go back to work for the railroad?' I says, 'Hell, yes.' He says, 'Well, be up to San Francisco Monday.' "

For the next three years Ray worked as a fireman on the SP while running the service station in his spare time and raising purebred sheep as a "side hobby—I like being outside and I like working with animals. I just liked the ranching life." In 1970 he sold the station and in 1985 the sheep business. The SP promoted him to the engineer's seat in 1971, and he came over to Amtrak, like so many of his colleagues, in 1987.

Like them, he enjoys the regular life of Amtrak crews. "I come out to Lovelock with Number Six on Tuesday, go back to Oakland with Number Five on Wednesday, and work in the Oakland yards on Thursday. Friday I go back out on Six, return Saturday on Five, and then I'll have Sunday and Monday off."

I began riffling through my pocket calendar. Shyly I said I'd like to ride with him from Lovelock to Oakland in the cab of the *Zephyr* next spring, if I might—and if I can work it out with Amtrak. Perhaps I had enough journalist's clout to do so. But that could take some doing, I added, because Ray's schedule might change (it did) and getting sleeper space on the *Zephyr* to Oakland on short notice wasn't easy. Like anybody else, a journalist has to take his chances with the reservations system.

"We'll work it out," Ray replied with a confident smile. "I don't mind because I want to see you do a nice job on your book. I get tired of these phony books and magazine articles by people who don't really know what's going on."

His generous confidence in me made me swell with pride. In fact, it brought to mind a favorite passage from Stephen Crane, who in "The Scotch Express" near the turn of the century captured, perhaps somewhat satirically, the essence of the locomotive engineer, the epitome of the blue-collar *mensch*:

It should be well-known fact that, all over the world, the engine-driver is the finest type of man that is grown. He is the pick of the earth. He is altogether more worthy than the soldier, and better than the men who move on the sea in ships. He is not paid too much, nor do his glories weight his brow, but for outright perform- ance, carried on constantly, coolly, and without elation by a temper- ate, honest, clear-minded man, he is the further point. And so the lone human at his station in a cab, guarding money, lives and the honor of the road, is a beautiful sight. The whole thing is aesthetic.

In the end, my cab excursion very nearly didn't happen. It's an ironclad Amtrak rule that a road foreman—a chief of engineers— must be in the cab every time a civilian rides, presumably to keep the ignoramus from pressing switches and grabbing levers and perhaps hurting himself. That year Amtrak was sorely short of road foremen in Oakland, and as the time for my journey grew closer, it appeared that an overworked foreman might not be available except for the short and comparatively uninspiring run between Sacramento and Oakland—if at all.

But when I saw Ray standing by his locomotives at Lovelock that morning, a broad smile wreathed his face as he gave me the thumbs-up sign and a sweeping, arching gesture that could mean only one thing: "We're going over The Hill," as California rail- roaders call the Sierra. Someone—Ray won't say who, although I suspect it was he—had devised the brilliant idea of deputizing Ray as an acting road foreman, a job he had held in the past. And so, after signing a waiver indemnifying Amtrak from liability for any injury I might suffer "on the property," I shook conductor Bob Pimm's hand and climbed up into the cab of F40 Number 360, a well-worn veteran a long way from home ("NEW ORLEANS" was stenciled in small letters on its frame above the front wheels). Pimm walked back down his train and boarded the crew-dorm car.

Inside, the cab of the F40 (or "unit," as railroaders call diesel locomotives) looks like the flight deck from a steel-and-iron fore- runner of the Boeing 747, except a locomotive engineer rules his domain from the right side while an airliner captain controls his machine from the left. The four-foot-high control console, from which myriad levers, switches and dials hang, sits on the engineer's left rather than directly in front of him. Between the control console and the fireman's seat is a steel floor broad enough for a couple of folding chairs. On the wall in the back of the cab hangs an array of electrical switches. In the center of the dashboard a low door leads to the nose of the locomotive. "CONDUCTOR'S OFFICE," said a crudely lettered sign above the door in Number 360. "That's the toilet," Ray said with a grin.

Briefly Ray took me inside the engine compartment behind the cab. Two feet from my nose, three thousand horsepower of thrumming diesel engine the size of a Volkswagen, its sixteen dinnerplate-sized cylinders arranged in a *V* of eight each, assaulted my senses. Though I could not hear the idling engine, its vibrations rattled my fillings and the heat scorched my skin. The experience, I thought, must be like standing inside Mount St. Helens at full eruption.

Had we been at Oakland starting the day's run to Chicago, Ray would have checked out all systems carefully. First he'd have testwhirled the large rotary hand brake on the rear inside wall of the engine compartment, doing the same inside the trailing locomotive (F40 Number 260, based in Chicago). He'd have examined brake valves, buttons, switches, fuel gauges, air hoses, electrical lines, headlights, the hoses from the sanders—tanks that dump dry sand on the tracks to improve wheel adhesion ("Gotta keep those sanders working") and in general "look over the locomotives to make sure all the right pieces are in."

This morning, however, Ray trusted the engineer who had brought the *Zephyr* from Salt Lake City to inform him about the condition of the units. With a clean rag Ray wiped the grime from all surfaces near the engineer's seat and spritzed a bit of space-age WD-40 lubricant on the whistle lever. Everyone in the cab donned plastic safety spectacles and earplugs—except me (I wear prescription glasses and have no need for ear protection). I climbed into the fireman's seat, and Chris took the folding chair in the center.

Ray studied his thick computer-printed sheaf of orders, called a "track warrant." It told engineer and conductor of temporary "slow orders" on the line, giving speed restrictions for track work and the like. "I want to be letter-perfect 'cause people are going to be reading this book," Ray said.

"Highball Number Five Lovelock!" Bob Pimm suddenly barked from the radio on the console. On the Southern Pacific and many other roads, *highball* is an old term meaning "proceed." The word is a survivor of mid-nineteenth-century railroading, in which signals were flashed to engineers by the raising and lowering of large wooden balls on ropes attached to a tall standard.

"Okay, we're out of here," said Ray, reaching for the whistle lever and loosing two long blasts. (To be accurate, a cluster of air horns, not steam-locomotive whistles, sits atop the locomotive, but modern enginemen still call them "whistles.") He opened his throttle a notch, and four feet behind me I felt an expectant surge of revolutions.

Slowly Number 5 gathered momentum. In a noisy, grimy, workaday locomotive cab the name *California Zephyr* does seem effete and frou-frou, and all the rest of the way to Oakland I fell in with the crew jargon, thinking of the train as "Number 5." In a couple of train-lengths Number 5 ambled past a motel where Amtrak crews used to bunk on their layovers but deserted because, they say, the landlady treated them poorly. Ray and Chris made a point of counting automobiles in the inn's drive. "Only one today!" Ray chortled, in a fine display of high-iron *Schadenfreude*.

As the train rolled slowly out of town, Ray "tested the air," checking the brakes throughout the train. Finally, satisfied that all his equipment functioned correctly, he opened the throttle a few more notches.

The control console suddenly warbled like an exuberant songbird. Without turning his head, Ray punched a large yellow button on the console with the side of his left hand. This was the "Alertor," a device connected to an electric field between the console and the cushion of the engineer's chair. If the engineer doesn't "make" and "break" an electrical connection by touching something on his console every twenty seconds, the Alertor trills a warning, making sure he's awake and alert. If there's no response, a light above the windshield flashes and an alarm sounds. If the engineer still doesn't respond, the brakes apply and stop the train.

The Alertor replaces the old "deadman," a flat steel pedal the engineer had to hold down constantly with his left foot. If he suddenly pitched over from a heart attack or a bullet from a trackside sniper, his foot would fall off the pedal, and if it were not pressed back down within ten seconds, the train would stop. All too many engineers used to disable the pedal with a stick of wood.

Every time Pimm radioed a message from back in the train, Ray acknowledged it aloud, and Chris repeated the message to make sure both he and Ray had heard it. Great concentration is required in this job. Those who think that all locomotive engineers have to do is touch a throttle and press the brakes while the rails guide their trains are much mistaken. Yes, the presence of a fireman— sorry, assistant engineer—helps keep the engineer awake. "An assistant engineer has more responsibility than a fireman," Chris said, "but I would hate to see the old term *fireman* disappear." In modern passenger railroading, however, assistant engineers ride only on runs exceeding four hours, and longer trips can be nerve-deadening to both crew members.

Locomotive cabs are noisy places, and not just from the yammer of diesel engines. *"SP detector milepost three-forty-six, detector working,"* a tinny voice chortled on the radio, returning seconds later to announce, *"SP detector milepost three-forty-six, no defects, no defects!"*

"Who's *that?*" I asked, surprised.

"Trackside hotbox detector," Ray replied. The passing locomotives of Number 5 had awakened two small silver-colored steel boxes, one sitting on each side of the track. Inside the boxes are sensors that measure the temperatures of the axle bearings on the train's wheels. An electronic voice transmitted to the locomotives informs the engineer if all is well with his train. An overheated axle bearing would have caused the voice to say, *"Stop your train! Stop your train!"* and give the location of the offending bearing.

"There are all kinds of detectors," Ray said. "There's a metal bar placed across the ties that looks for dragging equipment. Another checks for loose wheels. There's a big steel hoop that measures high or wide loads—shifted cargo—on freight trains." And they all nag the engineers in their metallic harridan's voices.

Several miles out of Lovelock Number 5 topped out at seventy-nine miles per hour. At high speed, locomotive wheels "hunt" back and forth on the track, the flanges searching for the inner edges of the rails in a high-speed sashay. The cab bucks and rolls like a lathered bronc; locomotive trucks are built for pulling, not for riding. So rough was the ride that I could neither take notes nor train a camera lens; I just held on to the window ledge. The jolting brought on a call of nature and I glanced longingly at the door under the dash. I was not, however, going to try to stay in the saddle of a pitching, bucketing toilet, and decided to wait until a slower stretch of track.

With a large digital stopwatch Ray measured the time the train took to pass two trackside mileposts, and shook his head. Locomotive speedometers are not always accurate—the constant vibration is hard on instruments. Engineers, however, must run at exact speeds, no matter what the speedometers say. When Ray's speedometer indicated eighty miles per hour, Chris's said seventy-seven. One or both—probably both—were wrong. From his satchel Ray pulled a screwdriver, opened the speedometer case and turned a screw to recalibrate the instrument. Chris did the same with his. Again Ray counted off the seconds between mileposts. "Dead on! Seventy-nine!" he called, flashing his smile and characteristic thumbs-up sign. Three times before the next stop, Sparks—seventy-three miles from Lovelock—the engineers checked their speedometers, once at seventy-nine miles per hour, again at seventy and once again at sixty.

Gray skies opened and Ray flicked on the windshield wipers, whose mechanisms went into action with a frenzied howl. He squirted WD-40 liberally on the gears, and their protest settled down to a grumpy mutter. As he settled back into his seat, Number 5 approached a siding. "Green over red!" Chris called. "Green over red!" Ray repeated. Through the fog, on the left side of the tracks, a tall signal post displayed two lamps, one over the other like a traffic signal. Green over red meant the track ahead was clear, and Number 5 could proceed.

Each time Number 5 swept by a signal light or speed-limit sign ("79-60" means seventy-nine miles per hour for passenger trains, sixty for freights), Chris called out the indicated color or speed, and Ray echoed him.

"Be sure to include in the book that we call out all speed boards and the colors of all signals—red, hard yellow, green," said Ray. "Those are the rules."

("Why *hard* yellow? What's the difference between that and plain yellow?" I asked conductor Pimm later. "Nothing," he replied. "It's an old Southern Pacific term to distinguish a steady yellow signal from a flashing yellow one, which they no longer use. In your book just say 'yellow.' ")

Most trackside signals come in pairs, the lamps of each member of the pair shining from a separate tall standard on the engineer's side of the tracks. Increasingly on the Southern Pacific, however, signal pairs are being replaced by a single standard to which are affixed lamps pointing in both directions. Such two-in-one signals are cheaper to erect and maintain than separate westbound and eastbound signal posts. Some engineers, Chris said, dislike the arrangement, because in heavy fog and snow it's harder to see a signal on the opposite side of the tracks. But double duty saves money for the Southern Pacific, and the engineers live with it.

As Number 5 flashed by a train stopped on the siding—a long, long coal train, also westbound—Ray examined it carefully, looking for signs of smoke from the wheels, open doors, shifted loads. His counterpart on the freight did the same for Number 5. Cabooses have for the most part joined steam locomotives on the scrap heap, and instead freight trains carry, on the last car, a small black box called a FRED. That means "flashing rear end device," although many railroaders use a different word in place of the first. FREDs, however, cannot perform the function of lookouts the way brakemen did in the cabooses, peering up at the train as it goes around curves and making sure all is well with cars and their loads.

The engineers still do that, carefully examining every foot of their train in their rearview mirrors whenever they lean into a curve.

As Number 5 swept past the four Southern Pacific locomotives at the head of the freight—Engine 8515 was in the lead—Ray picked up the handset of his radio and said, *"Eighty-five fifteen, your train looks good on the south side!"* Seconds later came the reply, *"Highball Amtrak Five!"*

Ray is punctilious about the etiquette of passing other trains. (Automobiles, too; so conscientious is he that at night he switches off the powerful headlights of his locomotive at points where the track runs cheek by jowl with Interstate 80 so that the glare does not dazzle the eyes of drivers of oncoming cars.) Some Southern Pacific engineers, Ray said, won't answer an Amtrak hail; "they're just being jackasses." A certain animosity still exists between freight-road and Amtrak engineers. In 1987, when Amtrak first hired its own operating crews, many engineers who had been running passenger trains elected to remain with the home roads and were bumped off their long-held runs by Amtrakers, some of whom, in their opinion, lacked sufficient engineer's-seat time in both the cabs and on the demanding run over the Sierra. "It's all groundless," said Ray, "especially with the older guys like myself. I'd had a fair amount of passenger service as well as twenty-six years of experience on freight."

Ray had spent most of his Southern Pacific career working out of San Luis Obispo, running 220 miles to Los Angeles and 152 miles to Watsonville Junction. "Of course I knew all that track like the back of my hand. But now, since I've been up here with Amtrak, I've made so many trips from Oakland to Lovelock I almost think I belong here." He spoke without a trace of irony.

Is there much difference between the jobs of a freight engineer and a passenger engineer? I asked. Ray's answer echoed the words of Wally Prince, the former Burlington Northern engineer to whom I had spoken way back in Galesburg. "There's a lot more responsibility when you think of the number of people you have on passenger trains," Ray said. "But the actual job of running a passenger train is easier."

For one thing, Ray said, instead of having to remember the controls and running characteristics of half a dozen or more freight locomotives of different models and manufacturers, an Amtrak engineer essentially runs the same locomotive all the time. With few exceptions, the standard Amtrak locomotive is an F40 made by the Electro-Motive Division of General Motors. "They all have exactly the same control panel, the same brake valves, the same everything. Only the whistles sound different."

The F40s, most of which are at least twelve years old and have gone through three or four complete rebuildings, are also extremely durable locomotives, Ray adds. "They're constantly on the go and we will have difficulty with them occasionally, but when you stop and think of how many millions of miles these engines get put on 'em, they're pretty trouble-free."

All the same, I said, the F40s are getting long in the tooth, and Amtrak has bought scores of new locomotives from General Electric. Ray nodded. "They've had a couple of 'em out here on tests, but they didn't really test out very well. I'd rather kiss my mother-in-law than work on one of 'em." As do those engaged in any other pursuit, railroaders prefer well-worn and familiar tools to the new and untried.

Whatever one may say about locomotives, there are considerable differences in the operation of freight and passenger trains. Loaded freight trains a hundred or more cars long weigh many thousands of tons. It's impossible to start up such a train all at once. Even four to six locomotives, twelve thousand to eighteen thousand horsepower, could not move that enormous inertia were there not plenty of slack in the spring-loaded coupling mechanisms—as much as six inches of "slop" at each end of a freight car.

To start their trains, freight engineers first back up their locomotives, pushing together the cars as if the train were an accordion. Once all the slack is taken up, the engines slowly move forward. One at a time each car begins rolling, the inertia of the train's mass overcome bit by bit as the slack is pulled out. It is not a smooth process; each car starts with an increasingly strong jolt. Until the FRED arrived, brakemen sometimes were knocked off their feet when the fast-disappearing slack reached the end of the train and yanked the caboose forward.

Shepherding a limber, loose-jointed, one-hundred-car-long monster weighing ten thousand tons and more around curves and up and down steep mountain grades without derailing cars or snapping drawbars is not a simple job. It takes patient, knowledgeable work with throttle, air brakes, dynamic brakes and sanders.

A passenger train, however, is a comparatively solid unit, with little slack between cars. If there were much slack, the cars would constantly jerk back and forth, as they do on a freight train. The presence of that minimal slack, however, means that a feathery touch with throttle and brake still is needed to start and stop passenger trains smoothly, without lurches that might jolt awake sleeper passengers and land lunch in the laps of dining-car patrons.

Whether their locomotives tow freight or passengers, engineers must contend with obstacles on the tracks—inanimate and animate. Things fall on the tracks, things are placed on the tracks, people fall on the tracks and people place themselves on the tracks.

Youngsters will dump just about anything on the rails they can carry, simply for the joy of watching it smashed to flinders. Once, Ray said, he hit an empty outhouse. Chris offered that his oddest victim was a fifteen-foot-high chicken advertising a fast-food restaurant. His locomotive struck it at high speed, pulverizing it into fiberglass feathers.

A few years ago another *Zephyr* engineer hit a motor home at seventy-nine miles an hour on a grade crossing near Salt Lake City. The only recognizable component left in the wreckage was the vehicle's frame. For ninety minutes the engineers and the entire on-board crew, sickened by the fear that their train had killed a whole family, searched the brush for bodies. The local sheriff's police brought dogs to join the hunt. When no corpses turned up, the searchers concluded that someone had tried to pull a fast one on a bank or insurance company by parking the motor home on the tracks and later claiming it had been stolen. No more vehicle, no more payments.

If someone wants to commit suicide, there is nothing an engineer can do. People bent on self-destruction will stand on the tracks watching calmly as death hurtles toward them. Others have topped up their old Ford Pinto gas tanks (which had a propensity for exploding in rear-end accidents), then parked the cars on the tracks with rear bumper facing an oncoming train just around a curve, and waved gaily as the engineer spotted them much too late.

Two or three times a year every newspaper carries a small, sad story about a van or car loaded with half a dozen teenagers losing a race with an oncoming train to a grade crossing. It's almost impossible for a driver to judge the speed of a large train approaching in the distance. A driver thinks he has fifteen or twenty seconds to gun his car around the gates and beat a five-minute wait while a long freight ties up a crossing, but discovers too late that the laws of physics put the locomotive there in five seconds. Think of an enormous Boeing 747 drifting to a landing. It seems to hang in the air, approaching the runway as if in slow motion, but it is actually boring in at almost 170 miles per hour. On the ground, the same trick of perspective applies to locomotives going nearly eighty miles per hour. From top speed a passenger train needs two miles to execute an emergency stop.

I thought back to an evening in Galesburg months earlier, when I had asked Wally Prince whether a train he engineered ever killed anybody.

"Several of them," he replied laconically.

The freshest incident had occurred just months before, when Wally was taking Number 6 out of Lincoln, Nebraska. A young man riding a motorcycle down the middle of the eastbound main heard the locomotive behind him, stopped and was trying to drag the motorcycle out of the way when the locomotive struck him at speed.

"Just before then I was between Omaha and Lincoln and a guy simply walked out in front of the train and we ran over him," Wally added. At this point in the conversation Wally's wife stood up from the table in the restaurant where we had been chatting and said quietly to her husband, "I'm leaving—you can tell him." She walked over to an empty table on the far side of the room, lighted a cigarette and stared out the window. Being the spouse of a locomotive engineer sometimes is not easy.

Was it suicide? I asked Wally.

"Nineteen-year-old kid. His friends said he was playing chicken. They'd been drinking all day. You're going sixty miles an hour and sometimes in the dark you can't see anybody walking across the tracks. When I saw him he kind of stopped and hesitated, and he looked like he was starting to go on, and he just barely—the left part of the engine caught him and spun him around and killed him. He was just a nineteen-year-old kid. I felt bad about it, but there wasn't nothing I could do." Wally's expression was set in granite.

Amtrak provides a counseling program for engineers involved in fatal accidents, but many of them, especially the veterans, decline aid. After the most recent accident, Wally said, "a counselor called me. He wanted to know if I was having any problems. I think I'd have told him if I was. I mean, I'm a professional. I didn't do anything to cause the accident. There was nothing I could do to prevent it. Therefore I feel I had no responsibility for that person's death. The warning signs were working. The whistle was blowing. The bell was ringing. The headlight was burning bright. And that guy made the decision to walk in front of the train. I felt bad about it because he was only nineteen years old, but you have to be a *professional*. That's my job."

When I told Ray Craig what his Midwestern colleague had said, he nodded somberly. "I killed four people when I was on freight, but with Amtrak I haven't killed anybody. It's not in our control. It bothers you for a few days."

He paused. "It stays in your mind. And even after a few days—

look, I can give you a picture right now of every person I've killed. It's just embedded in my memory."

He gazed into the distance. "The first one was a little tiny girl, two years and eleven months old, standing alongside the tracks waving. She wanted to wave at us as we went by. The only thing of it was she was too close. She didn't know. And I'll never forget that."

The child lived in a house a few yards from the main line, Ray said, and her parents were home at the time of the accident. She had wandered out of the backyard to say hello to the kindly men who drove the big trains to the city far away.

"I just had to put in my mind that it wasn't my fault, that there was nothing I could have done. I seen her a long ways away, a quarter of a mile. I put the train into emergency. We were doing about sixty, and we got slowed down to about thirty when we hit her, and then of course we still went on before we could stop. I wish we'd had a counseling program on the SP then."

An hour west of Lovelock, patches of green began to mark the course of the Truckee River as it paralleled the railroad like a long, undulating oasis in the desert. The Truckee rises on the eastern slope of the Sierra Nevada and is the first sign that California is near. As the miles rolled by, a few cows and horses emerged among the green patches, then shacks and tar-paper settlements. Repeatedly the tracks crisscrossed the twisting Truckee, hunting a straighter path to the Sierra.

Ever on the lookout for wildlife, Ray pointed out ducks and beaver dams on the river, and as we passed a junkyard showed me an old Cadillac he's had his eye on for a while, thinking he may someday rebuild it. "There's two '60 Mercurys in that lot there," Ray said at another point. "If I need parts I know where to find 'em." He inherited a Mercury of that vintage from his father, and still keeps it in the garage. Most of us look at automobile graveyards as eyesores on the landscape, but Ray considers them an integral part of the scenery. "Going to come back here and look around," he said as we passed a particularly offensive junkyard.

Chris pointed out a wooden structure guarding what appeared to be a minimum-security stalag coming up close by on the south side of the train. It was the watchtower of the infamous Mustang Ranch. Although the Amtrak route guide cites the brothel as a landmark, any mention of its function is carefully omitted. I smiled, remembering a Dutchman I had met on an earlier *Zephyr* trip.

He was an economist from Leiden and had been in this country for a year researching a book. He had a week to himself, so took the train West and, he said, liked it so well he planned to bring his girlfriend along next year and tour the Rockies. "Now that I've seen mountains," he said, "how can I go home?"

Though he knew Amsterdam, whose large red-light district operates with world-class public tolerance, he showed an inordinate interest in the Mustang Ranch, eagerly unlimbering his camera long before we passed it. When we finally swept by, he seemed disappointed, as if he expected beautiful naked whores to be disporting themselves outdoors on horseback. The enormous parking lot that surrounded the complex contained only a few paltry cars and trucks, and that early in the morning no one was out and about.

A few minutes later Number 5 entered the industrial outskirts of Sparks (Mile 2,176), rolling past a tire repair concern over which squatted a vast billboard that announced with letters as large as its taste was small: "THE WORLD'S BEST PLACE TO TAKE A LEAK." Slowly the train rolled past vast villages of huge steel buildings emblematic of Nevada's tax-free warehousing. Sparks, a longtime Southern Pacific division point, is becoming as much a distribution center for Western markets as it is a railroad town.

For Numbers 5 and 6 Sparks is a refueling stop. The trains pause here for fifteen minutes, gulping diesel fuel and water while passengers either rush the two lonely telephones under the yard tower or embark on a short, brisk walk, the only opportunity other than Denver and Salt Lake City to stretch one's legs on the journey from Chicago. Gingerly I climbed down from the cab—that's a ten-foot drop to the pavement—and set off to watch a switcher couple a

"Sparks car" onto the rear of the train. These are ancient Santa Fe Hi-Level coaches, look-alike contemporaries of the crew-dorm car, and they are used to ferry gamblers between Oakland and Reno, just three miles west of Sparks.

After we clambered back into the cab, Chris showed me a track warrant he had just picked up at the tower. During the rest of the trip, he said, we'll encounter two track gangs, two flagmen and three slow orders. "That's low for the rest of the way to Oakland," Chris says. If all goes well, we just might complete our trip On Time.

"Highball Number Five Sparks!" Bob Pimm's voice rattled over the radio. Two blasts of the horn and at 9:30 A.M. we were away, ten minutes late. Not five minutes later we pulled up by the Main Street sign that proclaims Reno (Mile 2,179) "The Biggest Little City in the World."

This road-show Las Vegas, its downtown neon gaudiness belied by a scruffy skid row that begins only two blocks away, has never been to my taste. But I am not a gambler of any sort; my idea of high-rolling is cashing in CDs and putting the proceeds into savings bonds. All the same, Reno is full of incident and much of it happens on the train.

"Ray, radio the police!" said Pimm. *"We have a disruptive passenger!"*

Ray picked up his handset and called the Southern Pacific police in Sparks and the city police in Reno. Both dispatched squad cars that arrived within minutes. A woman had boarded at Winnemucca early in the morning, quite drunk, and had repaired to the lounge car to consume surreptitiously the better part of a bottle she had brought with her. When she arrived at her destination in Reno, the chief did not step as smartly to help her off the train as she thought he should have, and she tried to kick him—but missed. She then threw her bag at his head, with no better results.

Clearly she had committed assault. But since nothing found its target, battery did not ensue. Since there was no contact, the cops simply hauled the woman to the Reno city jail to sleep off her binge, intending to release her with a warning when she sobered up. This kind of thing happens with such frequency that Amtrak crews often choose not to press charges for simple assault—else they'd spend a great deal of time in court.

"Ray, we'll be a couple more minutes," Pimm radioed. Several gamblers had boarded the Sparks car with a large private stock of refreshments—four cases of beer, a dozen bottles of liquor and fifty pounds of ice—presumably intending to consume at least part of it on the all-day trip to Oakland. Pimm confiscated the supplies temporarily, locking them away in a cabinet until Oakland. Most conductors would have looked the other way, Ray said, but Pimm has a reputation for toughness, for doing everything by the book. And I think Pimm was right. That much booze could have meant trouble for both crew and the other passengers.

While that little drama was playing itself out, Ray climbed down from the cab and engaged in quiet conversation with a little girl and her father at trackside. Suddenly Ray picked up the youngster, five or six years old, and whirled her about as she screeched with laughter.

"Highball Amtrak Five Reno!" Pimm suddenly radioed.

Chris stuck his head out the engineer's door. "Highball, Ray!" he called. Ray swiftly mounted the ladder and took his seat.

"Who was she?" I asked.

"Oh, a regular," Ray said as he opened his throttle. For months, he said, she had waved eagerly to him every day from the platform at the Reno station as he brought in Numbers 5 and 6, and he had returned the salute, as all engineers do. "Finally I got down from the cab and met Angel and her daddy," Ray said. "He's an Eskimo, I've heard. He was out of work and her mother had deserted the family, so I just took her under my wing. Every time I see her I ask her to say her ABCs." And at Christmas he brings a gift.

As the train slowly gathered speed, I couldn't banish the intrusive image of a "little tiny girl, two years and eleven months old," standing by the tracks and waving. Some things you never forget.

ELEVEN

F rom the Southern Pacific main line at Reno, the ghost of the old Virginia & Truckee Railroad curves southward down the foothills of the Sierra Nevada. Twenty-three miles from Reno lies Virginia City. There in 1859 miners struck the Comstock Lode, a $300 million deposit of silver ore that attracted hordes of treasure seekers and built enormous fortunes. With the Gold Rush of a decade earlier, it helped turn San Francisco from a collection of frame cottages into a fashionable city, paid much of the Civil War debt and financed the laying of telegraph cables under the Atlantic Ocean.

And there, ninety years later, arrived history's most remarkable railfan of all, Lucius Morris Beebe (1902–1966), one of the world's great eccentrics, gourmands, tosspots and reactionaries. Beebe, a towering (six-foot-three) and elegant boulevardier with the physique of a linebacker, was a hardworking journalist and author born to great wealth and social position. He was New York's first café society columnist and wrote thirty-five books, twenty-one of which dealt with railroading. Later in his career he became the flamboyant owner and publisher of the Virginia City *Territorial Enterprise*, the weekly where Mark Twain had first staked a claim to literary reputation. Railfans still remember Beebe with mixed affection, awe and caution.

The descendant of prominent Boston bankers, Beebe was gay, insouciant, snobbish, stylish and rich. He spent his boyhood at three of the East's nobbiest prep schools: St. Mark's, the Berkshire School, Roxbury. As an undergraduate at Yale he often rode the train from New Haven to New York in full evening dress with a gold-handled cane. Thrown out of Yale after a drunken escapade, he went to work for the *Boston Telegram*, each day producing a story of orgies in Back Bay bedrooms and Harvard dormitories, learning early on that the hijinks of high society built circulation. Later he took his degree at Harvard, where he wreaked vengeance on his former alma mater by writing scathing attacks for the *Crimson* on compulsory chapel at Yale.

Graduating in 1927, he signed on at the *Boston Transcript* as a contributor to its literary section, then in 1929, at age twenty-seven, joined the *New York Herald Tribune*. In his "biography" of that late, great daily, *The Paper*, Richard Kluger tells how, one evening a few nights after Beebe's hiring, editor Ogden Reid beheld his newest reporter in Bleeck's saloon: "He was wearing his usual nocturnal gear when out on the town: white tie and tails, top hat, red-velvet-lined opera cloak, heavy gold chain adorning his midsection, silver-tipped black stick; he was smoking a cigar less than a foot long but not by much."

"Quite a sight," Reid told Stanley Walker, the city editor, upon Beebe's departure. "Is he good for anything?"

Walker nodded. "I hired him as a sort of sandwich man for the More Abundant Life."

"The extravagance of his wardrobe was mirrored in the tangled wildwood of his prose," Kluger wrote in one of the most accurate assessments ever made of a newspaperman's work. "He avoided the vulgar tongue whenever he could get away with it. Such a style was not much suited for reporting on small fires—which he did on occasion while wearing a morning coat."

Beebe's prose, as overstuffed as a Victorian sofa, suited a more elegant task. From 1934 until 1949 he wrote a column called "This Is New York," about Manhattan's café society. (In fact, he coined the term "café society.") In it Beebe chronicled what he called "the nervous hilarity of the damned" in "Babylon-on-the-Make," writing of "calamitous potations," "vaguely anonymous spaniels" and "the purlieus of magnificence." Food and drink were "comestibles." He was both satirist and historian of the habits of the upper crust, and he could toss off a *mot* as wicked as any. A celebrated xenophobe, Beebe wrote that Paris was "filled with foreigners, many of them Frenchmen."

Not everyone admired him. Howard Vincent O'Brien of the *Chicago Daily News* wrote sourly that Beebe "makes a good living as a chronicler of people who don't matter . . . he neither resents injustice nor is scornful of folly." For Beebe's unconventional sexuality as well as flamboyance, Walter Winchell dubbed him "Luscious Lucius," and others called him "the orchidaceous oracle of café society."

Beebe took the same baroque approach to railroad journalism, his off-hours passion. Early on he fell in love with the opulent travel habits of the rich, especially on trains, and of the *Twentieth Century Limited* he gushed: "To thousands of people, the Century is the oriflamme of romance, a name to quicken the pulses, and its passing in the night a splendor."

Beebe loved to dwell on the sensational, as was demonstrated in his exaggeratedly liquor-soaked account of the driving of the Golden Spike. "Promontory was a scene of opulent disorder once the official ceremonies were over. . . . The ranking brass forthwith retired to Governor Stanford's car where wine flowed and 'a sumptuous luncheon was furnished forth.' When there was no more liquor left they hastened through the sagebrush to Dr. Durant's Pullman, 'that superb piece of cabinet work' and drank the doctor out of house and home in short order."

The cost of the revelry to the Central Pacific alone, Beebe wrote, was astonishing: $3,000, or almost $32,000 in late-twentieth-century dollars. "Just how much whiskey could be purchased for

$3,000 in 1869 may be left to the statisticians but the going price for best Kentucky proof spirits was somewhat less than $1 a gallon, while the maximum estimate of the celebrants involved including the four companies of the Twenty-First Infantry, Major Milton Cogswell commanding, and the band, has never topped 1,500. Even allowing for red fire, rockets and breakage to account for some part of the official largesse, it must have been a not inconsiderable occasion. Survivors for years were regarded with the same awe as survivors of Shiloh or the Battle of the Wilderness."

No wonder his contemporary E. M. Frimbo considered Beebe "somewhat unreliable" as a railroad historian. It's true that Beebe's—and others'—colorful prose about the great limiteds have caused latter-day readers to remember only the impeccable service and luxury aboard those trains for the wealthy, not the dull, dusty and dogged workaday locals most Americans rode. Reality always has a tendency to be obscured by myth.

It is impossible today to break open a Beebe book and fail to crack a grin over its casual (and sometimes suspiciously apocryphal) anecdotes. "On one of the Southern Pacific's overnight sleepers out of Tonopah," he wrote, "a passenger overheard two blacklegs in the adjacent stateroom plotting the assassination of [Nevada] Senator Tasker Oddie, who happened to be a friend. Unceremoniously he kicked in the door of their compartment and suggested they get off the car now, while the train was in full career. 'Who the hell are you?' was a natural question. The answer was 'Wyatt Earp.' "

In 1949 Beebe fell in love with the Old West when he and his companion, the editor and photographer Charles Clegg, arrived in Virginia City, "the ghost town that refused to die," to research a book on the picturesque Virginia & Truckee Railroad. "Lucius was smitten," Clegg later recalled in a passage that almost obsequiously echoed the style of his chum, "and after checking out the population as a little over four hundred people he turned to me and said, 'Keedo, do you realize that there is one saloon for every twenty men, women and children in this town? Do you recognize the absolute ultimate in Progress when you encounter it? Well, I do. Why, the alcoholic proof here is so high, and the moral tone so low, that we can be absolutely inconspicuous. Let's see if there is a house for sale.' "

In 1951 the two reestablished the *Territorial Enterprise*, whose circulation they soon built into the biggest of any weekly west of the Mississippi. Its editorial policy managed to be both rowdy and reactionary. One reader called it "pro-prostitution, pro-alcohol, pro-private-railroad-cars-for-the-few, and fearlessly anti-poor-folks, anti-progress, anti-union, anti-diet, anti-vivisection and anti–prepared breakfast foods." It fought efforts to move a brothel away from a school with the slogan, "Don't Move the Girls; Move the School."

While in Virginia City, Beebe dressed the part. Each day he stepped out of his office in broad-brimmed black hat, string tie, ruffled shirt, black clawhammer coat, frontier pants and boots, and repaired to the nearest barroom. Tourists and travel writers were entranced. Not all, however. Horace Sutton wrote unkindly in the *Chicago Daily News*: "As far as I can determine, Virginia City is Lucius Beebe surrounded by 19 saloons."

Beebe told another Chicago columnist that in Virginia City he divided his time between "entertaining perfect strangers with awful thirsts" and going out to photograph trains. In the latter pursuit he took along a basket lunch typically consisting of a thermos of martinis, two magnums of Cordon Rouge and sandwiches of pâté de foie gras.

In 1960 Beebe and Clegg sold the *Territorial Enterprise* and moved to San Francisco, where Beebe joined the *Chronicle* as a curmudgeonly columnist who artfully walked the thin line between liveliness and libel, complaining about how the twentieth century had brought on "the disasters of women's suffrage, the universal motor car, credit cards, international airports, repudiation of the national currency, tranquilizers, freedom riders and the one-ounce martini."

Repeatedly Beebe would try to sneak libelous calumnies into print, deeply offending his editors. Over periodic luncheons, many of them opulently hosted by Beebe, they kissed and made up.

Beebe's strategy, remembered Gordon Pates, the *Chronicle*'s managing editor, was to "stuff them with good food and paralyze them with strong drink and 'they will see things my way.' They usually did, too, until they sobered up."

Such high living brought on five kidney stone operations, periodic attacks of gout and a liver that, Beebe once boasted, had occasionally swollen to "ducal dimensions." In 1966 a lifetime of cholesterol and Chambertin finally caught up with him, and he died almost instantly of a massive heart attack.

Only in libraries can one find most of Beebe's books—just a few titles are still available, most from railroad-history reprinters—but one of his flamboyant legacies still endures out under the sun where it can be seen: his palatial private car, the *Virginia City*. In 1954 Beebe and Clegg visited what Beebe called "Pullman's used car lot" in Chicago and bought, for $325,000, a one-hundred-ton Pullman open-platform observation car. It had begun its career in 1928 on the *Overland Limited* and ended it during World War II on the Great Northern's *Oriental Limited.* Beebe and Clegg hired Hollywood designer Robert Hanley to redecorate the car with Venetian Renaissance reproductions and Victorian antiques, including furnishings that once had belonged to Leland Stanford, governor of California and one of the "Big Four" railway barons who founded the Central Pacific.

The result was a monument to opulence that featured three staterooms for two, a shower and Turkish bath, a dining room seating six, a spacious drawing room, a fifty-bottle wine cellar, and a radio telephone. Mirrored walls, faux marble, fireplace, chandeliers and fourteen-karat gold leaf moldings completed the ensemble. Beebe and Clegg shared it with a 185-pound St. Bernard named T-Bone Towser. ("After a person has become accustomed to his violently bloodshot eyes," Beebe wrote of the dog with characteristically casual grammar, "they hardly ever notice ours.")

The *Virginia City* was the site of a triumphant *beau geste* enshrined in a *New Yorker* profile. One morning after the car bore Beebe into Manhattan, Wolcott Gibbs of the magazine arrived at the rail yards to visit him. As Gibbs approached over the tracks,

Beebe, dressed in morning coat and striped trousers, greeted him from the brass-railinged platform by raising high his glass of champagne and calling out, "Welcome to Walden Pond!"

The car is now owned by a California firm that leases it for tours. It's regularly coupled to the rear of the *California Zephyr* between Oakland and Salt Lake City, and twice I've watched the elegant, low-roofed *Virginia City* following the tall Superliners around broad curves in the desert, gently rocking like a short but lordly bishop "slightly taken in wine," as Beebe would have put it. (This car was not, however, the culprit that gave the Amtrak crew such fits between Denver and Salt Lake City.) It is just as well that Beebe did not live another twenty years into a ripe old age. He would have found the survival of the passenger train gratifying, but Amtrak's democratic homogeneity appalling.

And yet there was no more endearingly enthusiastic and colorful champion of the nation's passenger trains and the people who made them run. Lucius Beebe, who harbored a soft spot in his gilt-edged heart for grimy engine crews, was simply Rail Lit's version of P. T. Bridgeport, the "Pogo" comic-strip character Walt Kelly modeled on Phineas T. Barnum. In his dialogue balloons Kelly rendered Bridgeport's luxuriant utterings in rococo turn-of-the-century wanted-poster type. Beebe was the same sort, a carnival barker with a yen for entertainment. In his colorful excess he performed a gallant service, keeping the faith for passenger railroading during the latter years of its long decline, hoping that it someday would rise from its ashes, yet acknowledging the unlikelihood that things would ever be the same.

"Once there was a splendor in the railroad's passage, a romance and wonderment that shall come not again, for the dead return not," Beebe wrote in his history of the Central Pacific just three years before his own death. "Only in museums can one see the great storm lanterns against which the night winds blew. . . . Their coal oil flames are one with the fires under the crown sheets of a thousand splendid engines, a thousand gleaming Palace cars that must remain forever a great blaze of memory in the folk-recollections of the nation."

• • •

"Get away from the window!" Ray Craig shouted from the engineer's seat as Number 5 closed at speed with a long freight train on the opposite track. Out of a fog of daydreaming I dove off the fireman's chair onto the deck just as the freight locomotives thundered past, inches away. Ray chuckled at my discomfiture, then turned solemn.

"That train's hauling a lot of lumber," he said. Such loads, he added, can shift, hanging off the side of the cars. Not long ago a dangling wooden beam smashed through the windshield and killed a Southern Pacific fireman in the locomotive of a train going the other way. The accident happened at night, Ray said, "when the trains were going so fast that the headlight didn't light up the loose lumber until it was too late."

Breathing hard, I gave up the fireman's seat for a folding chair in the center of the cab, which would suit me just fine for the rest of the trip. Barely had I settled down when Ray called "Hard yellow!" as a signal loomed around a curve two hundred yards ahead. Calmly Ray picked up his telephone and reported the signal to conductor Pimm back in the train. An engineer, Ray added as he throttled down, can proceed at no more than forty miles per hour when he sees a yellow signal, which indicates well ahead of time that the following block of track will be "protected" by a red signal at which the engineer must be prepared to stop. In a few minutes a deep red indeed did greet the train, and Ray throttled down to a crawl, his attention riveted on the rails ahead. On the left, next to the opposite tracks, we spotted several suitcase-sized rocks near but not on the rails, presumably having punched through the slide detector fence from the low hill above. Apparently the rocks had tripped the signals from green to yellow and red, and Number 5 continued to creep onward.

Near the same spot several months before, a mud slide had oozed down a nearby hill and blanketed the track in four feet of goo without snapping any of the warning fence's strands and tripping the signals. Long experience, Ray said, had taught him to keep his head up in heavy rain, and he spotted the slide just in time to stop his train before plowing into it and off the rails. After the *Zephyr* had switched to the opposite track and continued on its journey, "the trackmen needed a whole week to dig out the mud and get the rails back into shape," Ray said, just as Number 5 approached a green signal. He opened the throttle, and soon we had returned to a steady forty-five miles per hour.

"Five, Verdi!" Ray sang into the radiotelephone. As Number 5 flashed by each Southern Pacific depot, he called out the name of the station, keeping his conductor and the SP dispatcher informed of the train's location in the Roseville District of the SP's Western Region. We were now eleven miles west of Reno, climbing through the gorge of the Truckee River into the beginning of the Sierra, about to cross the state line into California. We had left behind the desert for deep stands of Ponderosa pine that marched far into the hills, lordly granite crags peeking above the tree line.

Una Gran Sierra Nevada—"a great snowy range"—the Spanish missionary Pedro Font called the mountains when he first saw them on a trip inland from the coast in 1772. He did not name them that; he was just echoing his countryman Juan Rodriguez Cabrillo, who had sailed past the Big Sur in 1542 and spotted some white-covered peaks inland, for which he used the words "Sierra Nevada" in his journal. Of course Cabrillo could not have seen the Sierra from the sea, and because the Coast Range seldom had snow, Font simply assumed the great inland range was what the earlier explorer had been talking about. And so this great mountain range was named sight unseen.

It extends in an unbroken reach 360 miles along what is now California's eastern border, dividing the watersheds of the Great Basin and the Pacific slope. The eastern face of the range looms abruptly from the desert, its ridges soaring four thousand to seven thousand feet above sea level. The interior summits, many capped by glaciers, rise gradually in height until they top ten thousand feet—and even fourteen thousand feet far to the south. The broad western face, guttered and furrowed by deep box canyons, dips down gradually for fifty miles to the Central Valley. From any

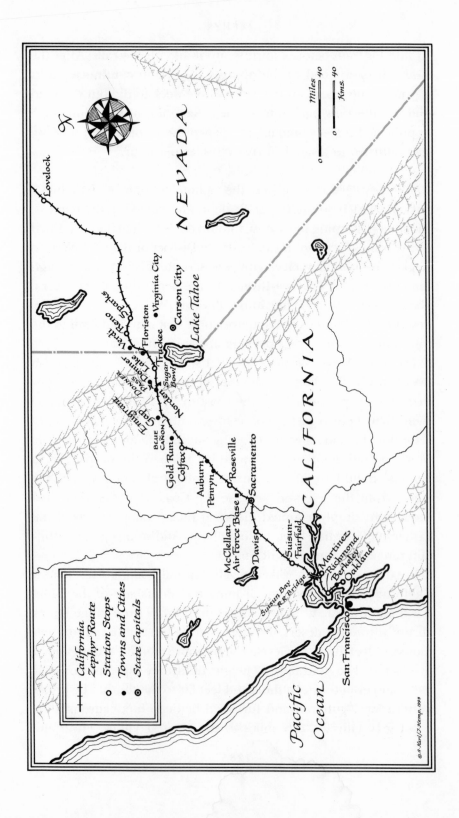

direction, the Sierra is one of the world's most formidable natural barriers. That a railroad, built with the crude tools of the nineteenth century, could breach these forbidding mountains seems almost impossible.

But it was done, in one of the grand engineering exploits of all time. In 1863 gangs of workers began to assault the Sierra eastward from Sacramento over a route surveyed by civil engineer Theodore Judah, who early on had to defend his dream against both competing transportation companies—steamboat, clipper ship and wagon—and his own tyrannical and greedy financial backers, Leland Stanford, Mark Hopkins, Collis P. Huntington and Charles Crocker. Before construction began, Judah was shunted aside and Crocker ran the show.

The natural obstacles were almost overwhelming, and the workers met them almost from the beginning. In 1864, at Bloomer not much more than thirty miles east of Sacramento, every inch of an eight-hundred-foot-long, eighty-five-foot-deep gap had to be blasted with black powder through astonishingly hard rock aggregate. The cut remains today as it was then, its rock so durable that it has not changed over a century and a quarter.

By 1865 Crocker had imported armies of workers, many of them Chinese from San Francisco and mainland China. Using only hand tools, the Chinese diligently chipped away inside the high tunnels, often advancing scarcely eight inches a day. In one two-mile stretch they carved seven bores through solid granite. Uncomplainingly they dangled from bosun's chairs over precipices 2,500 feet above the American River, drilling holes for explosives. By 1866 the workers had reached the line's summit, under which they drove a 1,659-foot tunnel, known to this day to railroaders and railfans alike as "the Big Hole."

And the snow! During the winter of 1866–67, forty-four storms dumped forty feet of snow on the Sierra. Snow slides carried away entire camps of workers. Hundreds of thousands of board feet of timber went into long, snakelike wooden snow sheds to protect the track from drifts. The work faltered but never stopped, and by August 1867 the summit tunnel was holed through, and workers from the west end could behold Donner Lake far below, where the ill-fated party had starved twenty-one years before. Almost before the snows arrived, rails had reached the Truckee River canyon, and the struggle began to lessen. The first Central Pacific locomotive nosed over the state line into Nevada on December 13, 1867, and by the next spring reached the site of present-day Reno. Soon the great race across the desert to link up with the Union Pacific commenced.

Today Number 5 ran west on Track No. 1, the original line of the single-tracked Central Pacific. In many places Track No. 2, constructed in stages between 1909 and 1925, only roughly parallels the original route; it is nearly a separate railroad in itself, with its own tunnels and snow sheds, now built of concrete rather than wood.

A few minutes over the California border, as Number 5 approached a short bridge spanning the Truckee River near the hamlet of Floriston, Ray observed, "You're always looking ahead. Not just two feet or fifty feet or a hundred feet. You're looking ahead a quarter mile, a half mile, for something to happen that you hope never happens. Once, a few summers ago, something did. It was a nice warm day, the kind where kids get out on that bridge and dive into the river. I was looking ahead, expecting kids to be there. Half a mile away I started whistlin', and sure enough, when we got within a quarter of a mile I could see kids were there.

"I'm still whistlin' when we get up to the bridge. There's three kids there. Two of 'em jump up on the railing and dive in. See, they always pretend like they're afraid—they always pretend. The third one really gets chicken, and he takes off and starts runnin' on the side of the tracks. We're doing forty-five, and we overtake him. We hit him in the arm and knocked him off the bridge, and he goes rollin' down the bank, and I thought we'd killed him."

Ray sighed. "We stopped and backed up the train, and when we got to the bridge the kid was standing by the tracks. We just bruised his arm—didn't even break it. He was in shock, though, and we bundled him aboard the SP private car that was on the back of the

train and took him on to Truckee. We called ahead for the paramedics, and"—Ray cut the story short as the locomotives thundered over the bridge—"now he lives happily ever after. Just a
bruise, but the rest of us had a heart attack."

On the other side of the bridge two adults and half a dozen small
boys waved eagerly at the train from copses of brush. As they had
done scores of times since leaving Reno, the engineers genially
acknowledged the trackside salute, each in his own way. Ray's was
a forefinger lifted halfway to his baseball cap, Chris's a brisk wigwag of his left palm. "The most important part of this job is
waving," Ray said with a fond chuckle.

It was near this spot that on a previous trip I had been walking
through one of the coaches on my way to the sleeper when the
brakes suddenly dropped into emergency, nearly pitching me forward into a heap as the train shuddered to a stop. I dashed down
to the vestibule and surreptitiously opened the window to see what
was going on. The conductors stood on the ground, conferring. I
returned to the lounge car just as Lela Janushkowsky emerged at
the other end from the dining car and said, in her unflappable way,
"Nothing to worry about—we just lost the last car." The rearmost
coach, the gambler's car, had broken off the back of the train;
apparently the knuckles of the couplers had not been quite locked.

Fortunately, Lela added, at the time of the break, nobody had
been walking through the vestibules between coach and diner, so
there were no injuries. It's an embarrassing occasion for a railroad
when a train breaks in two, but provided nobody's walking between
cars, it's not a disaster, even on steep inclines. The air brakes do
what they are designed to do—stop both halves of the train when
air pressure is lost.

With a casual smile Lela added, "This is only the second time in
my career a train broke in two. The first time, we were heading out
of Oakland when the locomotives separated from the train and
kept going out of sight while the cars stopped. I told the passengers, 'Don't worry! By the time they get to Martinez somebody will
tell them there's no train behind them!' "

How, you may ask, could the locomotives have kept going when air pressure was lost? Some engineers, I learned later from one of their colleagues, "have a nasty habit of 'plugging' the engine brake." Pressing down the locomotive brake handle prevents the locomotive brakes from applying. Normally, in braking for a stop, the engineers allow the train brakes to apply, but press down the engine brake so that the locomotives will pull slightly against the load behind, keeping the slack between cars stretched out.

When the engine brake is then released, a loud blast of air follows. On runs requiring frequent use of the engine brake, the blasts become annoying. Hence "some engineers will press down the handle and put a plug of wood or a coin in the brake linkage so it *stays* down. Trouble is, if the brakes go into emergency, the brakes on the engines won't apply."

"Plugging the brake" nullifies a safety device, and that's a serious no-no for both Amtrak and the Federal Railroad Admistration. Yet it's apparently done all too frequently. Still another Amtrak operating crewman said he once described the practice to a friend who rebuilds engine brake assemblies in the railroad's brake shop at Beech Grove, Indiana. "He said, 'Is that why I find all the loose change in the brake assembly when it comes to the shop?' "

Shortly later Number 5 ground past a yellow Southern Pacific maintenance truck parked by the roadbed, and Ray flashed the driver a brisk thumbs-up. If all is going well on a run, Ray often gives the thumbs-up sign to everybody. It's informal but unmistakable in meaning. What about official hand signals? Do conductors and engineers still exchange them? "No," Ray said, "except sometimes in the yards. We use the radio now. I wish we didn't use it so much. It's silly when the conductor may be only a few feet away and easily visible."

As Number 5 passed a whistle post—a trackside sign warning of a road crossing the tracks a few hundred yards ahead—Ray reached for the horn lever on the console and cranked out two long blasts, a short one, then another long toot. This is whistle code for "Approaching Grade Crossing."

A single long blast means "Air Brakes Applied When Standing." Two long blasts mean "Release Brakes, Proceed." (Or "Highball!") Two short blasts mean "Acknowledge." Three quick toots indicate that the train is "Backing up." A long series of short blasts announces "Emergency!"

Other than the highway crossing warning, whistle codes, Chris said, aren't used much anymore on the Southern Pacific, but Ray follows them still. He is a traditionalist in many ways, and he plays the diesel horn like a Satchmo in overalls.

As the *Zephyr* rolled into Truckee (Mile 2,214), Ray pointed out in its yards the Southern Pacific's army of snow-removal equipment. The first line of defense, Ray said, is the flanger, a car with adjustable steel wings that not only carve the snow from inside the flangeway—the area between the rails—but also push it away on the outside. "When the snow starts building up," Ray said, "they'll use a Jordan spreader. See over there?" The car looked like a gigantic headless bird, twenty-foot-long wings folded against its side. "If it gets bad enough, they'll use the rotary plow," he added, reminding me that back in Sparks we had seen a massive rail-borne snow-thrower squatting on a siding. The bulging control cupola over its circular maw, toothed with wide propeller blades, gave it the ugly mien of a science-fiction monster that tunnels through the earth.

Nestled in the Truckee River Valley, Truckee on this sunny spring morning still was choked with high banks of snow bulldozed over the winter from streets and lots. At the station the locomotives slowly ground past a single waiting passenger—a fair-haired young woman with backpack and kaffiyeh proclaiming her solidarity with the Palestinians—and I looked out at the town. It is an amiably postcardy tourist village, gateway to the resorts on Lake Tahoe ten miles to the south, and I smiled as I saw a row of "Painted Ladies"—Victorian homes trimmed in gaudy colors—on the main drag. They were very nearly a visual pun for a lost industry; Truckee, an old mining town, at one time contained more brothels than all of Nevada. I had begun to compose a lewd ditty about

"Lucky Chucky from Truckee" when the call came at 10:35 A.M.—just eleven minutes off schedule—from conductor Pimm: *"High-ball Number Five Truckee!"*

The grade steepened perceptibly. "Eagle!" Chris called as the brush along the Truckee River parted and a majestic bird soared upriver. This morning Ray and Chris counted four eagles along the river—"a record for me," Ray said. Riding in the locomotive going over The Hill, Ray said, is "just like going to the zoo. There's a lot of deer, and you'll see bears, once in a while a mountain lion, coyotes, bobcats, badgers, skunks, squirrels, chipmunks, all kinds of birds—but mostly deer." In the winter, he added, "deer, bobcats and coyotes run right up along the tracks, where the snow's been plowed real shallow. It's easy going for them." Unfortunately, Ray's locomotives strike many of the animals. When he can, he'll slow down so they can get out of the way, "even a dog," but often he's running behind time and can't throttle back. "That's the worst part of this job, killing all these deer and dogs."

"Five, Donner!" Ray barked into the radio as we approached the Stanford Curve, a long stretch of track that arches back on itself as it claws for altitude. From our vantage point we could see the line high up as it plunged into a tunnel, and in a few minutes Number 5 entered that curving tunnel. At the instant we emerged on a long ridge overlooking Donner Lake, still and deep blue far below, Ray turned and beamed a proprietary smile at me. The vista was so glorious that Jennie (Lady Randolph) Churchill's words on her first visit to Blenheim sprang to mind: "As we passed through the entrance archway, Randolph said with pardonable pride, 'This is the finest view in England.' " Anywhere, but especially high in the Sierra, a locomotive cab is like a fifty-yard-line, front-row-orchestra, picture-window seat upon wide-angle landscapes of the kind nineteenth-century Victorian romantics painted of the Old West. For the next twenty miles something unexpected and breathtaking always lay around the next bend.

Seconds later Number 5 slid into Tunnel 41, the "Big Hole," and for a quarter of a mile we fell silent in the roaring darkness, the tunnel walls magnifying the bellow of the locomotives. The cool air in the bore told me that Number 5 was the first train over The Hill that day. If a freight or two had preceded Number 5, our cab temperature would quickly have risen ten or fifteen degrees, thanks to the hot fumes from the multiple engines ahead. So smoky is the air at those times that engineers cannot see the end of the tunnel beyond. It's an eerie sensation. What lies ahead? Will the locomotive collide with something unseen? Running at thirty miles an hour into a gray, roiling void is uncomfortably spooky, and these engineers do it every day.

As we dove out of the Big Hole into daylight right under the gondolas of the Sugar Bowl ski lift soaring to the summit above, I began to share another sensation of uncertainty with the engineers. A warren of crossover tracks lies just before Norden, the huge old Southern Pacific summit station and yard that once sheltered against the snow scores of helper locomotives under wooden roofs. Today six inches of new snow covered the tracks, obscuring the crossovers. The engineers could not see where the switches pointed, "and that's a discomforting feeling," Ray said.

Still the snow was not deep. "It's only thirty-five percent of normal this year," Ray observed. "Usually up here at this time of year the snow is half the height of the cars. The SP hasn't used its rotary plow in years." It was hard to believe that forty years earlier, just a few miles west of this point, the snowpack had been so heavy that it provided a stage for one of the great railroad dramas of the twentieth century.

On January 13, 1952, snow had been falling steadily on the Sierra for four days and four nights. That morning, at a point a few miles west of the summit, the Southern Pacific's westbound *City of San Francisco*, carrying 226 passengers plus crew, plowed through a raging blizzard into a snowdrift between six and twelve feet deep, and locked fast. The SP dispatched rescue engines and rotary plows from both ends, but they too became snowbound. One engineer died when his rotary derailed, crushing him.

Meantime, the wind, raging at eighty to ninety miles per hour, blew solid sheets of snow onto the line. By the morning of the fourteenth both No. 1 and No. 2 tracks were so snow-choked that nothing could get through. U.S. 40, the only highway over the summit, had been closed earlier in the month after an avalanche had buried a truck and trailer near Donner Summit, and it would remain closed until early February. Now the national press focused in grisly fashion on the streamliner snowbound near the spot where, a little more than a century before, members of the Donner Party had consumed each other in despair.

Late on the fourteenth, the U.S. Army sent Weasels, World War II–era tracked snow vehicles, to the rescue, but they sank uselessly in the wet snow. On the morning of the fifteenth, a Pacific Gas & Electric Sno-Cat rendezvoused with a doctor and a dogsled team brought to the summit from Truckee aboard a rescue train, and struggled with its load up the steep hillside to the snowbound *City of San Francisco*. The little vehicle, however, was useless for evacuating 226 people. Later in the day a Coast Guard helicopter used a break in the storm to drop medicine, food and supplies.

On the morning of the sixteenth, fuel had run out. Cold seeped aboard the train, freezing toilets and rupturing pipes. But the storm had ended, the sun had emerged, and highway crews managed to dig a path from a lodge in Emigrant Gap a few miles east to a point on the road just below the stranded train. There rescuers helped the passengers, wrapped in blankets, down to the highway and into waiting automobiles. Not one perished.

Not for three more days was the empty streamliner finally pulled from the drifts, and not until January 27 was The Hill once again open for normal operations.

A few miles farther west, Number 5 slid across Emigrant Gap above the interstate highway uncoiling through the Ponderosa pines on a long tangent below, passed the old mining community of Blue Canon and wound slowly along the cliffs high above the spectacular canyon of the North Fork of the American River. Here and there bare ground peeked through the unusually shallow snowpack. Even here, in this ineffably beautiful place, the traveler can't

escape evidence of the many woes of modern-day California, woes
that have turned the state into a shell of its former promise as the
grail of the westering instinct, the culmination of the American
dream.

California's cities are built on sites so arid that water for them
must be piped in from far away—from out of state as well as from
the Sierra. The year 1992 was the sixth of the most recent drought.
Near its end, the water levels of the state's 155 reservoirs stood at
near-record lows—56 percent of average. The state, however, was
spared a nearly unprecedented seventh year of drought by the
above-average snowfall (175 percent of normal) that fell on the
Sierra during the winter of 1992–93. To be sure, the mountains
may need a few more such winters before the state's water tables
and reservoir levels return to their previous marks, and the end of
water rationing does not mean the end of water conservation.
Droughts do not disappear that easily.

Nor do their side-effects. So dry was the land around Oakland,
for instance, that the place had turned into a tinderbox by 1991,
setting the stage for the ruinous fire on October 20 of that year
which killed twenty-five people and destroyed 2,500 dwellings
valued at $1.5 billion. (I happened to be aboard the *California
Zephyr* that day, and as the train descended the western slope of the
Sierra, I thought the black pall in the sky air pollution from the San
Francisco Bay area. Not until that evening, when I sat in a Chinese
restaurant in Sacramento watching live television coverage of the
disaster, did I learn the reason for the smoke. The next day, fine
ash and soot spotted the roofs and windows of the *Zephyr* returning
to Chicago.)

When rain or snow does come, the soil is so parched that as
much as 10 percent of any moisture simply soaks into the ground
before it runs off into rivers. Rain often comes in such abundance
that the dry ground just cannot handle it. In many places, such as
San Diego County in southern California and Marin County north
of San Francisco, the soil is so unstable that heavy rains sometimes
trigger mud slides that destroy entire residential areas and carry
away highways.

Drought, however, is not the only natural peril that threatens California. Think of the inherent geological instability of a state built along one of the world's great earthquake zones. The 1991 Oakland fire came along almost two years to the day after the October 17, 1989, quake that killed sixty-two people—forty-two of them in the collapse of a section of Interstate 880 in Oakland—and caused an estimated $7 billion in damage. Though the quake was the worst in forty years, it likely was merely a precursor to the "Big One" seismologists think will strike the San Andreas Fault during the next quarter century.

If natural disasters were not enough, there's the human tendency to cock things up economically. The deepening national recession of the early nineties struck California hard, sending its perennially prosperous economy into free fall with deep cutbacks in defense spending, a collapsed commercial real estate market, plummeting home prices and a crippled construction industry. It was the worst fiscal crisis in the state since the Great Depression. A quarter of the state's banks lost money. Unemployment nudged 10 percent. Los Angeles teachers ate a 10 percent pay cut. Others elsewhere were laid off in droves. School libraries everywhere closed. The state's vaunted university system eliminated courses, raised fees and trimmed admissions. All these things, plus a huge influx of immigrants—many of them illegals from Mexico—who competed for jobs with less affluent members of the black community as well as for expensive social services that shrank as the state's tax base took large hits—contributed to the deadly Los Angeles riots of April 1992.

For many Californians, most of them middle-class and white, the nineteenth century's "Go West, young man" turned into "Get out while the getting's good." As the nineties wore on, more Americans were moving out of the state than moving in, heading for Oregon, Colorado, Idaho, Nevada, Texas, Washington and Arizona. It's true that the state's population of 31 million was still growing overall, but this was primarily because of the high birth rates of low-income Californians and foreign immigration, mostly

Hispanics and Asians. A large number of well-educated and skilled Americans in their prime working years, between thirty and forty-four years old, formed the cutting edge of the exodus.

Is the California dream at last ending? Is "Every man for himself" going to become the watchword in what once was called the Golden State?

In a few minutes the *Zephyr* passed the little town of Gold Run, all that remains of an enormous hydraulic mining site, culmination of still another historical drama—the period in American history popularly called the Gold Rush. Farther down the American River, in January 1848, while helping build a sawmill for a settler named Johann Augustus Sutter, a sawyer named John Marshall saw flecks of gold in the watery gravel of the millrace. Within weeks thousands of hopeful miners had flooded the place, standing with gold pans hip to hip in the river. By the end of 1849 more than 50,000 fortune seekers had arrived, and by 1855 some 120,000 congested the crags and valleys of the Sierra. While the majority were Americans, forty-niners also came from Europe, Australia, China and Latin America. Not all were prospectors; many were merchants and bankers, among them men named Huntington, Crocker, Stanford and Hopkins.

In the 1850s panning and digging no longer sufficed. To get at the gold in the rubble of fossil rivers, miners sought to dismantle whole mountains, and the best way to do so was to wash them away with high-pressure jets of water. Miners dammed streams in the high country, then brought down the water thousands of feet in flumes. So strong was the pressure of gravity that the water emerged from eight-foot-long hose nozzles called "monitors" at 120 miles per hour. With such artillery the miners bombarded the Sierra, eating away 130 billion cubic yards of mountains.

As the mine tailings washed downstream, they strangled streams and valleys. The Sacramento River, into which the American River empties, rose seven feet from its original sea-level elevation. Near San Francisco, mud clogged the Carquinez Strait between San

Pablo and Suisun Bays, hampering navigation. The Golden Gate ran brown with silt. Finally, in 1884, nascent conservationists succeeded in outlawing hydraulic mining.

For decades great swaths of the Sierra looked like moonscapes, its hillsides denuded of trees and its valleys choked with gravel and debris. Today a century of healing has largely softened the damage, and for most of the *California Zephyr*'s run over the Sierra only a sharp and knowledgeable eye can perceive its remnants. Except for a few hollows still choked with gravel and odd pools of water—all that remains of an entire hill—I saw little as I looked out through the windows of the cab onto the snowy landscape of Gold Run. Trees and brush had healed many of the scars, and a thin dressing of snow covered the rest.

Not fifteen minutes after departing Gold Run, Number 5 passed Cape Horn, the steepest slope on the train's route. The nineteenth-century newspaperman Frank Leslie described it aptly:

> Now comes Cape Horn, the jutting promontory that frowns at the head of the great American River Canyon. The train swings round on a dizzily narrow grade, with a wall of rock towering above and the almost vertical side of the abyss sweeping down to the narrow bed of the river. Between its walls there seems just space enough for the narrow stream to slide and no more—not a trail wide enough for a jackrabbit on either side.

Here, more than a century ago, Central Pacific construction crews lowered Chinese laborers in baskets from the summit of the ridge to hack a narrow ledge from the nearly sheer rock walls, a ledge other crews widened with pick and blasting powder until trains could navigate its narrow confines. Just across the American River Valley the little town of Colfax is visible, and in a few moments the train rumbled across Long Ravine Trestle on its outskirts.

Just before 1:00 P.M., with a "tooooooooot-tooooooooot-toot-tooooooooot," Number 5 rolled across a state highway into Colfax (Mile 2,278), the first sizable town on the west slope of the Sierra.

An old mining village that is now a shipping point for Tokay grapes, Hungarian prunes and Bartlett pears, Colfax used to be called Illinoistown. Not long after the Central Pacific's rails reached the place, the railroad's officials renamed it for Schuyler Colfax, Speaker of the House and Ulysses S. Grant's vice president. A scoundrel as famously greedy in his day as Michael Milken is in ours, Colfax taught the Central Pacific's owners the finer points of fleecing the government. One was the ploy of hiring yourself to build the railroad, then using federal money to meet your own inflated payrolls. So blatantly crooked was Colfax that Grant, whose administration became infamous for its tolerance of roguery, dumped him from his reelection ticket in 1872. Stanford, Crocker, Hopkins and Huntington, however, became millionaires.

Shortly after the train stopped, an assistant conductor ran up to the locomotive, bearing a large cardboard box. "Compliments of the chef," he said, handing up his burden to Ray. Opening the box, Ray grinned appreciatively. Inside lay plastic bowls of soup, crackers, cardboard containers of apple juice and two huge plastic platters of cut vegetables and lettuce—railroad crudités. "What do they think, we're a bunch of rabbits?" Chris said in mock complaint. The largesse was an agreeable gesture, and the enginemen appreciated it. Most service crews, Chris declared, don't give a hoot about the engineers, who sit up front out of sight and out of mind. And the Amtrak regulations declare that no free food, except coffee, is to be sent to the cab. If management finds out, Chris said, it'll try to make the chef pay.

Later I asked John Davis about the practice of feeding the locomotive crew. He does take care of his friends on the operating crew, as do many other chefs. "We won't send up steaks or hamburgers or fish or other revenue items," he said. "But why waste leftover soup and salad? It'll just be thrown out at the end of the run in Oakland." He shrugged, as if to say that sometimes those Amtrak bureaucrats in Washington just don't get it.

The stop at Colfax was brief, and once again Ray cracked the throttle. Slowly and steadily the grade lessened—the western slope of the Sierra is as gentle as the eastern face is sheer—and half an hour later Number 5 whispered through Auburn, another old Gold Rush town just north of Sutter's Mill. Once a sleepy little forty-niner village, it's rapidly becoming a thriving bedroom suburb for commuters to Sacramento, as evidenced by the many new houses—some of them palatial—nestled into the hills. Here mountainous terrain is exchanged for golden ranchlands and a taste of sunny California.

A few minutes later Ray pointed out a large dinosaur fossil in a rock outcropping over the tracks as we swept by, and not much farther down we traversed Bloomer Cut, that eighty-five-foot-high, 800-foot-long slash that had so slowed the builders of the Central Pacific. Ray reached into his satchel and pulled out a book—an oversized, illustrated railfan's volume called *Donner Pass: Southern Pacific's Sierra Crossing* by John Signor—riffled to a page and showed me a photo of the cut. A tiny teakettle-stacked locomotive of approximately 1880 vintage stood at the bottom of the cut, which appeared exactly as it does more than a century later. This is truly construction for the ages.

I shot Ray a sharp look. This is a grizzled professional railroader who, like so many of his confrères, claims not to care for railfans— yet not only carries blatant evidence to the contrary, but also bends over backward to accommodate a rail-buff writer. He gazed out the window innocently.

Scarcely three miles west of Bloomer Cut, at Penryn, is the true dividing line between the Sierra range and the great Central Valley of California. Officially, however, the Sierra begins fifteen miles farther west, in the flatlands six miles northeast of Sacramento at the present-day junction of Interstates 80 and 880. Why? The chicanery of the founders of the Central Pacific, who managed to move the mountains, at least on paper. The Pacific Railroad Act had appropriated $16,000 for each mile of railroad constructed on the flatlands and $48,000 for each mile in the mountains. The Big Four's engine in this ascent was Professor J. D. Whitney, for whom Mount Whitney is named, and who surveyed the rocks at nearby Arcade Creek, then announced they were the same color as those in the Sierra. Q.E.D., here is where the Sierra begins. This fraudulent announcement brought an extra half-million dollars into the coffers of the Central Pacific.

Just before 2:00 P.M. Number 5 rolled past the huge Southern Pacific classification yards and engine shops in Roseville, where hundreds of faded, muddy and rusty-looking SP and Rio Grande locomotives squatted forlornly on tracks awaiting repairs. ("This looks like the East German railroad!" my Dutch acquaintance from Leiden had said.) Why doesn't the SP paint its locomotives when overhauling them? I asked Chris. "It doesn't have the money," he replied, "and besides the locomotives have to go through so many tunnels the heat is going to blacken and fade the paint in just a few trips."

As Number 5 passed McClellan Air Force Base at sixty miles per hour, I glimpsed three boxcars inside the base boundary fence. They were stenciled "UNITED STATES AIR FORCE." "The Air Force is in the *railroad* business?" I said incredulously. "Yes," replied Chris, "but they never leave the base—they're just switched around in there."

At 3:00 P.M. Number 5 called at Sacramento (Mile 2,331), site of the California State Railroad Museum, perhaps the nation's prettiest. It is the home of a grand black monster, a restored Southern Pacific cab-forward locomotive with four pilot wheels, sixteen huge driving wheels, and two trailing wheels. The 4-8-8-2's enginemen sat in a little cabin up above the pilot truck in front of the boiler. The arrangement allowed the crew to ride through the long Sierra tunnels well ahead of the choking black oil smoke from the engine's enormous firebox. At the museum on just about any day, a tall, stooped, white-haired docent in his eighties, dressed in classic engineer's overalls, cap and red bandanna, stands before the locomotive. To children, small and large, he spins first-person yarns of life in the cab-forwards going Over The Hill almost half a century before. The presence of the locomotive and its veteran engineer almost makes up for next-door Old Sacramento, next to Fisherman's Wharf in San Francisco the gaudiest, sleaziest tourist trap west of the Black Hills of South Dakota.

As we crossed the Sacramento River I spied a preserved red-silver-and-gold set of Santa Fe F7 diesel locomotives on the museum grounds. A wave of nostalgia passed over me, for those F7s were just like the ones that pulled the Lionel toy trains of my boyhood. I had little time to reflect on them, however, as we sped across miles of flooded rice paddies toward our next stop at the university town of Davis (Mile 2,334). Its handsome pink Spanish-motif Southern Pacific station, surrounded by palms, announces the nearby presence of Southern California.

"Baa!" Just out of Davis, conductor Pimm saluted Ray over the radio as Number 5 passed a herd of sheep, referring to Ray's old career as a sheep-raiser. "Baa!" Ray replied dutifully, acknowledging the message with a smile I can only describe as sheepish.

For the next twenty minutes the *California Zephyr* sped at seventy miles per hour across the great ricelands and sugar beet farms of the Central Valley, the astonishingly flat plain, fifty miles wide and four hundred miles long, that lies between the Sierra and the Coast Range. I spotted high on the ceiling of the F40 cab a crude drawing of a man's head that looked like a water pail. "Buckethead" was the legend underneath. It reminded me that in boarding at Lovelock, I had seen the same graffito on the flank of the locomotive underneath the engineer's window. "What's that all about?" I asked Ray.

Out of Oakland, Ray replied, runs a large-skulled Southern Pacific engineer named Burkett, whom everyone calls "Buckethead." ("I call him that to his face," Ray said. "Gets under his skin.") To make fun of Burkett, another engineer covers locomotives with Buckethead drawings in indelible pen. "I once found sixteen Bucketheads in one locomotive," Ray said.

The practice echoes one from the past. Railroaders and hoboes once etched their Kilroys, some of them famously elaborate and distinctive, on locomotives and boxcars. They used chalk, however, not the indelible marker of our less considerate age.

Just before the brief stop at Suisun-Fairfield (Mile 2,371), someone threw a rock at the engine. Instinctively I ducked, though the engineers were unperturbed. "The cab windows are bulletproof," said Chris, as if reading my mind. "They'll stop .22 slugs or any stones kids can throw."

Ten minutes later, crossing the Suisun Marsh, Number 5 passed the National Defense Reserve Fleet—also called the Mothball Fleet—in Suisun Bay, where sixty-six moldering World War II Victory cargo ships huddle in storage along the shoreline. Viewed as technological wonders when they were built between 1942 and 1945, they are now considered old, slow and inefficient to load and unload. They have been earmarked for the scrap heap, as is perhaps the *Glomar Challenger,* the old spy vessel moored close by the railroad drawbridge across Carquinez Strait.

After thundering across the bridge, Number 5 passed old ferry slips and derelict canneries, forests of burned pilings sticking out from the water like bristles on an old brush, as well as an entangled maze of refineries. This is industrial California, and just beyond the strait is the port of Martinez (Mile 2,387), home of John Muir and birthplace of Joe DiMaggio.

At Crockett we passed through, and under, the California & Hawaii refinery, the last sugar cane processing plant in the continental United States. Bearing south along the shore of San Pablo Bay, birds pecking in the mud flats at low tide, we reached the next-to-last stop, Richmond (Mile 2,407), at 4:20 P.M., just fifteen minutes late.

I looked back through the rearview mirror just as conductor Pimm alighted from a coach directly in front of the station. He had been doing that at every stop since Lovelock, stepping down at the perfect spot. "How do you know where to stop the locomotives?" I asked Ray. "I don't know—I just do," he said, shrugging. Actually, Chris replied, long experience and knowing the length of his train tells him.

Just after departing Richmond, Number 5 passed along San Francisco Bay proper, offering a dramatic view of Alcatraz Island, the Golden Gate Bridge and the San Francisco skyline, their outlines limned brilliantly by the setting sun behind.

As Number 5 coasted past Berkeley and began to slow, I asked Ray for one more look at the Signor book, and he fished it from his satchel. Chris gazed askance, eyebrow lifted, at Ray as he handed me the book. "Foamer, eh?" Chris said. "Aaaah," replied Ray, "if I'm a foamer, you're a *certified* foamer!" "Certified?" Chris said. "You're *registered!* You own ten railroad videos—I've seen them!" Both grinned widely at each other across the locomotive cab.

TWELVE

At 4:45 P.M.—fifteen minutes ahead of schedule, thanks to an extra forty-two minutes of padding between the final two stops—the *California Zephyr* crept into Oakland (Mile 2,416), and tied up at the ramshackle former Southern Pacific station at 16th and Wood Streets. The place does not make an auspicious end to a grand transcontinental railroad journey. For one thing, the station lies spang in the middle of Oakland's notorious high-crime district. For another, it was severely damaged in the 1989 earthquake, has been condemned and is to be torn down for the rebuilt Interstate 880, which as a double-decker collapsed in the quake, trapping and killing scores of motorists.

"There is no there there," native daughter Gertrude Stein once wrote about Oakland, but that is as unfair a calumny as has ever been laid upon a hapless city. I have stopped in Oakland several times, and although its dark national reputation as a hotbed of poverty, street crime and drugs is partly deserved, many parts of the city are surprisingly attractive. The people, too. Oakland is not, as many Americans think, a hostile black town to be avoided. Although African Americans are its largest component, there also are Greeks, Portuguese, Italians, Mexicans, Vietnamese, Lebanese, Koreans and Chinese. And mongrel Irish-German-French-English-Americans. The city's downtown area snapped out of the doldrums of crime and neglect in the 1980s. Its port inhales and exhales goods from and to the Pacific Rim. It is full of working factories. Its transportation is first-rate—it hosts the Bay Area Rapid Transit as well as Amtrak, and owns an excellent airport.

And Oakland is home to a rail buff named Robert Nicol. He is an architect in his mid-fifties, and I spoke with him one morning between *Zephyr*s. The scene was his offices in an old building in downtown Oakland, where he has title to an entire floor, but rents out most of the structure to other tenants. He once was part owner of a large architectural firm, designing $20 million office buildings and apartment blocks, but, tiring of the administrative duties, sold his interest and now operates on his own. He calls himself a "family architect," explaining, "I take on the little stuff big architects don't want to bother with, such as quality home additions, remodeling and historical restoration."

A balding man of medium height with a graying brush mustache, Nicol is richly humorous, with a quiet laugh and wry wit. He clearly is a railfan of epic proportions. His architectural awards— he is a Fellow of the American Institute of Architects—cover one wall of his sunny office, but the others are devoted to large glass-fronted display cases containing scores of HO scale brass steam locomotives six to eleven inches long. "I've got six hundred fifty of them, representing the steam era from 1890 to the 1930s and early forties," he said proudly, leading me over to a case and pointing out a Shay geared locomotive, so diminutive that I had to remove my spectacles for a close-in appreciation of its delicate detail. These tiny, exquisitely crafted models are not a costly obsession but a shrewd investment. Good brass models appreciate in value steadily, and since Bob began his collection twenty years ago, its value has climbed well into six figures. Not all Bob's models are on display; he simply ran out of room, and has locked the others in storage elsewhere.

He doesn't keep them at home because his wife, Susann, wouldn't appreciate walls and walls of brass clutter, but she is something of a rail buff herself. She collects dining-car china, mostly from the old Great Northern Railway, and it is arranged in shadow boxes around the upper walls of the kitchen in their Alameda home, which once belonged to a cousin of Jack London. The place is like every other architect's home I have seen—in a perpetual state of restoration or remodeling.

Bob's railfan roots were driven early in Helena, Montana, where at age six he rode around the turntable—"It was like a merry-go-round"—on an 0-6-0 steam switcher in the Northern Pacific yards, thanks to the prominence of his grandfather, a state senator. As an adult he became both a model railroader and historical architecture buff, creator of the Alameda Victorian Preservation Society as well as a longtime charter member of the City of Alameda Historical Advisory Commission. In the early 1980s he merged his two passions into an enterprise that still takes up one day of his time each week. In 1988 he and his "gypsy model railroad club"—so-called because it moved from hobby shop to hobby shop—decided to seek permanent quarters. They found an old Southern Pacific passenger depot in neighboring San Leandro. Built in 1898, it served passengers until the mid-1960s and had last been used as an insurance claims office.

"The Southern Pacific told us, 'You can buy it for five dollars, but you've got to get it out of here,' " Bob said. Six months later the group found a suitable piece of land, a plot two blocks away from the old site. San Leandro gave them a twenty-year lease at one dollar per year, but the club had to come up with a $75,000 surety; if the members lost interest, the city didn't want a dilapidated white elephant on its hands. It took the club—now renamed the San Leandro Historical Railway Society, a tax-exempt nonprofit group—six months to raise the money for that and for the move. "We knocked on doors, and we also had a couple of wealthy members," Bob said.

When the time came to shift the building, he added, "We had to move it over an active railroad track, and we were nervous that something might go wrong with the operation while the building was still on the track." He didn't need to sketch a mental picture of what would happen if a fast freight came through. So one Sunday, during a time of little rail traffic—between 5:00 and 7:00 A.M.—the club gingerly, inch by painful inch, jacked up the station onto three building mover's dollies and trundled it across the tracks to its new home.

The club had not yet poured a new foundation, because before moving the depot the members had no idea of the condition of its underpinnings. The building had been constructed right on the ground, without a foundation, with asphalt paving butted up to the building's edge. "There was no way to look underneath," Bob said. "As it turned out, the floor joists were OK, though the ends had rotted out."

When Bob and I drove down from Oakland to see the station, much had been done, and much remained to be done. The group had won tax-exempt status because it was now a historical society, with part of the building—the waiting room—slowly being converted into a museum hosting artifacts from old Southern Pacific depots, junkyards and attics all over the Bay Area, reflecting the railroad's history. In various stages of disrepair an old baggage wagon, a Pullman conductor's uniform, several telegraph machines, even a double semaphore signal littered the office. Inside the old dispatcher's office stood the semaphore levers. Eventually the blades and electric signals of the semaphore will stand outside the station. "We'll signal red when the museum's closed, yellow when it's open to members only, green when it's open to the public."

The station is built entirely of long-lasting first-growth redwood, a beautiful, evenly colored lumber (second-growth redwood common today contains sap streaks, thanks to the small diameter of the logs). Scores of coats of paint had covered the inside walls. Rather than laboriously strip each coat—a messy, thankless and even toxic job—the club pulled the planks from the walls, ran them through Bob's electric planer and removed $\frac{1}{16}$ of an inch of wood from the inside, or rough side. The club then reinstalled the planks backward, with the painted side in and the newly planed inside out. The warm natural red color of the wood enhances the California authenticity of the place.

"We're looking for an old caboose or heavyweight passenger car to put behind the station for use as a meeting room," Bob said. "We're particular about the era the car comes from—the twenties or thirties. They're hard to find."

The pièce de résistance, Bob said, is going to be an elaborate model railroad, a HO scale re-creation of the SP line during the 1930s from Oakland over The Hill to Truckee. John Armstrong, "the Frank Lloyd Wright of layouts," who is now about eighty years old and a famous figure in model railroading, designed the empire. It eventually will occupy three separate levels, with corkscrew loops of track raising trains from one level to another behind a plaster mountain. Catwalks will enable spectators to see each level. The whole will be controlled by "engineers" operating the trains from inside a three-quarter-sized mockup of an SP cab-forward locomotive cab, the framing for which already was partly in place.

"It'll never be finished," said Bob, who is at the station every Saturday from seven-thirty in the morning to two in the afternoon. "It may look finished to the spectators, but there'll always be something to be done." Part of the joy of such a project is the labor that provides continuity to a mission.

Bob is no stranger to restoring railroad depots. The city of Livermore and the new owner commissioned him to restore the Livermore SP station in 1988. "They wanted to restore the station to exactly how it looked when it was built, including its original colors. To discover what they were, we hired a historian from the California Rail Museum at Sacramento to analyze the multiple coats of paint. He found the original pigments. The station had originally been painted olive drab, showing that it went back to the Central Pacific era," Bob said. The station's owners decided, however, to use Southern Pacific yellow and brown because of local feelings for the SP. "Politics is always involved in these restorations," Bob said with a sigh.

Bob knows Californians of his economic class are leaving in droves, but, like those stubborn farmers on the Great Plains, he refuses to follow. His roots are both deep and widespread. He's a native of La Jolla and a Berkeley graduate. His office is conveniently located in downtown Oakland, the BART subway and the freeway close by. And he is putting both money and sweat into restoring his home. "California has been good to me," he says simply.

He has licenses to practice architecture in Montana, Arizona, or Washington, but the goodwill he has built up as a California architect is not to be lightly dismissed. He does not advertise his services, relying on word of mouth to sell his reputation. Even during the recession, he has not lacked for work; the normal six-month backlog of commissions merely shrank to six weeks. Some of it is designing new houses to replace the old ones destroyed in the 1991 Oakland fire. "It's a moonscape up there still," he said.

Of the victims of that fire, he observed, "One-third will rebuild, one-third will sit back and wait, and one-third will leave." As for himself, "someday, like everybody else, I'll retire. But I'm not the type to run away from the problems here."

The changes in California, he admitted, have affected some aspects of his life. He never used to secure doors, but now he locks everything. He sends his daughter to a private school, away from drugs and violence and academic cutbacks. All the same, he said, there are "no alarm signals telling me to get the hell out of here. I'll move only if and when the bullets start flying."

I have saved for last the most interesting aspect of Robert Nicol, at least from my point of view. This award-winning architect, influential civic leader, devoted historical preservationist and enthusiastic railfan was born deaf—totally deaf.

Tutored privately until third grade at home, where he received intensive speech therapy (he still takes it, mostly from his wife, who is hearing), he is an expert lip-reader and speaks clearly, with a slightly muffled enunciation typical of the long-term hearing-impaired, yet in a well-modulated voice most uncharacteristic of any deaf person. He is remarkably sensitive to music and plays the organ in his home; when he was a child, he said, his teacher made him set his front teeth on the upright key cover while she played, so that his body could be attuned to the vibrations. "It was like the Indians in the 1800s who put their teeth on the railroad tracks so they'd know when the buffalo were coming," he explained.

By and large, deaf people are isolated through no fault of their own from the hearing community, but Bob Nicol has chosen to live and work entirely in the hearing world. As I took my leave, I felt that if Californians like him remain, there is considerable hope for the state. He represents the lesser-known side of the contradictory frontier dream, that desire for roots as well as a yen for rootlessness, that yearning for a sense of community that transcends the self and joins Americans to each other. Bob Nicol keeps the faith, too.

And so does the city of Oakland. In rebuilding after the 1989 earthquake, its inhabitants seem to possess all the never-say-die spirit of Chicagoans after the Great Fire of 1871. On a foot trip through the downtown business section, Bob had pointed out great fissures in masonry walls, external evidence of internal damage that had caused the local authorities to close building after building in block after block. "Condemned," he said time and again. "Condemned."

Yet everywhere workmen scrambled over scaffolds, bolting together handsome old structures that had been on the verge of collapse. You *can* put Humpty Dumpty back together again, the city seemed to say. If to some outlanders those who remain in the quake-prone Bay Area are living in a state of deep denial, they also are displaying the same steadfastness, the same faith in themselves as had those obstinate plainsmen back in Nebraska and Iowa. Maybe they are only grasping the tattered remnants of the frontier impulse. Call them fools or call them farsighted, theirs is a noble tenacity. If they and their neighbors in San Francisco could build upon the disaster of 1906, so can they overcome that of 1989, and, in perhaps infinite progression, so can their children and their children's children.

They are building two new railroad stations to replace the old one—a $13.5 million terminal in Oakland's flossy Jack London Square on the bay, and a smaller six-million-dollar structure in neighboring Emeryville. Not only will the *Zephyr* call at these stations, but also the *Coast Starlight*, the *San Joaquin* to Bakersfield and the new *Capitol*—the Sacramento–to–San Jose speedster that began service in late 1991 with six trains each day, and surprised even the rail industry with its quick acceptance by Californians sick of contending with jammed freeways.

As it opened California a century and a half ago, the railroad could well lead the resurgence of the California Dream. New trains came to the Los Angeles metropolitan area beginning in 1992, too, as a brand-new commuter network was born. Like the passenger train, California is a resilient creature. Its past prosperity has given it a cushion. Its infrastructure—highways, bridges, railroads—is in far better shape than that of the East. Its balmy climate will not change. Its suburban "edge cities" are thriving. It sits on the verge of the Pacific Rim, likely to be the world's market basket for the next century. And the immigrants? Immigration built California and may yet save it.

Making reluctant and lingering farewells to Ray and Chris, I climbed down from the cab and patted the F40 on its dusty flank. Ray and Chris leaned out the window and waved, Chris with a wigwag and Ray with his one-fingered salute. Tomorrow Chris would return to the extra board to be called when needed, while Ray would run the Amtrak switcher in the yards. The next day Ray would drive Number 6 back over The Hill to Lovelock on one more round trip, then take the weekend off with his wife and grandchildren in Alameda.

But my trip had not ended; I still had to say good-bye to the crew and get across the bay to San Francisco.

I joined the throng flooding past the cars to the parking lot, where a bus waited. Very few of the passengers looked familiar; since Lovelock early that morning, the manifest had nearly turned over completely, most of it at Reno and Sacramento. A good number of riders had debarked at Richmond, some of the savvier veterans catching a fast Bay Area Rapid Transit subway for San Francisco, others taking BART to points on the bay south of Oakland.

I looked for Jackie Park, the novelist, but she already had disappeared, presumably met by Random House's San Francisco publicist. Nor could I find Mildred McCaskey, the elderly alcoholic who had given Don Cushine such a rough ride during that first hour out of Chicago. I hoped her "rich baby daughter" had picked her up and taken her home. I didn't envy the daughter.

Down the platform a few familiar passengers struggled with their baggage—the gazelle-like Air Force noncom, for one. She had changed her skintight catsuit for shapeless fatigues before hopping into a taxi, duffel on her shoulder. The young man in the green Mohawk, its spikes sadly blunted and askew after three days on the train, peered about bleary-eyed, his censored T-shirt now right side out and proclaiming the mood that undoubtedly enveloped him. The beautiful Québecoise and a black-capped chauffeur wheeled her crippled husband to a long white limousine—no doubt armor-plated, as befitted a drug lord, even an imaginary one. Then I saw the numbers on the rear bumper; it was a rental livery, the kind you can hire at any big-city airport.

Bob Heath waved from the doorway of his sleeper as I strode by. "What're your plans tonight?" I asked.

"It's a good crew," he replied, knotting the top of a linen duffle. "There are good crews and bad. Some people you don't want to see away from the train. Good ones, they're your family. So we'll all get together tonight for a couple of cocktails, some dinner, a little dancing at a nightclub maybe. And by and by we'll look at our watches and say, 'Well, we've got to get up early,' and go back to our hotel and turn in. We've got to be back in the yards at eight A.M. tomorrow to get ready to take Number Six back to Chicago."

Lela Janushkowsky and Reggie Howard stood head to head by

the lounge car, bidding smiling good-byes to two elderly ladies, regular passengers on the *Zephyr* by the look of the scene. Both Lela and Reggie would ride the train into the yards and call at the crew base, where they'd settle their accounts. The crew stays at a hotel near Jack London Square, while Reggie, a member of management, overnights alone at a slightly more upscale hostelry.

"I hope I don't come out by more than twenty dollars off this time," said Lela, whose accounts have been askew by as much as $175 on one trip. Riding herd on meal checks in a busy seventy-two-seat diner is difficult, and she has to make up any discrepancies with her own funds. Once she has signed the accounts in the commissary, she'll catch a late train back to her home in Sacramento. Another steward will go out with the Chicago-based crew on Number 6 tomorrow.

John Davis was headed for the yards, too, to turn in unused supplies. Because he had to return to the train very early the next morning to replenish its provender before the 10:20 A.M. departure for Chicago, he'd call it a night well before the others. As I passed the diner, he stuck out his hand from the doorway. "When're you coming to eat with me again?" he asked. "Soon, soon, I hope!" I replied, and I meant it.

The last San Francisco–bound passengers were threading aboard the bus, and I broke into a run, not wanting to be stranded. As I stepped aboard, the driver pulled the door shut behind me. Just as the bus pulled out, Ray yanked the whistle cord twice, and the *California Zephyr* slid slowly out of the station toward the yards. "So long, Number Five," I whispered to myself, as if the train were a living beast.

During the first nine years of its career, the original *California Zephyr* tied up in the long, dark train shed of the Southern Pacific Mole, the ferry terminal both the SP and the Western Pacific had been using as a transfer point for their transcontinental rail passengers. There the *Zephyr*'s passengers boarded ferries for San Francisco. In 1958 the last passenger trains departed the Mole, by then more than eighty years old and crumbling, and riders had to take buses from the Western Pacific's Middle Harbor Road yard for the ten-minute journey across the Bay Bridge between Oakland and San Francisco.

This evening the bus ride was hardly onerous, even though it's a pain to switch from the roomy Amtrak reclining seats to motor coach chairs, packed as tightly together as those on a short-hop DC-9. The ride across the bay, however, is brief, and by daylight Yerba Buena Island and the shipyards to the south offer diverting sights. Today a flotilla of destroyers and frigates approached the bridge from the north while a couple of supertankers slid under it from the south.

As the bus plunged out of the tunnel through Yerba Buena Island, the skyline of San Francisco spread out before us, its lights beginning to wink on as the sun dipped toward the horizon behind. So far as the railroad is concerned, San Francisco is a cul-de-sac, almost an afterthought. Long-distance passenger trains do not call there; even the Los Angeles–to–Seattle *Coast Starlight* stops nine miles to the southeast at San Jose, where passengers for Nob Hill must switch to a Caltrain commuter local.

The glory of San Francisco, once the jewel in California's crown, is fading. The port is moribund and factories have disappeared. The financial movers and shakers long ago left for Los Angeles, and most of the great ships from the Pacific Rim call across the bay at Oakland and Martinez. Tourism is now the city's biggest industry. And behind the sleaze of Fisherman's Wharf and the glitter of Ghirardelli Square, its slums ring with the cries of the unemployed and the homeless, drug addicts and persons with AIDS. Even in the better neighborhoods environmentalists war with small businessmen and supercilious gay waiters exchange hostilities with homophobic Middle Americans. Added to this multicultural urban angst, weird cults, bizarre fads and unconventional, wide-open sexuality spook conservative tourists.

Liberal ones, too. Once, at a time when I did not know San Francisco well, my elder son—then a college senior—and I spent a night in a budget hotel whose name I had plucked blindly from the *Mobil Travel Guide*. Most of the other guests seemed to be economy-minded young adults, a step up in age from the backpack crowd. The place was small, clean and shabby-genteel, in a neighborhood within walking distance of downtown. It had functional although ancient plumbing, and the twin beds bore both new mattresses and new coverlets. The aroma of fresh oil-based paint from the woodwork in the hall did linger in our room, but all in all, it seemed a bargain for the low nightly price.

On the way there, however, the cabbie had offered a few words of warning, and that should have tipped me off. "Don't walk the streets at night around here," he had said, "and keep your hands on your wallets."

My son and I, however, had not ridden into town on a turnip truck. I'm a big-city newspaperman and he was a student at a college in an Eastern slum neighborhood. We were familiar with the rudiments of urban survival, and when we set out in search of a cold beer late in the afternoon, the sun was still bright.

Almost immediately misgivings overtook me. Scarcely had we walked half a block when we passed a pimply-faced young man in black leather jacket, engineer boots and long silver chains lounging against a parked car. As he made eye contact, he boldly thrust forward his pelvis. As we walked by he said nothing, and we responded in kind. A few feet beyond, a grubby old man urinated into an alley, and a shapeless middle-aged woman in a torn housedress scurried across our path, twitching and gibbering to herself.

Then two young women of unmistakable profession ankled by in tight knit tube dresses whose upper as well as lower hems skirted the bounds of propriety, even for San Francisco. "Hiiiiii," said the pair in unison. "In town for a good time?" I smiled, shook my head, and propelled my son past on the sidewalk.

"How does it feel to be accosted by hookers?" I asked him a few moments later.

"Dad, those weren't prostitutes!" he replied, in astonishingly innocent tones. "They were just being *friendly*."

I took a deep and surprised breath. For a sophisticated Eastern almost-college-graduate, I thought, my son displayed great gaps in his education. And so, I learned later that day, did I. That evening, an old friend, a San Francisco transplant from Chicago, picked us up at the hotel for dinner. As we climbed into her car, she said in a horrified tone, "Do you have any *idea* where you're staying? This is the *Tenderloin!*"

If in its squalor San Francisco is world-class, so, however, are its auras of nineteenth-century romance and of timeless endurance. With New York, London and Paris it remains one of the most cosmopolitan cities on earth. Its residential areas are gorgeous, especially those near the Presidio, Seacliff and Lincoln Park. For all its warring special-interest groups, it is a tolerant and egalitarian place. The arts are thriving, and so is gastronomy; I have never eaten better seafood anywhere. The city's high dark hills, the Golden Gate Bridge, tendrils of fog at dawn and sunset, the forbidding rock of Alcatraz all may be hackneyed postcard fare—but they still thrill the eye.

The bus chugged into the scruffy Transbay Terminal in the center of the financial district. Two dozen passengers tumbled off, gathered their bags and disappeared into the evening.

A finger gently tapped my shoulder. I looked around and up into the smiling bearded face of Bob Locher, with whom I had plotted the perfect crime while rolling across Colorado just the day before. Our conversation seemed a long time ago, in a distant land.

"And where are you bound?" I asked.

"The Lost Coast," he said, "for a little exploring." About 170 miles north of San Francisco, California's coast-hugging Highway 1 loops inland for fifty miles, returning to the sea at Eureka. The mountainous area west of that loop, largely wilderness, is called the Lost Coast, and the small towns there are accessible only by narrow roads. "I'll take the bus up to Ukiah and rent a car there."

He thrust out a hand. "You've got my card. Be sure to get in touch so we can get to work on that mystery. Or I'll call you at your office."

With a wave Bob turned on his heel, then stopped and looked back. "When we get back home, come flying with me," he called.

Staring at his back as it receded into the gathering dusk, I suddenly was visited by a familiar sensation, one that washes over me after every long railroad journey. It is simply a pleasant weariness, warmly tinged by the traveler's agreeable expectation that although an adventure is ending, a new one soon will begin.

Hailing a taxi, I lit out for my hotel and a new Territory.

AUTHOR'S NOTE

More than thirty years ago, when I was an undergraduate at Trinity College in Connecticut, I heard a story about Sigmund Freud that has stayed in my memory all that time.

One day Dr. Freud was told a story about Franz Rosenzweig, a distinguished, massively gifted Talmudic scholar who lived in Frankfurt. Rosenzweig suffered from a degenerative disease that gradually paralyzed him. Yet he kept working on his essays, his translations and his correspondence, even when his malady sent him to his bed. Soon he could neither move nor speak. He simply lay still as death. The only muscles that would respond to his command were those of his eyes.

He and his wife discovered a way for him to keep working. They devised an alphabet of wooden blocks and arranged them at the foot of his bed. By following her husband's gaze over the blocks, Mrs. Rosenzweig could assemble his thoughts into words and sentences. It was a slow and laborious way to communicate, but the scheme worked. Though Rosenzweig's body was paralyzed, his mind was unaffected.

He even undertook a new translation of the Hebrew Bible in collaboration with his friend Martin Buber, and kept on writing witty essays and genial correspondence. The work was difficult and painstaking, and after almost every paragraph Rosenzweig would lie exhausted in a puddle of sweat. But in this fashion he kept on working until he died.

Freud's reaction to the story? With a shrug he said, "What else could he do?"

I was stunned. What an absurd reaction to such an inspiring story! Dr. Freud, I thought, must have been an extraordinarily cold man, examining other human beings from a glacial distance. All the same, that punch line remained in my mind: "*What else could he do?*"

When I conceived this book, I thought I could produce it in my usual independent fashion, the way I had always done as a journalist—without the intervention of hearing people, except for help with the occasional phone call. For a quarter of a century I had been almost obsessively proud of my ability to function autonomously as a deaf person in a fiercely competitive hearing world. And for the most part that wasn't inordinately difficult. The jobs of critic and editor—working with books and other people's words—didn't require much assistance. That ubiquitous journalist's tool, the cassette tape recorder, was all that I needed to help me conduct formal interviews of authors. Afterward, a transcript filled the voids left by the imperfect art of lip-reading.

Early in my travels on the *California Zephyr*, however, I discovered that I'd never be able to rely on lip-reading to gather the information necessary for a lively and thoughtful book. For example, urban black English is not easily understood by a lip-reader most comfortable in the white suburban speech patterns with which he grew up. Nor are foreign accents, New Yorkese, tight-lipped Western expressionlessness and a host of other visual Babels easy for me to deal with. On a train I would encounter them all, and more.

Slowly I realized that I would have to ask for help, by securing the services of an interpreter. Not the familiar sign-language translator one sees on the television screen, but an oral interpreter who speaks in a manner easy for lip-readers to understand. Not slowly and in exaggerated form, but deliberately, crisply enunciating every word, speaking from the lips instead of deep in the mouth and throat.

The idea depressed me. For half a century I had functioned utterly on my own. I had never leaned on anybody. Now I was surrendering to my deafness, admitting that I could not do alone what other journalists did. I was giving up my independence, my self-reliance, my pride.

But I kept remembering the last line of that story: "What else could he do?" Slowly I realized that Dr. Freud may not have been such a frosty fellow. In that tale, at any rate, he was simply being practical and hardheaded. When one is faced with a number of choices so limited that they can be counted on two fingers, taking the obvious course is hardly an act of valor.

And so, on most of the trips I took aboard the *California Zephyr* for this book, I brought along an interpreter.

I was pleasantly astonished. With somebody else to do the hearing for me, I discovered, gathering information of all kinds was much, much easier than straining to understand. And not just because of the interpreters' aid with people difficult for lip-readers to handle. Because I couldn't overhear what people were saying out of my line of sight, I had been missing a great deal. And think of the public-address announcements on the train, the radio messages in the locomotive. I had been unaware of background sound.

With someone else to be my ears, I missed nothing.

My interpreters were friends and family members who, for their labor, received a free all-expenses-paid train trip. They were not professional interpreters, who are much more accurate and sophisticated than amateurs. Professionals are trained not to inject themselves into exchanges between deaf and hearing, but to keep their personal feelings out of the interaction. They also must repeat every word as it is spoken; they must not take the easier route of a watered-down summary.

As a self-employed writer, however, I could not afford to pay a professional fifteen or twenty dollars an hour for a trip that might last ten days. Hence I had to make do.

Only on a few occasions, however, did an interpreter's amateur approach cause a problem. Once was when he heard the train chief's call for medical assistance. My journalist's reaction was to jump right up and go to the scene. "But it's none of our business," my interpreter pleaded. He couldn't understand that sticking one's nose into other people's business is the essence of journalism. Nevertheless, I stood up and dragged him to the scene, where he did a fine job of interpreting while at the same time nervously tugging on my sleeve and saying, "That's enough. Let's go!"

Another episode occurred when a large Austrian tourist took loud and nasty exception to a conductor's moving him to another seat to make room for a family to travel together. We were standing right next to tourist and conductor in the vestibule of the car, but my interpreter was so fearful that violence might ensue that she refused to translate until later, when the scene was over and the freshness of the words had disappeared from her memory.

All the same, there were definite advantages to amateur interpreters. For one thing, their personalities—which tended to be sunny and confident—made up for their lack of professional skills. I chose each because he or she was friendly and outgoing, able to coax shy people out of their shells. That is a talent I do not have, and which professional interpreters are forbidden by their code from exercising. The amateurs' easy, casual social skills turned out to be invaluable in the lounge car and in the dining car.

Each interpreter brought a different sensibility to the trip. One, a female relative in her seventies, offered considerable insight into the concerns of the elderly aboard a train. Another, a college graduate in his early twenties, performed the same service from the youthful point of view. None was a railfan, hence brought a fresh and critical eye to his travels, offsetting my buff's tolerant eagerness.

My interpreters also provided a timesaving gambit. When I traveled alone, fellow passengers often refused at first to believe that I was a writer researching a new book. To many minds, deaf people aren't supposed to be capable of such a task. Breaking down their disbelief often took hours. I instructed my interpreters to introduce our mission with the words, "*We* are working on a book"—which, technically, was perfectly accurate. By the time my subjects realized, from the direction of our conversation, that *I* was the writer, the ice had been broken.

Did I lose my independence? Of course not. In their jobs hearing journalists use all kinds of tools: tape recorders, laptop computers, telephones, research assistants and "legmen," on-the-street helpers. My interpreters turned out to be just another tool, a kind of automatic two-legged tape recorder with instant replay and some other useful features.

With them I crossed a frontier of my own and opened a new one of possibility. Given the themes of this book, I should not have been surprised. Implicit in the lure of the West is the promise of a new beginning, and that can be found within as well as without. We Americans, after all, are very good at reinventing ourselves.

ACKNOWLEDGMENTS

For their suggestions and succor I owe much to James Axtell, Stephen Becker, Stan Brandt, Jan Harold Brunvand, Ross Capon, Robin Daughtridge, Bob Glover, John Kirkwood, Colin Kisor, Deborah Abbott Kisor, Judith Kisor, Thomas Kott, Robert C. Locher Jr., Robert Nicol, Jacquelyn Holt Park, Wade Pellizzer, Craig Peterson, Pam Potter, Wally Potter, Jack Schnedler, Charlotte Searl, Scott Stewart, John Stroud and Carol Whitehead.

Special thanks for their research assistance to Terri Golembiewski and Judith Halper of the Chicago *Sun-Times* editorial library; Anne Feiler of the Chicago Public Library; Wayne Coffey of the Denver Public Library; Charles Albi, director of the Colorado Railroad Museum; Ellen Halteman of the California State Railroad Museum Library; and Linda Thatcher of the Utah State Historical Society.

Thanks also to Linda Scott, who transcribed voluminous interview tapes, and to the aforementioned Charles Albi and locomotive engineers Corbett Price Sr. of Amtrak and Steve Patterson of the Santa Fe for reading early versions of the manuscript and catching egregious blunders. (Any remaining errors are, of course, mine alone.)

Deep thanks and a salute to these Amtrakers: Marcia Bradfield, Sandi Brown, Ray Craig, Don Cushine, John Davis, Jim Deely, Ron Dippner, Mimi Earley, Alfredo Gomez, Deborah Hare, Bob Heath, Reggie Howard, Lela Janushkowsky, Sam Jenkins, Curtis Keeton, Pat Kelly, Mike Kemp, Gregg Konstanzer, Sue Martin, Linda Grant Niemann, Terry O'Hara, Kurt Olsson, Robert Pimm, Noel Prell, John Muhammad, Michael Parker, Wally Prince, Glen Sullivan, Giana Swift-Franklin, Peter F. Turrell, John Weeks, John Welch, Brenda Yater and Chris Younger.

My gratitude to my editor, Paul Golob, for rerailing my engine whenever it strayed from the track, and to my agent, Eugene H. Winick, for his faith and good advice.

Finally, thanks to the Ragdale Foundation, a writer's sanctuary where much of this book was written.

INDEX

accidents, 160
  Advance Flyer and *Exposition Flyer* crash, 79–82
  derailments, 183, 209
  engineers and unavoidability of, 269–72, 284
  in stations, 47–48
Across the Plains (Stevenson), 69–70
Adams, John Quincy, 173
Adams-Onís Transcontinental Treaty (1819), 173
Advance Flyer, 79–81
Adventures of a Biographer (Bowen), 101
air brakes, 84, 289
airline industry, 12, 60, 101
"Alertor," 263–64
All Aboard! The Railroad in American Life (Douglas), 50

All Aboard with E. M. Frimbo (Whitaker and Hiss), 8
altitude sickness, 167–68
Alzheimer's disease, 169, 170, 171
"Amboxes," 147
American Indians, 173–74, 244
American Notes (Dickens), 69
American River, 297
American Sign Language, 106
Amtrak
  and airline industry, 12, 60, 101
  black employment, 42, 231–33
  car construction, 46
  and car maintenance, 218
  car shortages, 11, 83
  chef training, 23, 24, 45, 167
  creation of, 11
  crew schedules, 237

Amtrak (*cont'd*)
  and drug smuggling, 182
  and employee tips, 166
  employment cutbacks, 237, 238
  engineers, 83, 267, 271, 299
  federal operating subsidy, 57
  and food service, 23, 40, 44–45
  and homosexual employment,
    216–17
  labor shortages, 216
  locomotives, 259, 261, 268
  mail service, 147
  meal reimbursement, 258
  minority employment, 42
  operating crews, 22, 70–71,
    218, 267
  operation of *California Zephyr*,
    15, 19, 34, 79, 83, 154–55
  private-car hauling, 156–57,
    239–41, 242
  prohibition of animals, 222–23,
    224, 225
  and safety devices, 290
  service crews, 8, 11–12, 14, 19,
    22, 32, 36, 100
  and sexual harassment, 234
  shoe-shine service, 230
  sleeping-car reservations, 99
  sold-out trains, 57, 99, 207–8
  speed limits, 94
  station rebuilding, 54, 55, 56,
    57
  success of, 11, 12–13, 57, 238
  timetables, 93–94
  toilet systems, 125–26
  track rebuilding, 78
  train numbers, 25–26
  and train supplies, 25, 27,
    34–35, 299
  women's employment, 42,
    204–5
Andrews, Laura, 85, 86, 88, 91
animals on trains, 222–27

Arguelles, Cesar, 132
Armstrong, John, 309
assistant conductors. *See*
  brakemen
assistant engineers. *See* firemen
Auburn, Calif., 299–300
Aurora, Ill., 201
Auto-Train, 222

Balanced Rock, 243
Baltimore & Ohio Railroad,
  36–37, 56, 128
Bass, Jane E., 205
bathrooms, 123–26
Bay Area Rapid Transit (BART),
  313
Beauharnais, Josephine de, 201
Beebe, Lucius Morris, 277–83
Belli, Melvin, 51–52
"Big Hole" (Tunnel 41), 287–88,
  292–93
blacks, 18–19, 52, 305–6
  Amtrak employees, 42, 231–33
  Pullman employees, 227–30
Blaine, William W., 81, 82
Bloomer Cut, 300
Bonneville, Lake, 249–50
Bonneville Salt Flats, 249
Boomer: Railroad Memories
  (Niemann), 214–15, 216
Bowen, Catherine Drinker, 101
brakemen ("assistant
  conductors"), 70, 214–16,
  218, 269
Broadway Limited, 11, 118, 171
Broderick, Byron, 212–13
Brotherhood of Sleeping Car
  Porters, 227
Brown, Sandi, 203–4, 205–7,
  208–9, 210
Buber, Martin, 320
Buchanan, James, 244–45
Budd, Edward G., Sr., 16

Budd, Ralph, 16
Budd Company, 16
"builder's plate," 6
Burlington & Missouri River
    Railroad, 96
Burlington Route. *See* Chicago,
    Burlington & Quincy
    Railroad
Burlington Northern Railroad,
    154
Burnham, Daniel, 54, 56
Byers Canyon, 180–81

Cabrillo, Juan Rodriguez, 285
Caen, Herb, 120–21
California, 182, *map* 286, 294–97,
    310, 312
California State Railroad Museum
    (Sacramento), 301
California Zephyr, 25, 109, 112
    Amtrak's operation of, 15, 19,
        34, 79, 83, 154–55
    coach seating, 62–63
    creation of, 16, 17
    derailment of 1988, 209
    original train, 15–16, 17–18,
        94, 149, 155, 314
    route of, 151, 153, 155, 184,
        251–52
    scenery, 17, 94, 102, 184
    service crews, 18–20, 22, 166,
        238
    timetable, 93–94
Canadian Pacific Railroad, 154
Cape Horn, 298
Capitol, 312
Capitol Limited, 56
Cardinal, 54
Carquinez Strait, 297–98
car washers, 151
Cascade Tunnel, 154
Cassidy, Butch (George LeRoy
    Parker), 206, 243–44, 253

Castle Gate, 243
Central Military Tract Railroad,
    95
Central Pacific Railroad
    construction of, 288, 298
    costs of, 251, 279
    federal subsidization of, 299,
        300–301
    meeting at Promontory with
        Union Pacific, 153, 251, 279
    route of, 251–52
Central Station (Chicago), 56
Central Valley, 302
Chandler, Raymond, 200
chefs, 22, 32, 85, 193, 299
    Culinary Institute training, 23,
        24, 45, 167
Chicago, Ill.
    railroads and, 95, 130–31
    railroad stations, 55–57
Chicago, Burlington & Quincy
    Railroad ("Burlington
    Route"), 94–95, 96, 153–54
    Advance Flyer and *Exposition
        Flyer* crash, 79–82
    California Zephyr train, 15–16,
        94
    food service, 37
Chicago & Aurora Railroad, 95
Chicago Daily News, 51, 81,
    82–83
Chicago Museum of Science and
    Industry, 16
Chicago & North Western
    Railroad, 95
Chicago Sun-Times, 24
Chicago Tribune, 82–83
Chicago Union Station, 17, 49,
    59, 61
    construction of, 56
    rebuilding of, 55, 56–58
chief of on-board services, 22,
    29–30, 34, 66, 71

Christie, Agatha, 101–2, 177, 178
Churchill, Jennie (Lady
    Randolph), 292
Cincinnati Union Terminal, 54,
    55
City of New Orleans, 56, 103
City of San Francisco, 293, 294
Civil War, 37, 277
Class (Fussell), 162–63
Claytor, Graham, 238, 242
Clegg, Charles, 280, 281, 282
Clyman, James, 251
coach attendants, 238
coach seating, 62–63
Coast Starlight, 109–10, 312, 315
Cogswell, Milton, 280
Cold War, 158
Colfax, Schuyler, 299
Colfax, Calif., 298–99
Colorado, *map* 152, 154, 174,
    211
Colorado Railroad Museum
    (Golden), 196
Colorado River, 174, 184, 196,
    211, 219
Comstock Lode, 277
conductors, 22, 69–70, 71, 228,
    232, 275
Conrail, 11, 53
Considine, Bob, 94
Craig, Ray, 258–59, 299, 303–4,
    312, 314
  on accidents, 269, 271–72,
    284–85, 288–89
  and disruptive passengers, 274,
    275
  on engineering, 260, 261,
    267–68, 288, 290, 293,
    303
  hearing loss, 259
  on locomotives, 268
  prior occupations, 259–60,
    261, 302

  and safety devices, 262, 263,
    264–65
  on snow removal, 291
  and speedometers, 265
  and track signals, 266, 284
  on track warrants, 262–63
  and whistle codes, 291
  on wildlife, 272, 292, 300
Crane, Stephen, 260–61
crews, 260
  assaulted by passengers, 275
  blacks, 18–19, 42, 227–30,
    231–33
  collegiality among, 70–71,
    231–32, 237, 299
  composition of, 22
  from freight railroads, 70, 218,
    267
  and homosexuality, 216–17
  and passenger illnesses, 168,
    169
  passenger relations, 100, 124,
    166
  pay levels, 71, 258
  personnel cutbacks, 237, 238
  pillaging of supplies, 41–42
  professionalism of, 11–12,
    19–20, 32
  and racism, 42, 231, 232–33
  railfans among, 8
  regional differences among,
    11–12, 100
  rotation among trains, 19, 237
  and sexism, 42, 234–35
  staffing levels, 19, 36, 238
  and timetables, 73
  and tipping, 166, 229
  and train numbers, 25
  women, 18, 42, 43, 218,
    234–35
Crocker, Charles, 287, 297, 299
Culinary Institute of America, 23,
    24, 45, 167

Cushine, Don, 77–78
and disruptive passengers, 77,
133, 134, 313
on personnel cutbacks, 238
as track worker, 78–79
as train chief, 79, 124–25,
126–27
as train manager, 77, 79,
132–33, 150

Davis, John, 22–23, 120, 131,
132, 212, 314
and clean-up procedures, 38,
40, 88
on cooking, 47, 85–89, 91,
140
cooking career, 24–25
Culinary Institute training, 23,
24
and equipment malfunctions,
38–39
and galley supplies, 25, 26, 27,
28, 35, 40–41, 45–46, 49, 88,
193–94
and operating crews, 299
on passengers, 90–91
"deadman," 264
deafness, 14, 118, 311, 320,
322–23
Dearborn Station (Chicago), 55
Denver, John, 195
Denver, Colo., 154
Denver, Northwestern & Pacific
Railroad, 153–54
Denver Post, 157–58
Denver & Rio Grande Western
Railroad, 150
and Amtrak, 154–55, 161
California Zephyr train, 15–16,
155
history of, 153, 191, 196
Rio Grande Zephyr train, 155
Southern Pacific merger, 151

Denver & Salt Lake Railroad,
154, 191
Denver Union Station, 142–43,
145, 146
Denver Zephyr, 16
derailments, 183, 209
Desert Wind, 34, 67, 248
Dewey, Thomas E., 51
Dickens, Charles, 69
DiMaggio, Joe, 303
dining cars, 23
history of, 36–38
profitability and, 37–38, 44–45
seating in, 89, 136–38, 139, 167
service crews, 32, 36
supplies, 25, 26–28
waiters, 32, 38, 164, 165–66
Dinsmore's American Railroad
Guide, 128
discrimination
gender, 205, 234
racial, 52, 231, 232–33
Donner, George, 250–51
Donner, Tamsen, 250–51
Donner Lake, 292
Donner Party, 250–51, 287–88,
294
Donner Pass: Southern Pacific's
Sierra Crossing (Signor), 300
Donner-Reed Trail Monument,
250
dormitory cars, 125, 132
Dotsero Cutoff, 191–92
Douglas, George H., 50, 54
Dowd, C. F., 129
Drug Enforcement Agency
(DEA), 182
drug smuggling, 182–83
drug use, 30–31
"Dry Salvages" (Eliot), 66–67

Earley, Mimi, 204–5
Earp, Wyatt, 280

El Capitan, 125
electricians, 42–43
Eliot, T. S., 66–67
Empire Builder, 13, 60, 189
engine brakes, 290
engineers, 22, 83–84, 260–61
    and accidents, 84, 269, 270–72,
        284
    on freight trains, 267, 268–69
    hearing loss, 259
    on passenger trains, 267–68,
        269
    and safety devices, 263–64,
        266, 290
    service crews and, 299
    and train speed, 265
Erie Railroad, 53
Exposition Flyer, 16, 95
    Naperville accident of 1946,
        80–82

farmers, 114–15, 116
Farnham, Thomas J., 250
Fast Mail, 147
Federal Railroad Administration,
    290
feminism, 235
firemen ("assistant engineers"),
    70, 264
flag stops, 235–36
Flashback (film), 209
"flashing rear end device"
    (FRED), 266, 269
Flathead Tunnel, 154
Florida, 173, 222
"foamers," 6–7
Font, Pedro, 285
Food and Drug Administration
    (FDA), 40
Ford, Ernest, Jr., 229
Francis, Dick, 188
Fraser, Colo., 171

freight railroads, 266
    Amtrak trains and, 11, 154–55
    crews and pay, 71
    engineers, 267, 268–69
Fremont, John C., 173–74
Freud, Sigmund, 319, 320, 321
Frimbo, E. M. (Rogers E. M.
        Whitaker), 7–8, 10, 280
Fussell, Paul, 162–63

Galena & Chicago Union
        Railroad, 95
Galesburg, Ill., 94
galleys, 39
Gardner, John, 53
General Electric Company, 268
General Motors Corp., Electro-
    Motive Division, 268
Gibbs, Wolcott, 282–83
Gilmore, Art, 232
Glenwood Canyon, 194–96
Glenwood Springs, Colo., 197,
    198, 201–3, 209
Golden Gate Bridge, 195–96
Gold Rush, 277, 297
Gomez, Alfredo, 40, 45, 90,
    164–67
Gore Canyon, 184
Gosiute Indians, 250
Gould, Jay, 241–42
Granby, Colo., 171
Grand Canyon, 174
Grand Central Station (Chicago),
    56
Grand Central Terminal (New
    York), 50, 54
Grand Junction, Colo., 212
Grant, Ulysses S., 299
Great Basin, 249
Great Depression, 16, 296
Great Northern Railroad, 37
Great Plains, 115–16, 201

Great Salt Lake, 249, 250
Great Salt Lake Desert, 251
Greeley, Horace, 251
Green River, 236
Greenwich Mean Time, 129
Gross Reservoir, 159–60

Hankins, Tom, 99–100, 238, 239
Hanley, Robert, 282
Harvey, Fred, 36
Hastings, Lansford W., 251
Heath, Robert, 174–75, 210, 248
    and animals on trains, 225–27
    on crew relations, 231–32, 237, 313
    on racism, 231, 232
Helper, Utah, 242–43
Hi-Level coaches, 125, 274
Hillerman, Tony, 188
Hiss, Tony, 8
homelessness, 52
homosexuality, 214, 216–17
Hopkins, Mark, 287, 297, 299
Hopper, Dennis, 209
"hotboxes," 239–40
    detectors, 264
Hot Sulphur Springs, Colo., 180
Howard, Reggie, 248, 313–14
    as chief of services, 28–29, 33–34, 46, 66, 88, 132, 160
    and crew relations, 216–17, 233
    on dining cars, 32
    and disruptive passengers, 30–31, 133–34, 161–62
    and movie screenings, 101, 102, 255
    on racism, 233
    railroad career, 31–32
    on sexism, 234
    on toilet malfunctions, 124

and train supplies, 29, 34–35, 41–42
Humboldt River, 252
Huntington, Collis P., 287, 297, 299

Illinois Central Railroad, 56
Illinois Central Station (Chicago), 56
Illinois Zephyr, 70
Interstate 70 highway, 194–95, 196
Interstate 880 highway, 296, 305
Iron Road to the West (Stover), 128
Isabella I (queen of Castile), 200
Israeli-occupied territories, 254–55

Janushkowsky, Lela, 23, 43–44, 85, 91, 248, 289, 313–14
    and crew relations, 42–43, 232–33
    and dining-car passengers, 47, 87, 89, 113, 136–38, 141, 212, 235
    on food service, 44–45, 47, 135–36
    and galley supplies, 26, 27, 28, 35, 40, 49–50, 255–56
    on racism, 232–33
    railroad career, 44
    on stewards, 177
    on tipping, 166
Jenkins, Linda, 234
Jenkins, Sam, 231
Job Corps, 24
Johnson, Lyndon B., 24
Johnston, Albert Sidney, 244–45
Jones, Casey, 130
Judah, Theodore P., 287
Justinian I (emperor of Byzantium), 200

Keeton, Curtis, 29–30
Kelly, Walt, 283
Kemp, Mike, 70, 71–73
Kluger, Richard, 278
Konstanzer, Gregg, 240–41

Lake Shore Limited, 41, 49
Lake Shore & Michigan
    Southern, 128
land grants, 96–97
La Salle Street Station (Chicago),
    56
Leonard, William Ellery, 98
Leslie, Frank, 298
Livermore, Calif., 309–10
Locher, Bob, 101–2, 178–82, 183,
    184, 185–91, 317
Locomotive God (Leonard), 98
locomotives, 95, 155, 268, 270
    operation of, 261–62, 263–64,
        265, 289–90
    in stations, 49
Loewy, Raymond, 57–58
London, England, 54
Loomis, Robert, 214
Los Angeles, Calif., 296, 312
Lost Coast (California), 317
Louisiana Purchase, 173
lounge cars, 47, 97, 103–4, 107,
    108
luggage, 182, 205
luxury trains, 15, 17

Macalester College, 254–55
McCarthy, Joseph R., 43
McCaskey, Mildred, 74–77, 79,
    133–34, 139, 313
McClellan Air Force Base, 301
McCook, Neb., 116
MacKenzie, John M., 53–54
mail service, 147–49
Map 21-A, 38, 39, 132
Marin County, Calif., 295

Mark Twain Zephyr, 16
Marryat, Frederick, 36
Marshall, John, 297
Matthews, Anne, 116
Middle Park, 173–74
Miles of Smiles, Years of Struggle
    (Santino), 229
mining industry, 211, 297–98
Model Railroader, 10
model railroaders, 10
Moffat, David, 153–54, 180,
    191
Moffat Tunnel, 154, 160–61
Mormons, 245, 246–47, 248
Mount Macdonald Tunnel, 154
Muir, John, 303
Mustang Ranch, 273

Naperville, Ill., 79
Napoleon I (emperor of France),
    201
narrow-gauge railroads, 153
National Defense Reserve Fleet,
    303
National Weather Service, 171
Nebraska, 117–18
Nebraska Zephyr, 16–17
Nero (emperor of Rome), 200
Nevada, 252, 273
New Castle, Colo., 211
newspapers, 120, 121–23
New York, N.Y., 54, 130–31
New York, Susquehanna &
    Western Railroad, 53
New York Central Railroad, 7, 9,
    11, 128
New Yorker, 8, 282
New York Times, 80–81, 129
Nicol, Robert, 306–11
Niemann, Linda, 214–15, 216,
    217–18
Nixon, Richard M., 11
Norman, William S., 205

Northern Pacific Railroad, 37
North Western Station (Chicago),
55

Oakland, Calif., 295, 296, 305–6,
311–12
O'Brien, Howard Vincent, 279
Oddie, Tasker, 280
Offutt Air Force Base, 118
O'Hare Airport (Chicago), 59
Olsson, Kurt, 223–24
Omaha World-Herald, 120
operating crews. *See* crews
Osborn, Cyrus, 17, 196
Overland Limited, 17
Overland Route, 155

Pacific Railroad Act (1862), 300
Paglia, Camille, 235
Panama Limited, 56
Park, Jacquelyn Holt, 213–14,
313
Parker, Michael, 203–4, 205–7,
208, 209, 210
passengers, 60, 100, 101, 142,
206–7
alcohol and drug use, 29–31,
58, 134
computer lists of, 33, 34
and dining car, 89, 136–38,
139, 141, 167
and food service, 23, 36, 38,
90–91
illnesses, 168–71
and lounge car, 97, 104, 107,
108
porters and, 229–30
racism, 231, 232
sexual activity, 108–11
sleeping-car, 34, 229
and theft, 176–77
and tipping, 90, 166, 229
and toilet malfunctions, 124

passenger trains
Amtrak and, 11–12, 32, 34, 57,
154
decline of, 18, 19, 56–57, 196
emergency stops, 270
engineers, 267–68, 269
history of, 10–11, 16, 17–20,
58, 80
mail trains and, 147–48, 149
revival of, 12–13, 57
Pates, Gordon, 282
Pennsylvania Railroad, 11
Pennsylvania Station (New York),
52, 54
Philadelphia, Wilmington &
Baltimore Railroad, 37
Pimm, Bob, 261, 263, 264, 292,
302, 303
and disruptive passengers, 274,
275
on track signals, 266
Pioneer, 34, 120
Pioneer Zephyr, 16
"polacking," 35
Popper, Deborah, 115–16
Popper, Frank, 115–16
porters, 227–28, 229–30
Prell, Noel, 28–29, 103–4
Prince, Wally, 83–84, 267,
270–71
private rail cars, 156–57, 239–42
Promontory, Utah, 153, 251, 279
Provo, Utah, 245–46
Public Service Company
ofColorado, 196
Pullman, George M., 37, 227–28
Pullman Company, 228, 230
conductors, 228
porters, 227–28, 230
waiters, 228–29

racism, 42, 231, 232–33
railfans, 5–7, 8, 9–10, 278

railroads, 13, 95, 211. *See also*
freight railroads; passenger
trains
in California, 312
and dining cars, 36–38
federal land grants, 96–97
mail service, 147–49
stations, 50, 52–60
timetables, 128–31
Railway Post Office (RPO), 148,
149
Randolph, A. Philip, 227
Random House, Inc., 213, 214
Red Canyon, 192
Reed, James Frazier, 250–51
Reid, Ogden, 278
Reno, Nev., 274
repeaters, 185–86, 187
Richards, Jeffrey, 53–54
Rio Grande Ski Train, 146, 164
Rio Grande Zephyr, 155
Rocky Flats nuclear plant, 158–59
Rocky Mountain National Park,
171
Rocky Mountains, 154, 159, 183,
201
Rogers, Will, 36
Roman baths, 200
Romo, Altagracia, 41, 45, 86, 88,
91
Rosenzweig, Franz, 319–20
*Route Guide to the California
Zephyr*, 79
"Royal Gorge" route, 191
Ruby Canyon, 218–19

Sacramento, Calif., 301
Sacramento River, 297
St. Pancras Station (London), 54
Salt Lake City, Utah, 246, 247
San Andreas Fault, 296
San Diego County, Calif., 295
Sands, Bobby, 45

San Francisco, Calif., 277,
311–12, 314–17
San Francisco Chronicle, 120–21,
281–82
San Francisco Zephyr, 155
San Joaquin, 312
San Leandro Historical Railway
Society, 307–9
Santa Fe Railway, 36, 37, 153
Santino, Jack, 229, 230
Sayers, Dorothy, 101–2
Scherer, Lynn, 213
"Scotch Express" (Crane),
260–61
service attendants. *See* waiters
service crews. *See* crews
sexism, 42, 205, 234
sex on trains, 108–11
sexual harassment, 234–35
Shoshone hydroelectric plant, 196
Sierra Nevada, 261, 285–87,
299–300
"Big Hole" tunnel through,
287–88, 292–93
exploration of, 285
mining in, 297, 298
snowfall in, 287, 293, 295
Signor, John, 300, 303–4
Skinner, B. F., 53
Skonieczny, Matt, 99–100, 238–39
Skull Valley, 250
sleeping cars, 13, 34, 67, 99, 108,
124, 175–76
smoking, 103–4, 117, 119
snow-removal equipment, 291,
294
Soldier Summit, 244, 245
Southern Pacific Mole (Oakland),
314–15
Southern Pacific Railroad, 252,
263
City of San Francisco train, 293,
294

Livermore station, 309–10
merger with Denver & Rio
    Grande Western, 151
overhaul of locomotives, 301
route of, 155
track signals, 266
whistle codes, 291
South Station (Boston), 50
Sparks, Nev., 273
"Sparks cars," 273–74
Standard Time, 128, 129–30
Stanford, Leland, 282, 287, 297,
    299
Stanford Curve, 292
Starrucca House (Susquehanna),
    53
station agents, 50–51
Steam Up (Treacy), 58–59
Stein, Gertrude, 305
Stevenson, Robert Louis, 69–70
stewards, 22, 29, 165, 177, 178,
    179
Stone Gone Mad (Park), 213, 214
Stover, John F., 128
Styron, William, 213–14
Sullivan, Glen, 109–11
Superliner cars, 12–13, 100
    dining cars, 89
    galleys, 39
    lounge cars, 104, 107
    sleeping cars, 67, 108
    toilet systems, 125, 126
Susquehanna, Pa., 53
Sutherland, Kiefer, 209
Sutter, Johann Augustus, 297
Sutton, Horace, 281

thermal springs, 200
Theroux, Paul, 7–8
30th Street Station
    (Philadelphia), 55
Thomas, Clarence, 140
Thompson, Utah, 235, 236

Thoreau, Henry, 130
Time, 82
time zones, 129–30
tipping, 90, 166, 229
tourism, 201, 315
"track warrant," 262–63
travel agents, 68
Treacy, Eric, 58–59
Truckee, Calif., 291
Truckee River, 272, 288
Truman, Harry S., 51
tunnels, 154, 158, 159
    "Big Hole," 287–88, 292–93
Twain, Mark, 277–78
Twentieth Century Limited, 7, 11,
    37, 279
Twin Cities Zephyr, 16

Union Pacific Railroad, 288
    meeting at Promontory with
        Central Pacific, 153, 251,
        279
    route of, 151–53, 155, 251
United States
    acquisition of Florida, 173
    time zones, 129–30
United States Air Force, 301
United States Army, 244, 294
United States Coast Guard, 294
United States Congress
    and Amtrak, 44, 126, 241
    and mail trains, 147
    and Standard Time, 130
United States Mail, 148, 149
USA Today, 120
Utah, 247–48, 249
Ute Indians, 173–74

Victoria Station (London), 54
Virginia City, Nev., 277, 280, 281
Virginia City (rail car), 282–83
Virginia City Territorial Enterprise,
    277–78, 281

Virginia & Truckee Railroad, 277, 280
Vista-Dome cars, 17, 18, 97, 196
Vonnegut, Kurt, Jr., 104

waiters ("service attendants"), 32, 38, 164, 165, 166, 228–29
Walker, Stanley, 278
Walton, Sam, 115
Ward, Artemus, 156
Washington Union Station, 54, 55, 56
Wesley, John, 201
West, Mae, 162
Western Pacific Railway, 16, 155, 251, 314
Where the Buffalo Roam (Matthews), 116
whistle codes, 290–91
Whitaker, Rogers E. M. See Frimbo, E. M.
Whitney, J. D., 300
Wiley, Alfred, 82

Winchell, Walter, 279
Winnemucca, Nev., 253
Wisconsin, 128
women
employees, 18, 42, 43, 204–5, 234–35
passengers, 52, 107

Yampa Hot Springs, 198–200
Younger, Chris, 262, 263, 273, 275, 289, 304, 312
on accidents, 269
on firemen, 264
on food, 258
on locomotives, 301, 302–3
on service crews, 299
and speedometers, 265
and track signals, 265, 266
on track warrants, 274
on whistle codes, 291
on wildlife, 292

Zephyrettes, 18

HENRY KISOR is the book-review editor and literary columnist of the *Chicago Sun-Times*. A graduate of Trinity College and the Medill School of Journalism at Northwestern University, he began his newspaper career at the Wilmington (Delaware) *Evening Journal* in 1964. He joined the staff of the *Chicago Daily News* a year later and became book-review editor in 1973. After moving to the *Sun-Times* in 1978, Kisor has earned numerous prizes and citations, most notably his selection as a finalist for the Pulitzer Prize for criticism in 1981. He has served as an adjunct instructor at the Medill School of Journalism and also writes regularly on travel and personal computers. His first book, *What's That Pig Outdoors?: A Memoir of Deafness*, was published in 1990 and was named a Booklist Editor's Choice for 1990. He lives in Evanston, Illinois, with his wife, the children's author and critic Deborah Abbott Kisor. They have two sons, Colin and Conan.